The Thaw Collection

Master Drawings and Oil Sketches

THE THAW COLLECTION

Master Drawings and Oil Sketches
Acquisitions Since 1994

FOREWORD BY Charles E. Pierce, Jr.

PREFACE BY Eugene V. Thaw

THE THAW COLLECTION BY William M. Griswold

CATALOGUE BY
Cara Dufour Denison
William M. Griswold
Kathleen Stuart
Jennifer Tonkovich

WITH CONTRIBUTIONS BY
Colin J. Bailey · Rhoda Eitel-Porter ·
Egbert Haverkamp-Begemann · Evelyn J. Phimister ·
Jane Shoaf Turner

THE PIERPONT MORGAN LIBRARY
New York

Exhibition at The Pierpont Morgan Library, New York

27 September 2002 – 19 January 2003

The Thaw Collection: Master Drawings and Oil Sketches, Acquisitions Since 1994 is made possible by
Janine Luke and Melvin R. Seiden, David Rockefeller, Parker and Gail Gilbert, and Annette de
la Renta, with additional assistance from Jane Forbes Clark, Ronay and Richard Menschel, Mrs.
Charles Wrightsman, Agnes Gund and Daniel Shapiro, and Stephen and Carla Hahn.

This publication was made possible in part by the Franklin Jasper Walls Lecture Fund.

LIBRARY OF CONGRESS CATALOGING-IN-PUBLICATION DATA

The Thaw collection: master drawings and oil sketches, acquisitions
since 1994 / foreword by Charles E. Pierce; preface by Eugene V. Thaw;
introduction by William M. Griswold; catalogue by Cara Dufour Denison
. . . [et al.]; with contributions by Egbert Haverkamp-Begemann . . . [et al.].
    p. cm.
Catalog of an exhibition held at the Pierpont Morgan Library, New York,
Sept. 27, 2002–Jan. 19, 2003.
Includes bibliographical references and index.

  ISBN 0-87598-137-2

1. Drawing, European—Exhibitions. 2. Oil sketches—Europe—Exhibitions.
3. Thaw, Eugene Victor—Art collections—Exhibitions. 4. Thaw, Clare—
Art collections—Exhibitions. 5. Art—Private collections—New York (State)—
New York—Exhibitions. 6. Art—New York (State)—New York—Exhibitions.
7. Pierpont Morgan Library—Exhibitions. I. Denison, Cara D. II. Haverkamp
Begemann, Egbert. III. Pierpont Morgan Library.

  N6754 .T57 2002
  741.94'074'7471—dc21

              2002029320

ISBN 0-87598-137-2

COVER: Rembrandt Harmensz. van Rijn, *The Bulwark De Rose and the Windmill De Smeerpot in
Amsterdam* (No. 6)

FRONTISPIECE: (Carl Christian) Constantin Hansen, *Columns of the Temple of Neptune at Paestum*
(No. 100)

Acknowledgments

Sigrid Achenbach, Marie Lødrup Bang, Colleen Becker, Laura Bennett, W. Mark Brady, Melissa Cacciola, Constantino Centroni, Martin Clayton, Denis Coutagne, Richard Day, Antonino De Angelis, William Drummond, Inge Dupont, Jacques Fischer, Charlotte Gere, Mechthild Haas, Rena Hoisington, Christian von Holst, Ruth S. Kraemer, Armin Kunz, John Lishawa, James Mackinnon, Antoine Maisani, Peter Märker, Karin Mayer-Pasinski, Michael McAuliffe, Marianne Roland Michel, Asher Miller, J. Michael Montias, Anna Ottani-Cavina, Robert Parks, Ann Percy, Régine Rémon, Herbert W. Rott, Elsa Marie Saint-Germain, F. Carlo Schmid, Hinrich Sieveking, Franz Smola, Nicola Spinosa, Timothy Standring, Susan Stein, Nancy Spiegel, Claus Virch, Wheelock Whitney III, Timothy Wilcox, Klaus Wolbert, Laura Zukerman

Table of Contents

Foreword

During the fifteen years that I have been director of the Morgan Library, few things have given me as much pleasure as my friendship with Eugene and Clare Thaw. What began as a professional relationship between a director and a major collector has deepened into a rich and rewarding personal friendship. At the same time, their generosity to the Library has grown to such an extent that they must be regarded as the greatest patrons of this institution since the death of the founders. This past year, in particular, has been an *annus mirabilis.* In February, The Thaw Conservation Center opened to great acclaim, and now, in September, we have another exhibition of works in the Thaw Collection. When I wrote in 1994 that Gene considered his third exhibition of master drawings his last in this field, it was an occasion for celebration tinged with regret. Gene regarded the 1994 exhibition as a summing up of what he had learned, thought, felt, and accomplished in his long, distinguished career as dealer and collector. But, as the present exhibition and catalogue affirm, the third exhibition was not the last. We are all grateful because Gene and Clare have continued to acquire beautiful drawings for their collection and have broadened its scope.

The Thaws have continued to add to their collections of works by favorite artists with drawings by Claude, Degas, Delacroix, and Ingres as well as one of Rembrandt's most exceptional landscape drawings. There are a few new Italian drawings, but a fine group of seventeenth-century Dutch drawings and numerous German acquisitions attest to a broadening of taste. The German works are mainly from the early nineteenth century, in accordance with Gene's conviction that the Library should expand its collection of nineteenth-century drawings.

If strengthening the collection of nineteenth-century master drawings is a most welcome ongoing practice, two new aspects of the Thaw Collection can be considered radical departures from the collecting tradition established by Pierpont Morgan. Nearly half of this exhibition consists of oil sketches, mainly of landscapes painted from nature during the late eighteenth and nineteenth centuries. This fascinating phenomenon, until recently barely observed and rarely collected, is represented by a remarkable and representative selection ranging from the French and English to German and Scandinavian schools. This new field of collecting logically and consistently extends Gene's great interest in landscape drawings of earlier periods (Rembrandt, Claude, and later Morisot and Seurat). Many of these oil sketches are the same size and format as most drawings, which afforded artists the opportunity to express the wonderment of nature in a new, resourceful medium. The systematic collecting of a specific group of oil paintings takes the Morgan in a new, vital direction. Such a step had to be taken at the initiative of the private collector.

Clare and Gene Thaw have opened yet one more avenue for the Morgan. Every museum must decide sooner or later whether it wishes to identify itself wholly with particular periods that are receding inexorably, or rather extend its vision to more recent eras. The momentum of tradition usually precludes a spontaneous decision to move toward modern times. As early as 1985 the Thaws had added to their collection four drawings by Picasso and three by Matisse as well as a sketchbook by Pollock and drawings by De Chirico, Ernst, Klee, and Mondrian, extending their collection firmly into the twentieth century. This tendency has been maintained in the present exhibition with works by Léger, La Fresnaye, and Morandi. To form a comprehensive or representative collection of twentieth-century art at this time would be an unrealistic proposal, but Gene and Clare have made it possible to prevent the older collections from becoming isolated from later developments and our own time.

Clare and Gene insist that this exhibition of recently acquired drawings and oil sketches will be their last. To the areas in which the Library's collection already was strong they have added works of the utmost rarity and beauty. In other areas, notably the nineteenth and twentieth centuries, they have played a critical role in opening new avenues. Their generosity altered the complexion of the Library, and their perspicacity has made possible the exploration of new decades to come.

I should also like to thank the following individuals whose efforts have made this exhibition and catalogue possible: Patricia Tang and Leslie Chang of E. V. Thaw & Co.; Cara Dufour Denison, Egbert Haverkamp-Begemann, Kathleen Stuart, and Jennifer Tonkovich of Drawings and Prints; Karen Banks, Patricia Emerson, and Genna Patacsil of Publications; Jerry Kelly, who designed this catalogue; Patricia Reyes, Reba Fishman Snyder, and James Donchez of Conservation; Marilyn Palmeri and Joseph Zehavi of Photography and Rights; and Lucy Eldridge and Patricia Courtney of the Registrar's Office.

CHARLES E. PIERCE, JR.
Director, The Pierpont Morgan Library

Preface

Here, in our fourth Morgan Library exhibition, we are including so-called plein-air oil sketches on paper. They are part of a larger group that we began to collect in order to have something on the walls of our New York apartment, since most of our drawings remained permanently at the Library after our last exhibition. Having begun for purely decorative reasons, Clare and I were rapidly caught up by the growing interest in this hitherto neglected area of art history. It seemed an interest very close to drawings and, as William Griswold will propose, quite appropriate to the collecting interests of the Library.

Most of the sixty-two drawings shown here as additions to the Thaw Collection have never actually been lived with at home by my wife and me. During this period, when our time has been spent primarily in Santa Fe, New Mexico, new drawings generally went straight to the Library, and our collecting can honestly be said to have been directed more strongly toward the Library's needs. The choices, however, always reflected our personal tastes and passions.

Bill Griswold's infectious enthusiasm helped me to overcome any qualms and to bid at auction more than I had planned for the great Rembrandt townscape from the Chatsworth and Michael Currier collections. During our 1994 exhibition a kind letter of approval came from Seymour Slive of Harvard, but he said there ought to be a Jacob Ruisdael in the Thaw Collection. Sure enough, one became available, as did a fine Koninck landscape and a rare van den Eeckhout figural wash drawing from a group once thought to be by Vermeer. Thus my earlier avoidance of seventeenth-century Dutch draftsmen, with the exception of Rembrandt, seems no longer to be the case. Now that an old friend, Professor Egbert Haverkamp-Begemann, has graciously accepted to step in for Bill Griswold, who left us for the Getty, my interest in Dutch and Flemish drawings and lots more will be helped by the best advice one could have.

As with earlier efforts of ours, we have tried to strengthen the Library's holdings. We sought more German Romantics, more strength in some visionaries of the nineteenth century, like Victor Hugo, Odilon Redon, and Samuel Palmer. Here once again is a toehold for the Library in the twentieth century. Now that we can look backward from a new century, it has been our fervent hope that another collector will someday try to fill out the Library's twentieth-century drawings.

Working with the Morgan in our collecting enterprise, originally Clare's idea, has been one of the great satisfactions of my life. I am grateful to Charles Pierce, the Director, and to the staff of the Publications and the Drawings departments for all their encouragement and their hard work producing this, the fourth Thaw catalogue. They have given to Clare and me our few minutes of fame and our chance to leave some small legacy to future lovers of master drawings.

EUGENE V. THAW

The Thaw Collection

Eugene Thaw's formidable knowledge of art history, keen sense of quality, and deep understanding of the goals of museums and private collectors are inextricable from his success as a dealer in paintings, drawings, and sculpture. It is inevitable, perhaps, that he and his wife, Clare, should also have begun to collect for themselves. In the decades since the early 1950s, when they acquired their first drawing, a figure study by Giambattista Tiepolo, they have assembled one of the finest holdings of drawings and watercolors in private hands.

Collecting always has been influenced by personal taste, and the drawings assembled by the Thaws naturally reflect their preferences with regard to artists, periods, and schools. Mr. Thaw has described the difference between "a print lover's and bibliophile's approach in which drawings are kept in mats and boxes" to that which "devolves . . . from a taste for paintings" (New York and elsewhere 1975, p. 13). His approach unquestionably is the latter. Many of the drawings in the Thaw Collection are highly finished, and almost all have magnificent frames.

It never was their intention that the collection be comprehensive. Instead they have focused upon the work of specific draftsmen and types of drawings that particularly appealed to them. They have emphasized the incunabula of drawing—sheets datable to the fifteenth and early sixteenth centuries—on the one hand, and works from the eighteenth to the first half of the twentieth centuries on the other, largely bypassing the later Renaissance and much of the seventeenth century. They have collected in depth the work of favorite artists Claude Lorrain and Rembrandt, from a period they otherwise have eschewed; Watteau, Giambattista and Domenico Tiepolo, and Goya, from the eighteenth century; and Friedrich, Turner, Géricault, Delacroix, Daumier, Degas, and Cézanne, from the nineteenth.

On the occasion of the first exhibition of their drawings in 1975, the Thaws announced their intention eventually to present the collection to the Morgan Library. Since then it has been exhibited twice—in 1985 and 1994—and in 1996–97 an overview of their holdings was presented at the Royal Academy in London. The exhibitions at the Morgan Library have been devoted primarily to recent acquisitions and thus trace the development of the collection over almost four decades. Each show has been markedly different from the one that preceded it, as the collection has evolved owing both to changing opportunities in the market and to Mr. and Mrs. Thaw's ongoing discovery of new areas of collecting.

The 1975 exhibition was the most narrowly focused. It included nine drawings each by Claude Lorrain and Giambattista Tiepolo, eight by Degas, seven by Domenico Tiepolo, six by Rembrandt and Delacroix, five by Watteau, Guardi, and Goya, and four by Géricault, Daumier, and Cézanne. Also in the first exhibition were a magnificent double-sided drawing by Rubens; *Pear Tree in a Walled Garden* by Samuel Palmer; two sheets by Ingres and Corot; *Saint Rémy, Workers in the Field* by van Gogh; and the first of what was to become a remarkable series of drawings by Redon.

The second show comprised newly acquired works by a number of the same artists, along with seven sheets by Fragonard. Among a small number of works datable to the fifteenth and sixteenth centuries were an extremely rare study by Mantegna and one sheet each by Hans Sebald Beham and Goltzius as well as a selection of drawings and watercolors by such later masters as Fuseli, Blake, Constable, Kobell, Dahl, and Moritz von Schwind. The first exhibition had included no twentieth-century drawings.

The Thaws regarded the 1994 exhibition, *The Thaw Collection: Master Drawings and New Acquisitions,* as their last in the field. With their move to Santa Fe, their interest had shifted to Native American art, and they had begun to assemble the collection now housed in a special wing of the New York State Historical Association in Cooperstown. The third exhibition of their drawings thus was intended as a summing up of what they had achieved during the previous forty years and comprised a broad overview of the periods and schools.

There were, to be sure, some spectacular new additions. Among the acquisitions since 1985 were two sheets each by such favorite artists as Rembrandt, Fragonard, Hubert Robert, Goya, Ingres, Delacroix, Degas, Cézanne, and Matisse. The show also included superb sheets by David, Morisot, Renoir, Cross, Modigliani, Chagall, and Giacometti—none of whom previously had been represented in the collection. Among the fifteenth- and sixteenth-century drawings that had been added in the past nine years were Altdorfer's *Two Lovers by a Fountain in a Landscape,* Cranach's *Portrait of a Man in a Black Cap,* Bartolommeo di Giovanni's *Adoration of the Magi,* and Fra Bartolommeo's *Barren Trees.* There were no new drawings by Watteau and just one each by Claude Lorrain, Daumier, Redon, and Picasso —each of whose works the Thaws already had collected in considerable depth. In other areas, however, they had made notable additions. While Turner had long been a favorite, and the collection had for some time comprised outstanding works by Constable and Palmer, between 1985 and 1994 the Thaws added, not only a new watercolor by Turner, but additional—and, in some cases, their first—sheets by such British artists as Alexander Cozens, Romney, Fuseli, John Brown, John Robert Cozens, Girtin, and Ruskin. They also had bolstered their representation of works by Dutch and Flemish artists other than Rubens and Rembrandt. The 1994 exhibition included sheets by Maerten van Heemskerck, Jacques de Gheyn, Jan Brueghel, Roelandt Savery, Saenredam, and van Dyck, none of whose works had figured in any earlier presentation of the collection.

In the years that followed, Mr. and Mrs. Thaw went on to explore other areas of collecting, including the bronze artifacts produced by the nomadic peoples of the Ordos region in what is now Mongolia. They did not, however, cease to acquire drawings, as they had predicted they would in 1994. Since then, they have added more than sixty drawings to the approximately 250 they already had given to the Morgan Library. This catalogue describes and reproduces these most recent acquisitions.

Just as each of the three earlier catalogues differed in emphasis from the one that preceded it, this volume marks a further evolution. This has been prompted by the Thaws' desire to build upon existing areas of strength or weakness in their own collection, by their wish to add works by artists underrepresented at the Morgan Library, by their developing interest in such fields as German draftsmanship of the early nineteenth century and the landscape oil sketch, and by their readiness to seize such exceptional opportunities as the possibility to purchase at auction Rembrandt's outstanding *Bulwark De Rose and the Windmill De Smeerpot in Amsterdam.* Those who are familiar with other catalogues of the Thaw Collection therefore will discover a range of works by artists whose drawings were not included in any of the earlier shows.

During the past eight years, the Thaws have acquired relatively few works by the artists whom they previously had acknowledged to be particular favorites. In addition to the famous Rembrandt, there is a Roman view by Claude Lorrain, a superb group portrait by Ingres, and two sheets by Delacroix. Degas's *Three Studies of a Dancer* is the largest and perhaps the most important of the Thaws' fourteen works by the artist. And the exhibition includes no fewer than three new drawings by Redon.

François Desportes's *Study of a Pointer* and Étienne-Louis Boullée's visionary architectural rendering, *Interior of a Library,* further round out the Thaws' holdings of eighteenth-century French art. They have added to the collection their first drawings by Victor Hugo, Théodore Rousseau, and Eugène Boudin, together with additional works by such nineteenth-century French artists as Granet, Millet, Pissarro, Fantin-Latour, Cross, Seurat, and Toulouse-Lautrec. Other significant acquisitions in the field of Impressionist and Post-Impressionist art include illustrated letters by Manet and van Gogh.

Relatively few Italian drawings have entered the collection since the last time it was shown, but two—Carpaccio's *Virgin and Child and Two Female Saints* and Stefano della Bella's large watercolor, *A Feast at the Cascine, Florence*—are of signal importance. The collection also now includes sheets by Domenico Campagnola and Giovanni Paolo Panini, together with a second drawing by Giovanni Benedetto Castiglione.

In the introduction to the catalogue of the first exhibition, Mr. Thaw noted that he "would not at all mind owning a flat landscape page by [Philips] Koninck" (New York and elsewhere 1975, p. 15). The collection now comprises a superb example—formerly the property of Morgan Library benefactors Rudolf and Lore Heinemann—as it does a magnificent brush drawing, *Seated Youth in a Hat, with His Chin Cupped in His Left Hand,* by Gerbrand van den Eeckhout and a landscape in black chalk and gray wash by Jacob van Ruisdael. The most significant addition to the Thaws' holdings of British drawings is Palmer's *Oak Tree and Beech, Lullingstone Park,* created during the 1820s. There also are individual sheets by John Robert Cozens, David Roberts, Edwin Henry Landseer, and Richard Doyle.

An area in which the collection has become particularly strong is German Romanticism. To the Thaws' holdings of five drawings by Friedrich have been added some sheets by his contemporaries, including Koch, Runge, and Fohr. They have acquired their first drawing by Menzel, as they have rare sheets by the Danish painters Christoffer Wilhelm Eckersberg and Vilhelm Hammershøi. Notable additions to the Thaws' holdings of twentieth-century drawings are sheets by Sickert, Klee, and La Fresnaye.

About 1995 Mr. and Mrs. Thaw began to assemble a collection of late eighteenth- and nineteenth-century oil sketches on paper. This was in many respects a logical extension of their long-standing interest in drawings. For centuries artists have used oil and tempera on paper as a part of their preparatory process. This practice is reflected in such earlier works in the Thaw Collection as Cranach's *Portrait of a Man in a Black Cap,* the *Head of a Bear* attributed to Frans Snyders, Desportes's *Study of a Pointer,* and Agasse's *White Horse.* The habit of sketching outdoors, introduced by such painters as Thomas Jones and Pierre-

Henri de Valenciennes, parallels the development of plein-air sketching in other materials, including chalk and watercolor. The very spontaneity of so many landscape sketches in oil on paper relates them to the most rapidly executed drawings.

The Thaws' first foray into the field was the acquisition of nine sketches by Valenciennes, which they intended to take the place of the watercolors by Cézanne that formerly had hung on the walls of their home but are now kept at the Morgan Library. True collectors, they wished to probe deeper. They bought more oil sketches, and today they own one of the finest and most comprehensive collections of paintings on paper anywhere in the world. To the core group of works by Valenciennes they have juxtaposed works by such other early innovators as Michallon, Denis, and Bidauld. They have acquired oil sketches by artists already represented in the collection—among them, Granet, Constable, Lear, Delacroix, Corot, Dillis, Dahl, and Rousseau—and they have purchased a number of sketches by the German and Scandinavian contemporaries of the Romantic draftsmen whose works they simultaneously were adding to their collection of drawings. In addition to Dillis and Dahl, they have acquired sketches by Carus, Rottmann, Lucas, Hansen, and Lundbye. Finally, although the few exhibitions that have focused upon the oil sketch have tended to emphasize the first generation or so of painters who worked en plein air, the Thaws also have bought works in oil on paper by such later nineteenth-century artists as Desgoffe, Paul Flandrin, Benouville, Giovanni Battista Camuccini, Cels, Harpignies, and Auguste Bonheur.

The importance of the Thaws' contribution to the collection begun by Pierpont Morgan and augmented by such other benefactors of the Morgan Library as Janos Scholz, Rudolf and Lore Heinemann, and Alice Tully cannot be overestimated. Many fill particular gaps in its holdings. If it were not for the Thaws, the Morgan might never have been able to acquire a drawing by Mantegna or Cranach or Altdorfer, whose works rarely now come on the market. Their compositional study by Carpaccio complements the fine double-sided study of heads, in brush on blue paper, that Pierpont Morgan purchased in 1910. Their three works by Fra Bartolommeo and double-sided sheet by Tintoretto strengthen the Library's already extensive holdings of Italian Renaissance draftsmanship, while their drawings by Heemskerck, Goltzius, Jan Brueghel, Savery, Jacques de Gheyn, Rubens, Jordaens, and van Dyck all greatly enhance its collection of works by Netherlandish and Flemish artists.

The Thaw Collection includes twelve sheets by Claude Lorrain and eleven by Rembrandt. There are six drawings by Watteau and ten by Fragonard. The Thaws' ten sheets by Giambattista and Domenico Tiepolo, together with those by Guardi, Piranesi, and Piazzetta, have helped to make the Library the principal center in North America, if not the world, for the study of eighteenth-century Venetian drawing. The eight sheets by Goya that the Thaws have given or promised have provided much greater depth to the Library's small holdings of Spanish draftsmanship.

Until fairly recently the Morgan had few nineteenth-century drawings. The Thaw Collection has profoundly altered this aspect of its holdings, prompting the Library's curators to make further acquisitions in the field. It is thanks to the Thaws that the Library has so fine and representative a selection of works by Turner and Palmer. Their two sheets by Constable and works by Alexander and John Robert Cozens also have enriched the Library's collection of drawings and watercolors by British artists. The Library previously had almost no German drawings of the early nineteenth century. With the Thaws, its collection of works by Friedrich, Runge, and their contemporaries is one of the finest in the United States.

The impact of the Thaws' gift upon the Library's holdings of nineteenth-century French drawings is still more extraordinary. The numbers speak for themselves. There are six by Ingres, six by Géricault, more than a dozen by Delacroix, fourteen (including a sketchbook) by Degas, five by Daumier, two each by Gauguin and Seurat, three by van Gogh, eight by Redon, and seven watercolors, a large pencil drawing, and an intact sketchbook by Cézanne.

Mr. and Mrs. Thaw have collected drawings for almost half a century. The series of no less than four exhibitions records their quest for quality and their expanding vision. Their generosity toward the Morgan Library makes the institution the beneficiary of their knowledge and insight and the public ultimately the recipient of their munificence.

WILLIAM M. GRISWOLD

DRAWINGS

VITTORE CARPACCIO

Venice (?) 1460/5–1525/26 Venice

I Virgin and Child and Two Female Saints

Pen and brown ink, brown wash, over red and black chalk; brown ink border along upper edge and on both sides; upper edge and sides marked for transfer. Lower left corner made up. 7½ x 9 in. (190 x 235 mm). Watermark: None.

PROVENANCE: Francesco Dubini, Milan (Lugt 987a); Dr. Rasini, Milan; by descent to Cesare Rasini, Polynesia, until 1965; Thomas Williams Fine Art Ltd., London, 1997.

LITERATURE: Morassi 1937, p. 25f., pl. 8; Tietze and Tietze-Conrat 1944, p. 154, no. 624; Arslan 1952, p. 109ff.; Laclotte 1956, p. 231, n. 3; Fiocco 1958, p. 33; Lauts 1962, no. 35 (Drawings), pl. 91; Miotti 1962, fig. 31; Pignatti 1963, p. 51; Muraro 1966, pp. 59–60; Zampetti 1966, p. 76; Cancogni and Perocco 1967, p. 95, under no. 22, repr.; Pignatti 1972, no. 24, repr.; Muraro 1977, pp. 59–60, repr.; Sgarbi 1994, p. 162, repr.

EXHIBITIONS: Venice 1963, no. 16, repr.; London 1998, no. I, repr. in color.

Best remembered for his lively narrative cycles for Venetian *scuole* as well as for his religious works of deep sentiment and great originality, Carpaccio is considered among the foremost painters of the fifteenth century in Venice. He was a highly accomplished and prolific draftsman.

The present drawing is Carpaccio's late compositional study for his panel painting of about 1500–1512 depicting the *Virgin and Child with Four Saints* (Fig. 1, now in the Musée du Petit Palais, Avignon, but formerly in the Musée des Beaux-Arts, Caen). For the painting the group in the foreground consisting of the seated Virgin, the Christ Child, John the Baptist, and the two adoring female saints—probably St. Elizabeth and the Magdalene on the left and right, respectively—was expanded to include two flanking male saints.

The complex and somewhat bizarre landscape background provides the setting for three hermit saints, Augustine, Jerome, and one generally identified as Anthony Abbot, all of whom are described with Carpaccio's typical anecdotal detail. Augustine is seen in the distance at center left, standing by the shores of a lake and speaking to the small child that according to legend made him aware of the futility of attempting to understand the Holy Trinity. St. Jerome, recognizable by the accompanying lion, stands on the rocky arch at the upper left; and Anthony Abbot is seated just inside a small hut surmounted by a cross.

Two additional drawings related to the Avignon painting are known, one formerly in

FIG. 1. Vittore Carpaccio, *Virgin and Child with Four Saints*, Musée du Petit Palais, Avignon

the Gathorne-Hardy collection and now in the National Gallery of Art, Washington, D.C. (Lauts 1962, no. 9, [Drawings], pl. 89), the other in the Uffizi, Florence (Lauts 1962, no. 16, [Drawings], pl. 90). Both studies focus almost exclusively on the disposition and interaction of the foreground figures, omitting most of the background. The present drawing is one of the earliest in European art to integrate figures into a finished landscape.

REP

3

DOMENICO CAMPAGNOLA

Venice (?) 1500–1564 Padua

2 *Apocalyptic Scene with Fallen Buildings*

Pen and brown ink, laid down on Udny's mount. 11⅝ x 10¼ in. (296 x 259 mm). Watermark: Encircled mounts surmounted by a cross (?), similar to Briquet 11912 and 11914. Inscribed on the mount in Udny's hand, *Titian;* in Esdaile's hand, *Fall of a City by an Earthquake;* on verso, in Udny's hand, *This a Genuine Drawing of Titian / representing the fall of a City by an / Earthquake.*

PROVENANCE: Robert Udny, London and Teddington, Middlesex (Lugt 2248; his mount); William Esdaile, Clapham Common, London (Lugt 2617); his sale, London, Christie's, 20 June 1840, lot 421, as Titian ("A subject from the Apocalypse, a pen and bistre; from Udney's collection"); sale, London, Christie's, 11–13 December 1985, lot 178, repr. in color as Campagnola; private collection, Boston; Thomas Williams Fine Art Ltd., London, 2000.

LITERATURE: Oppenheim 1986, passim.

EXHIBITION: New York 2000, no. 2, repr. in color.

It seems that by the age of ten the precociously talented Domenico Campagnola already had been apprenticed to (and evidently adopted by) Giulio Campagnola (ca. 1482–after 1515)—a figure of considerable importance in the context of Venetian landscape draftsmanship. Domenico's early drawings naturally reveal a profound debt to the work of his master. They also reflect the direct influence of Titian, with whom he also may have studied, and to whom this drawing was once attributed. After moving to Padua about 1520, Domenico became the leading painter in the city.

This recently acquired sheet may well belong to the 1530s, when Domenico's powers of invention and execution were at their peak. Though evidently an earthquake is represented, the subject is enigmatic. Crowded into the lower third of the sheet is a ruined townscape, void of any sign of human life, with several medieval and Renaissance buildings, such as a fortified tower at center, a basilica and a rusticated palace facade at left, and a domed rotunda reminiscent of Bramante's Tempietto in Rome at right. In the foreground tempestuous waves wash the sinking town. Presumably Campagnola experienced the 1511 Friuli earthquake that also shook Venice and Padua, though Oppenheim notes that the scene is an artist's fantasy rather than a realistic account of such an event (Oppenheim 1986, passim). The drawing may be related to a series of twenty-two studies with scenes from the Apocalypse by the artist preserved at Windsor Castle (Popham and Wilde 1949, nos. 161–82). Recently Martin Clayton noted that the Windsor Apocalypse series and a number of other drawings by Campagnola that have been on the market in recent years are close copies of a fourteenth-century fresco cycle by Giusto de' Menabuoi (flourished 1349–ca. 1390) in the apse of the baptistery in Padua (Clayton, in preparation). He further suggests that the present drawing is a reinterpretation of Giusto's fresco *The Seventh Angel Emptying His Bowl with the Wrath of God Which Causes a Great Earthquake that Divides the Great City (Babylon/Rome) into Three Parts* (Rev. 16:17–20). The corresponding fresco differs quite substantially from the present sheet in depicting a flying angel emptying a cruet onto three distinct heaps of collapsing, rather simplified cubic houses (Lievore 1994, p. 54, fig. 35). Consequently, some doubt as to the proposed connection must remain.

REP

4

5

STEFANO DELLA BELLA

Florence 1610–1664 Florence

3 *A Feast at the Cascine, Florence*

Pen and brown ink, brush and watercolor, accented with gum arabic, touches of white gouache, heightened with gold and silver, over traces of black chalk, on two sheets of paper joined vertically; framing lines in pen and brown ink and brush and brown wash. 10⅞ x 31½ in. (276 x 799 mm). Watermark: None. Signed and dated in pen and brown ink, *SDB/1630.*

PROVENANCE: Carlo Lotteringhi della Stufa, Florence; Bob P. Haboldt & Co., New York and Paris.

LITERATURE: Nugent 1925–30, II, 1930, p. 314; Viatte 1974, p. 9; New York 1995, no. 7, repr.

EXHIBITIONS: Florence 1922, no. 371; Florence 1931, no. 11; Florence 1965, no. 15, repr.; William M. Griswold, in London 1996–97, no. 19, repr.

One of the most talented and prolific Italian draftsmen and printmakers of the seventeenth century, Stefano della Bella trained as a goldsmith prior to entering the workshop of the Florentine painter Giovanni Battista Vanni, probably in 1623. About the same time, Stefano appears to have discovered and begun to emulate the prints of Jacques Callot, a native of Nancy who had been a pupil in Florence of Remigio Cantagallina and subsequently entered the service of Grand Duke Cosimo II. Stefano was only eleven years old when Callot returned to France in 1621. It is therefore unlikely that the two ever met, but Callot's distinctive late mannerist style was to have a tremendous influence upon the work of the younger artist. Stefano's first etching is datable about 1627. Six years later he traveled to Rome to continue his education, and by the time he left Florence for a ten-year sojourn in Paris in 1639, he was an internationally acclaimed, stylistically independent printmaker.

Stefano della Bella produced more than a thousand etchings and several thousand known drawings—most of them relatively small and made in preparation for his prints. This large, brightly colored, and highly finished drawing, executed on two sheets of paper that have been pasted together and heightened with gold and silver, is altogether exceptional in Stefano's oeuvre. Signed and dated 1630, and therefore made three years before the artist's departure for Rome, it is comparable in style and degree of finish to five drawings in Florence, Paris, and Rome, also executed toward the beginning of the artist's career, although on an appreciably smaller scale and in pen and ink on vellum

(Gabinetto Disegni e Stampe, Uffizi, Florence, acc. nos. 5907–8 S; Musée du Louvre, Département des Arts Graphiques, Paris, acc. no. 292; Istituto Nazionale per la Grafica, Rome, acc. no. F.C. 116967; see Viatte 1974, nos. 2–3, repr.; Isola 1976, no. 7, repr.).

The large size and high finish of this sheet imply that it was made as an independent work of art rather than as a study for a print, and its style reflects the breadth of Stefano's visual culture. The individual figures are very close in spirit to those of Callot and betray Stefano's familiarity with that artist's prints. At the same time, however, Stefano's comparatively naturalistic approach to the representation of landscape and his interest in scenes of everyday life, evident in his depictions of the picnickers on the left and the cardplayers on the right, suggests the influence of such contemporary Netherlandish printmakers as Esias van de Velde (Florence 1965, p. 48, under no. 15).

The drawing depicts a company of elegantly dressed men and their entourage engaged in a variety of pleasurable pursuits. In addition to eating, drinking, and playing cards, a number of men play pall-mall, a game akin to croquet that was popular throughout Europe in the first half of the seventeenth century; a strikingly similar depiction of a game of pall-mall by the Dutch artist Adriaen van de Venne is preserved in the British Museum, London (Royalton-Kisch 1988, no. 31, repr.). In Stefano's watercolor the setting may be the Cascine, a park on the outskirts of Florence. If so then the view would be toward Florence, with the Arno River on the right.

WMG

7

GIOVANNI BENEDETTO CASTIGLIONE

Genoa 1609–1664 Genoa

4 *Two Shepherds with a Flock of Sheep*

Brush and red-brown oil paint, partly colored in opaque light blue pigment, heightened with white gouache (partly oxidized), on paper. 15½ x 21 in. (394 x 532 mm). Watermark: None. Inscribed in pen and brown ink at upper center, *17.*

PROVENANCE: Dr. and Mrs. Rudolf J. Heinemann, New York; sale, London, Christie's, 4 July 2000, lot 119, repr. in color.

Arguably the most influential artist in seventeenth-century Genoa, Castiglione was equally important as a painter, draftsman, and printmaker. He is documented as having studied around 1626 with the late mannerist painter Giovanni Battista Paggi (1554–1627) but also may have been a pupil of Anthony van Dyck (1599–1641) in Genoa, thus gaining knowledge of the latter's and Rubens's warmly colored and loosely executed oil sketches. Castiglione's earliest surviving signed and dated work, *Jacob's Journey* (private collection, New York), was painted in 1633 in Rome. In the 1640s the artist returned to Genoa, where, with the exception of another visit to Rome and shorter stays in Mantua at the court of Duke Carlo II Gonzaga and in Venice, he remained until his death. Though Castiglione also received several important commissions for altarpieces, pagan and biblical pastoral scenes executed for private patrons were his specialty. His most commonly treated subjects, such as *Noah Guiding the Animals to the Ark,* the *Flight of the Israelites from Egypt,* and *Abraham Journeying to Canaan,* provided the opportunity to paint picturesque groups of animals, turbaned Orientals, and still-life details. This romantic aspect of his oeuvre anticipates the development of the rococo style as exemplified in the work of Giovanni Battista Tiepolo (1696–1770), François Boucher (1703–1770), and Jean-Honoré Fragonard (1732–1806).

This sheet is typical of the artist's late manner and may have been produced as one of a loosely connected series of drawings on the theme of the pastoral journey, all thought to date from the early 1660s (Philadelphia 1971, p. 125, under no. 114). Several comparable studies are in the royal collection at Windsor (for instance, Blunt 1954, p. 35, no. 111, pl. 14). Another, depicting a *Pastoral Journey with Flocks and Herds at a River,* is in the Metropolitan Museum of Art (New York 1996, p. 43, no. 41, repr.). Castiglione is celebrated for the virtuosity of his brushwork and his characteristic, highly original dry-brush technique. The novel effect was achieved by the oil that saturates the paper, blurring the edges of the brushstrokes and enhancing their subtlety. Here he first sketched the composition with a brush dipped in a mixture of red-brown pigment and linseed oil. Using a higher concentration of pigment, he then reworked the composition, boldly reinforcing outlines with short flicks of the brush. Finally he set off the landscape background by adding patches of light blue and white along the horizon.

REP

Attributed to FRANS SNYDERS

Antwerp 1579–1657 Antwerp

5 *Head of a Bear,* ca. 1625–40

Brush and oil in shades of brown, with touches of red and white, on paper; minor losses in upper left and lower right corners. The support is a page from a ledger written in seventeenth-century Dutch script. 13 x 10½ in. (325 x 250 mm). Watermark: None.

PROVENANCE: Private collector, Paris, purchased ca. 1903; Fred R. Kline Gallery, Santa Fe, 1999.

The bear growls at the viewer, baring large white teeth and powerful jaws. This drawing imparts a decidedly Flemish exuberance that reflects the artist's familiarity with the work of the great animaliers of the period, in particular, that of Frans Snyders. When one compares this work to the lions' heads in Snyders's *Two Young Lions Pursuing a Roebuck* (Fig. 1; Alte Pinakothek, Munich), a painting thought to have been completed in the 1620s, similarities of style and spirit can be clearly observed. Snyders applied the paint in loose, broad strokes and imbued the giant felines with a ferocity that also pervades the present drawing.

The freshness and vigor with which this work was executed suggests that it was invented by the artist and represents his own, highly personal interpretation of a threatening ursine visage. The head, however, is not unique, for it corresponds in considerable detail—particularly in the angle at which it is tilted as well as in its exposed jaws and glistening teeth—to bears' heads in the work of other animal painters of the period, many of whom were well acquainted with Snyders's considerable oeuvre.

The work of Snyders's pupils Jan Fyt (1611–1661) and Pieter Boel (1622–1674) display compelling similarities with this work. A drawing of a bear's head attributed to Fyt in the Hermitage, St. Petersburg (inv. no. 755; Dobroklonsky 1955, p. 157) as well as one of a bear that appears in a copy of Boel's *Still Life with a Swan* (sale, London, Sotheby's, 13 December 1978, lot 257) approximate the present subject. Moreover, as Fred Kline pointed out (correspondence, 19 May 2000), Jan van Kessel used the same prototype in *The Bear and the Honeypot,* one in a series of small paintings illustrating Aesop's fables (sale, New York, Sotheby's, 25 May 2000, lot 108). These examples point strongly toward a prototype that may well have been invented by Snyders himself. Indeed Hella Robels (correspondence, 17 October 1999) and Christopher White (correspondence, 22 July 1999) are inclined toward the view that the drawing is the work of the renowned Flemish master.

The highly unconventional support is a page from a ledger belonging to an unknown merchant. It is covered, recto and verso, in cursive Dutch script that is only partly legible (see Appendix A for a transcription). According to the historian of art and economics Michael Montias, the script yields interesting, albeit fragmentary, information. The unnamed Amsterdam

FIG. 1. Frans Snyders, *Two Young Lions Pursuing a Roebuck* (detail), Alte Pinakothek, Munich

merchant to whom the ledger belonged owned what would be called a dry-goods wholesale business today. He sold various commodities, including a variety of types of cloth and rope and other unidentifiable goods, in Nuijs, Nijmegen, and Venlo, and conducted business with several members of Amsterdam's commercial community. Among the merchants named is Pieter Jacobsz. De Goijer, whose death on 12 February 1636 provides a terminus ante quem for the page prior to its use by the artist (Montias, verbal communication, 4 January 2002). How it came into the possession of an Antwerp artist is a question that may never be settled.

EH-B

REMBRANDT HARMENSZ. VAN RIJN

Leiden 1606–1669 Amsterdam

6 *The Bulwark De Rose and the Windmill De Smeerpot in Amsterdam*

Pen and brown ink, brown wash, on light brown-toned paper; some delicately scraped highlights to the roof at the left; framing lines in brown ink along lower edge and on both sides. 5¼ x 8 9/16 in. (134 x 218 mm). Watermark: Fragment of an orb surmounted by three crosses. Numbered on verso in graphite at lower center, *51 HoleG. 845.*

PROVENANCE: N. A. Flinck, Rotterdam (Lugt 959), ca. 1660; William Cavendish, second or third duke of Devonshire, Chatsworth House, Derbyshire, 1723 or 1754; by descent within the family; Trustees of the Chatsworth Settlement (inv. no. 1031); their sale, London, Christie's, 3 July 1984, lot 65, repr. in color (to Richard Day Ltd. for Currier); Michael S. Currier, Santa Fe, 1984; his sale, New York, Christie's, 28 January 1999, lot 114, repr. in color.

LITERATURE: Lippmann 1882–92, I, no. 57; Michel 1893, p. 485; Hofstede de Groot 1906, no. 845; Lugt 1915, pp. 138–77, pl. 70; Lugt 1920, pp. 76–77, fig. 37; Benesch 1935, p. 42; Benesch 1954–57, VI, no. 1263, fig. 1490; Thompson 1957, no. 1031, repr.; Slive 1965, I, no. 57; Brussels and elsewhere 1968–69, under no. 116; Benesch 1973, VI, no. 1263, fig. 1569; Broos 1981, p. 132, n. 7.

EXHIBITIONS: London 1929, no. 605; Manchester 1961, no. 92; Washington and elsewhere 1962–63, no. 92, repr.; London 1964, no. 110, repr.; Amsterdam 1969, no. 93, repr.; Washington 1990, no. 65, repr. in color; Amsterdam and Paris 1998–99, pp. 196–97, repr. pp. 113 (in color) and 198.

One of an unparalleled group of twenty-seven landscape drawings by Rembrandt formerly in the collection of the dukes of Devonshire at Chatsworth, this superb sheet is arguably the finest of the drawings by the artist in both the Thaw and Morgan collections. This series of landscape drawings, which must have survived together in an album in the artist's studio until his death, passed into the collection of Nicolaes Flinck (1646–1723), whose mark appears at the lower left of the present sheet. He inherited his collection of some five hundred drawings from his father, Rembrandt's pupil Govaert Flinck (1615–1660). In 1723 the second duke of Devonshire bought drawings directly from Nicolaes Flinck. The group of Rembrandt landscape drawings, which may actually have been purchased only in 1754 by the third duke (since they lack the second duke's collector's mark), remained intact for more than two centuries, until a dozen sheets were dispersed at auction at the Chatsworth sales of 1984 and 1987.

Frits Lugt identified the present drawing as a panoramic view from the top of the Amsterdam city wall (a 5-kilometer earthen rampart covered with grass), facing southwest, toward the bulwark De Rose. This bulwark is the last of a series of three bastions on the southwest side of Amsterdam, situated just where the fortifications begin to curve toward the north.

On the right is an old-fashioned mill, popularly called De Smeerpot (the Grease Pot) in Rembrandt's time. Built in 1614 as a corn mill and renamed De Vechter (the Fighter) in 1630, it was used to grind rye and wheat when Rembrandt recorded it. It was an example of what is termed a post-mill; unlike the more modern tower mill, it did not have a movable cap. In order to face the wind, the entire upper section of its wooden body had to be

13

turned using the wooden poles or struts so deftly indicated by Rembrandt's quick pen strokes.

At the center and lower right, immediately to the left of De Smeerpot, are two groups of houses, both set, like the mill, below the level of the bulwark and city wall, so that only the tops of the roofs of the group closest to the viewer are visible. From a position farther along the city wall, Rembrandt studied both groups of houses from a closer viewpoint in a drawing in the Museum of Fine Arts, Budapest (ca. 1649–52; see Benesch 1954–57, VI, no. 1264, fig. 1491 [1973 ed., fig. 1570]).

On the left of the present drawing is a long, low, shedlike building with one or two doors providing access to a footpath that ran along the inner base of the entire city wall. This shed was built about the same time as the mill and was part of a rope factory situated on the canal named after it, the Lijnbaansgracht. The lower footpath, closed to traffic at the end by a long pole, is cast in shadow by the darkly washed roofs and walls of the western facade of the factory building (or ropewalk), which also sits below the level of the city wall. In the distance, Rembrandt placed two small figures along the high horizon to impart a sense of scale and context to the competing levels and elements of the composition as well as to emphasize the spatial recession. In the far right, to the right of the central group of houses, one can just glimpse the roof of the Pesthuis (Plague House) on Overtoomsevaart, directly south of the city.

Experts agree on a date of ca. 1649–52 for the present drawing. Its remarkable freshness and its quick but confident handling—with a complete lack of corrections in white gouache—suggest that it was made on the spot. In the fluid treatment of wash and economical use of line and blank areas of paper (unmarred by later additions), it is comparable to other virtuoso Chatsworth landscapes of around 1650, such as the *View of the Bend in the Amstel near Kostverloren* and the *View on the Amsteldijk near the Trompenburg Estate*, both still in the collection of the duke of Devonshire (see Washington 1990, nos. 67 and 69, both repr. in color).

JST

PHILIPS KONINCK

Amsterdam 1619–1688 Amsterdam

7 *Flat Panoramic Landscape with Scattered Farm Buildings and a Windmill*

Pen and brown ink, brown wash, and watercolor washes in shades of green, gray-blue, rose, and yellow, over faint indications in black chalk; framing line in brown ink. 4⅝ x 9 ⁷/₁₆ in. (117 x 240 mm). Watermark: Strasburg lily above the letters *WR* (similar to Briquet 7210: Neuweilnau 1585). Signed and dated on verso in red chalk at upper right, *p – ko 1671;* numbered in graphite at lower left, *216*.

PROVENANCE: Thomas Dimsdale, London (Lugt 2426); possibly Samuel Woodburn, London (no mark; see Lugt 2584); possibly his sale, London, Christie's, 17 June 1854, lot 418 (to Marzen for 3 guineas); J. E. Fordham, Melbourn Bury, near Royston, Cambridgeshire; his sale, London, Christie's, 9 April 1910, lot 89 (to Sabin for 30 guineas); sale, Amsterdam, Frederik Muller and Co., 11–14 June 1912, lot 136, repr.; princes of Liechtenstein, Vaduz; Galerie Feilchenfeldt, Zurich, 1949; Prof. Leopold Ruzicka, Zurich; Dr. and Mrs. Rudolf J. Heinemann, New York; their sale, London, Christie's, 1 July 1997, lot 211, repr. in color.

LITERATURE: Gerson 1936, pp. 66, 139, no. Z.7; Sumowski 1979–92, VI, no. 1363, repr., and under nos. 1509ˣ, 1510ˣ, and 1513ˣ; Broos 1981, under no. 44, n. 10; Paris 1993, under no. 63 (incorrectly conflating a reference to the present sheet with a chronologically related drawing in the Albertina, Vienna).

EXHIBITIONS: Zurich 1949–50, no. R 53, not in catalogue; New York 1973, no. 6, repr.; Cambridge and Montreal 1988, no. 51, repr.

Signed with the artist's monogram and dated 1671, this panoramic view of Dutch lowlands is typical of Koninck's late period, when he frequently resumed the use of watercolor washes, a technique first employed by him in the 1640s. Compared with the more abstract and graphic landscapes presumed to have been executed early in his career, drawings made during the last two decades of his life, such as the present sheet, have dark brown washes that are applied so broadly that they tend to obscure the underlying pen lines. The result is a landscape drawing with a profound sense of depth and space— one that is far more pictorial than the earlier views—a sweeping panorama as impressive as the idealized Dutch landscape paintings that constituted Koninck's most important contribution to seventeenth-century Dutch art.

This drawing features a standard compositional formula that also was developed and perfected in the artist's early work. Cut midway by the horizon line, such compositions divide into two halves, with the sky above and a broad, flat landscape below. The countryside is depicted from a slightly elevated viewpoint and is structured by contrasting areas of darks and lights as well as an alternating pattern of horizontals and diagonals (usually a river or canal winding toward the distant horizon), often with one central structure, like the windmill here, piercing the horizon line very slightly. The windmill is comparable, for example, to the silhouetted church tower in *Panoramic Landscape with Travelers,* a signed and dated painting of 1647, in the Victoria and Albert Museum, London (see Sumowski 1983–90, III, no. 1043, repr.). As he did with watercolor, Koninck regularly returned in the 1670s to this early compositional solution. In this case the dark *repoussoir* of the foreground helps draw the eye toward the brightly lit canal and fields in the distance.

Although Koninck's panoramas, both painted and drawn, are assumed to be imaginary rather than actual views, many are reminiscent of the landscape of Gelderland. Gerson and Sumowski have compared the present view with other panoramic landscape drawings from the 1670s in the British Museum, London (see Sumowski 1979–92, VI, no. 1509ˣ, repr.), the Museum der bildenden Kunst, Leipzig (see Sumowski 1979–92, VI, no. 1510ˣ, repr., and Paris 1993, no. 63, repr.), the Musée Condé, Chantilly (see Sumowski 1979–92, VI, no. 1513ˣ, repr.), and the Albertina, Vienna (see Sumowski 1979–92, VI, no. 1511ˣ, repr.). Sumowski further called attention to an apparently autograph replica of the present composition, formerly on the Amsterdam art market (sale, Amsterdam, Sotheby's, 14 November 1988, lot 121, repr.).

Unlike the three signed drawings by Philips Koninck in the Library, which bear traces of his signature in pen and ink on the verso (acc. nos. I, 213c; I, 213; and I, 213b), this example carries his characteristic monogram in red chalk, which he used as a mark of both authorship and ownership.

JST

GERBRAND VAN DEN EECKHOUT

Amsterdam 1621–1674 Amsterdam

8 *Seated Youth in a Hat, with His Chin Cupped in His Left Hand*

Brush and brown wash; framing line in brown ink. Water damage at lower left. 5⅝ x 4⁷/₁₆ in. (142 x 112 mm). Watermark: None. Numbered on verso in graphite, *162*.

PROVENANCE: Jacob de Vos Jbᶻⁿ, Amsterdam (Lugt 1450 on verso); his sale, Amsterdam, Roos, Frederik Muller & Co., 22–24 May 1883, lot 162; Pieter Langerhuizen Lᶻⁿ, "Crailoo," near Bussum, the Netherlands (Lugt 2095); his sale, Amsterdam, Frederik Muller & Co., 29 April–1 May 1919, lot 257, repr. (to Goldschmidt for 1350 fl.); Adolph Goldschmidt, Berlin and Basel, 1919; sale, New York, Christie's, 12 January 1995, lot 253, repr. in color; Bob P. Haboldt & Co., New York and Paris, 1995.

LITERATURE: Lugt 1921, p. 389; Henkel 1942, under no. 10 (the model identified as Titus, ca. 1655); sale, London, Sotheby's, 21 May 1963, under lot 33; Rotterdam and Paris 1974, under no. 33; New York and Paris 1977–78, under no. 35; Sumowski 1979–92, III, no. 782ˣ, repr.; Frankfurt 2000, under no. 49.

EXHIBITIONS: Chicago and elsewhere 1969–70, no. 167, repr. (ca. 1650–60); London 1996–97, no. 18, repr. in color.

This drawing, executed entirely with the brush, belongs to a unique group of at least seventeen drawings in exactly the same style and medium, most of them representing a single male figure in one of various poses (e.g., seated, smoking, reading). To the sixteen sheets published by Sumowski (1979–92, III, nos. 782ˣ–97ˣ, all repr.) can be added a drawing of a *Youth Carrying a Basket,* now in the Städelsches Kunstinstitut, Frankfurt-am-Main (see Frankfurt 2000, no. 49, repr.). As has been noted by several scholars, the unusual technique, with its exquisitely modulated tones of brown wash, may have been inspired by brush drawings by Rembrandt, such as the *Sleeping Hendrikje,* ca. 1655, in the British Museum, London (see Benesch 1954–57, V, no. 1103, fig. 1323 [1973 ed., fig. 1394]). Rembrandt, however, used his brush, which he allowed to run dry, almost as if it were a pen with a broad nib. By contrast, the liquid effects achieved by the washes in the present drawing and related sheets are entirely different in character and artistic intention. On the evidence of costumes, Sumowski dated the entire group of brush drawings to ca. 1655, exactly contemporary with Rembrandt's drawing of Hendrikje.

The same model as in the present sheet, in identical costume and very similarly posed, appears in another, somewhat larger drawing from the group, formerly in the collection of Mr. and Mrs. Walter C. Baker and now in the Metropolitan Museum of Art, New York (see Sumowski 1979–92, III, no. 783ˣ, repr.). What may well have been one of these two sheets was included in the Goll van Franckenstein sale (Amsterdam, de Vries, 1 July 1833, Album Q, lot 16): *"Een Jongeling, rustende met het hoofd op de linkerhand. Meesterlijk met bruine inkt, door G. VAN DEN EEKHOUT."* It was bought for 43 fl. by Samuel Woodburn, a known source of drawings for Jacob de Vos Jbᶻⁿ, the first certain owner of the present study (who also possessed the Metropolitan version, which figured as lot 161 of his sale). The artist's rendering of the youth's left hand is especially effective in the Thaw rendition: he added a ring to provide another point of focus and cleverly left the paper blank in parallel streaks to

convey the folds of the skin in the figure's bent-back wrist. One wonders if the subject, with his subtly smiling eyes directed straight at the viewer, might not have been trying to stifle a grin—an impression all the more compelling when he is compared with the daydreaming youth in the Metropolitan drawing, who stares blankly, absorbed in his thoughts. The young man seen carrying a basket on his shoulder in the new drawing in Frankfurt is most likely the same model.

None of the known drawings in this technique is signed, dated, or directly connected with a painting, but there is considerable evidence to support the traditional attribution to van den Eeckhout, which dates to at least the third quarter of the eighteenth century, when two drawings from the group appeared in Dutch auctions under his name. More-over, two other drawings—the related study in the Metropolitan Museum and the *Boy Reading,* now in the Musée Cognac-Jay, Paris (see Sumowski 1979–92, III, no. 788[x], repr.)—were reproduced as color facsimiles commissioned by Cornelis Ploos van Amstel (1726–1798) from Juriaan Cootwijk (1714–1798). These were published by Christian Josi (before 1765–1828) in the *Collection d'imitations de dessins d'après les principaux maîtres hollandais et fla-mands, commencé par C. Ploos van Amstel . . .* (Josi 1821), his supplementary edition of Ploos van Amstel's famous *Prentwerk,* which appeared in Amsterdam between 1765 and 1787.

The drawings are also stylistically compatible with several other sheets attributable to van den Eeckhout, and similar figures appear in the artist's paintings from the early to mid-1650s. Especially comparable is the signed *Study of a Sleeping Boy,* in the Rijksprentenk-abinet, Amsterdam (see Sumowski 1979–92, III, no. 634, repr.), which is executed in black chalk and gray wash. Sumowski's dismissal of this last stylistic connection, based on dif-ferences of medium, seems unfounded.

JST

JACOB (ISAACSZ.) VAN RUISDAEL

Haarlem 1628/9–1682 Amsterdam

9 *Ruined Cottage*

Black chalk, brush and gray wash; framing line in black ink. 7⅞ x 10¾ in. (200 x 275 mm). Watermark: Foolscap, seven-pointed collar atop an inverted *4* and three rings (cf. Heawood 2036, pl. 290). Signed with the artist's monogram in point of brush and gray wash at lower right, *JVR* (ligated).

PROVENANCE: Sybrand I Feitama, Amsterdam, or his son, Isaac Feitama, Amsterdam; the latter's son, Sybrand II Feitama, Amsterdam, 1709; his sale, Amsterdam, de Bosch, 16 October 1758, Album L, lot 44 (to Hoet for 25 fl.); Gerard Hoet the Younger, The Hague, 1758; his sale, The Hague, Franken and Thol, 25–28 August 1760, Album M, lot 801 (to IJver for 25 fl.); Johan Goll van Franckenstein the Elder, Amsterdam, ca. 1760; his son, Johan Goll van Franckenstein the Younger, Amsterdam (no mark; see Lugt 2987), 1785; his son, Pieter Hendrik Goll van Franckenstein, Amsterdam, 1821; his sale, Amsterdam, de Vries, 1 July 1833, Album S, lot 9 (to Hulswit for 90 fl.); Hendrick van Cranenburgh, Amsterdam; his sale, Amsterdam, Roos, 26 October 1858, Album B, lot 30 (bought for 61 fl.); Emile Galichon, Paris (no mark; see Lugt 1058–59); his sale, Paris, Hôtel Drouot, 10–14 May 1875, lot 143 (to Galichon for 415 fr.); Louis Galichon, Paris (Lugt 1060), 1875; his sale, Paris, Danlos, 4–9 March 1895, lot 146 (bought for 520 fr.); J. P. Heseltine, London (Lugt 1507); his sale, London, Sotheby's, 27–29 May 1935, lot 193 (to Reitlinger for £7.00); H. S. Reitlinger, London (Lugt S. 2274ᵃ), 1935; his sale, London, Sotheby's, 22–23 June 1954, lot 699; Curtis O. Baer, New Rochelle, ca. 1954; his daughter, Yvette Baer, Atlanta, 1976.

LITERATURE: Feitama 1746–58, no. 1297 ("*1 Bouwvallige schuur, omtr. Aᵒ 1670. Op dezelfde Notitie* ['*op oudste Notitie, omtr. Aᵒ 1690 gesteld op*']"; valued at 3.0.0 fl.); Josi 1821, II, n.p. (under "J. van Ruysdael"); de Vries 1915, no. 126; Huffel 1921, no. 144; Lugt 1921, p. 186; Giltay 1980, no. 15, repr.; Broos 1987, p. 210; Davies 1992, pp. 75–76, repr.; Slive 2001, no. D95, repr., and p. 654.

EXHIBITIONS: Cambridge 1958, no. 33; Poughkeepsie 1976, no. 41, repr.; Washington and elsewhere 1977, no. 71, repr.; The Hague and Cambridge 1981–82, no. 71, repr.; Washington and elsewhere 1985–87, no. 42, repr.

Van Ruisdael was particularly interested in themes of growth, decay, mortality, and re-birth, which he explored through hidden or explicit emblematic subject matter. The present picturesque motif of a crumbling cottage, for instance, has been interpreted as a symbol of the transience of life and the futility of human effort. Although the drawing, dated ca. 1653–55 by Jeroen Giltay, probably was made in preparation for a painting of the subject, no such work by van Ruisdael has been traced. An original oil version of the composition by the artist must have existed, however, as is suggested by the survival of at least four painted copies: one by Emanuel Murant (1622–ca. 1700) in the Rijksmuseum, Amsterdam (see Amsterdam 1976, p. 403, repr.), and three anonymous later copies, one formerly in the Museum of Fine Arts, Boston, and now in the collection of Warren R. Walker, London (see Slive 2001, no. dub120, repr.), another in the Musée des Beaux-Arts, Nîmes (see Nîmes 1940, no. 374), and the last with the dealer Douwes in Amsterdam in 1926 (possibly identical with versions with the dealer Vitale Bloch, The Hague, in 1964 and with the Munich dealer Julius Böhler in 1969). Some of the later painted copies may, however, have been based on the color facsimile (*prenttekening*) of the present work en-graved by Cornelis Brouwer (1733?–1803), who was employed by Cornelis Ploos van Ams-tel (1726–1798) on his famous *Prentwerk* project from 1775. While not among the original forty-five facsimiles published by Ploos in Amsterdam between 1765 and 1787, it was one of eight additional prints by Brouwer included in Christian Josi's supplemental edition, the *Collection d'imitations de dessins d'après les principaux maîtres hollandais et flamands, commencé par C. Ploos van Amstel . . .* (Josi 1821; see Laurentius et al. 1980, no. 110).

This sheet is one of an important group of thirty-eight drawings by van Ruisdael that belonged to the well-known Dutch collector Sybrand II Feitama (1694–1758). It features, as no. 1297, in Sybrand's manuscript *Notitie der teekingen van Sybrand Feitama* (1746–58; Rijskbureau voor Kunsthistorische Documentatie, The Hague), among a dozen drawings by van Ruisdael acquired by his grandfather Sybrand I Feitama (1620–1701) or possibly his father, Isaac Feitama (1666–1709). The twelve drawings came into the family collection in or before 1690, some of them possibly from Dirck Dalens (1657–1687), who may have acquired them directly from the artist's estate after his death in 1682.

It is evident from the detailed descriptions in Sybrand's *Notitie* that in the last years of the seventeenth century and the early years of the eighteenth, both the elder and younger Sybrand (and probably Isaac) commissioned artists to "embellish" the van Ruisdael drawings (as well as sheets by other artists in the collection) with the addition of figures, wash foregrounds or backgrounds, or monograms. The "creative" transformation of drawings, which were often referred to as *opgemaakt* (finished) or *verbeterd* (improved) in early-eighteenth-century sale catalogues, was then a common practice, since contemporary collectors considered sketchy or unwashed drawings to be incomplete and therefore less valuable (Broos 1989, p. 37). Eight of the drawings by van Ruisdael in the Feitama collection were described as *opgemaakt* in the *Notitie;* Giltay suspects that many more may have undergone such "finishing touches." Indeed, the three tiny marginal figures on the lower left and center right of the present sheet may have been drawn by another hand. Among the artists responsible for such "improvements" were Dalens, Dirck Maas (1656–1717), Isaac de Moucheron (1667–1744), Johannes Verkolje (1650–1693), and Simon Fokke (1712–1784). That the staffage is different in all four later painted copies would seem to confirm that van Ruisdael's original composition lacked figures.

JST

CLAUDE GELLÉE, called CLAUDE LORRAIN

Chamagne, near Mirecourt, 1600–1682 Rome

10 *View of Rome from Sta Croce in Gerusalemme*

Black chalk. 7⅛ x 10¾ in. (181 x 260 mm). Watermark: None.

PROVENANCE: Prince Don Livio Odescalchi, nephew of Pope Innocent XI (cited in Odescalchi's inventory of 1713, p. 69, part of the parchment-bound album described as "Altro libro in foglio coperto di carta pecora con ottant'uno disegni di Claudio Gellé Lorenese"—see Roethlisberger 1968, I, p. 55); by descent; Georges Wildenstein, 1960; Norton Simon, Pasadena, 1968.

LITERATURE: Roethlisberger 1962, no. 21, repr.; Roethlisberger 1962a, pp. 139, 147, repr.; Roethlisberger 1968, I, no. 449, II, repr.; Roethlisberger 1971, no. 4, pl. 4 in color.

EXHIBITIONS: Princeton and elsewhere 1973, no. 4; Tokyo 1998, no. 69, p. III, repr.; New York 2000–2001, no catalogue.

The style of this nature study suggests that it was part of the artist's Tivoli sketchbook, so called because it was the book Claude took with him on sketching trips to Tivoli during these relatively early years in Rome. Around the time of the artist's death, some of his sketchbooks were disbound and a selection of the best individual sheets were placed in a special album, known as the Odescalchi Album because it was in the collection of the Odescalchi family in Rome. This album originally was composed of sixty leaves, including twenty-four nature studies, twenty-one compositional studies, and fifteen figure drawings. Not only are they among the artist's best drawings, they have a remarkable freshness and immediacy owing to their preservation in the album for almost three centuries. This particular sheet, which is the most recently acquired drawing by Claude in the Thaw Collection, is the third to have come from the Odescalchi Album. The earlier two acquisitions were *Heroic Landscape* and *David and the Three Heroes* (repr. New York 1994, nos. 22–23). Unlike these highly finished, large drawings, the view of Rome was executed with an almost modern economy of means. It is also one of Claude's very rare urban panoramic views. Marcel Roethlisberger (1962, no. 21) has identified the view as follows: To the right of the apse of Sta Croce are the ruins of the ancient Sessorium, and to the left, those of the Amphitheatre Castrense. The dome of SS. Marcellino e Pietro, the Colosseum, the Senate's palace, and the dome of St. Peter's can just be made out in the distance. A second sketch on the top of the sheet is a broadly sketched view of the Campagna. The artist took more interest in the panorama of the city.

This sheet—the twelfth work by this artist to be acquired for the Thaw Collection—most likely dates to the late 1630s. During this period the artist drew extensively from nature, going to Tivoli or into the Campagna with sketching parties composed of other artists in Rome, including Nicolas Poussin (1594–1665), Joachim van Sandrart (1606–1688), and Pietro da Cortona (1596–1669).

CDD

FRANÇOIS DESPORTES

Champigneule 1661–1743 Paris

11   *Study of a Pointer*

Oil on paper prepared with a brown oil wash, laid down on canvas. 25¼ x 18⅞ in. (641 x 479 mm). Watermark: None visible through lining.

PROVENANCE: Sale, Paris, Palais Galliera, 30 May 1973, lot 8, repr.; Claus Virch, Paris; Adrian Ward-Jackson, London, 1981; Jean de Bestegui, Paris; Adrian Ward-Jackson, London.

Often credited with adding a Flemish influence to French baroque art, the renowned still-life and animal painter Desportes was trained in the atelier of Nicasius Bernaerts (1620–1678), who had studied with Frans Snyders (No. 5), directly linking Snyders's style with that of Desportes. Desportes first distinguished himself painting portraits at the Polish court. After the death of King John III Sobieski in 1696, however, he returned to France. In 1699 he was received into the Académie with his *Self-Portrait as a Hunter,* now in the Louvre. An unusual *morceau de réception* in which the artist depicted himself with his favorite dog, the work nevertheless attracted the attention of Louis XIV, who in 1700 commissioned Desportes to make portraits of his own favorite hunting dogs. These portraits, commissioned for Marly, were completed in 1702 and now hang in the Musée de la Chasse et de la Nature, Paris. In order to depict the dogs as naturally as possible, Desportes took up hunting and accompanied the king in the forests around Versailles, Fontainebleau, and Marly. The artist became the premier animal painter in France and popularized this typically Flemish genre among the upper echelons of French society. His work provided the impetus and inspiration for younger artists such as Jean-Baptiste Oudry (1686–1755). His popularity was so widespread that he remained in England for six months when he delivered some still lifes to the earl of Stanhope in 1712.

At his death Desportes left some two thousand paintings as well as numerous pencil drawings and oil sketches made directly from nature. More than six hundred were purchased in 1784 by the comte d'Angivillier, then directeur des bâtiments du roi under Louis XVI, for study at the porcelain factory at Sèvres. The most remarkable of these are oil sketches of landscapes and animals made as preparations for the artist's hunting scenes, a broad selection of which formed the basis of an exhibition in the early 1980s (Paris 1982–83). Painted directly from nature, in the immediate vicinity of Paris and the Seine valley, these works are extraordinarily immediate, fresh in color, and uncomposed. In fact more oil sketches than drawings have survived, attesting to Desportes's preference for color, which

FIG. 1. François Desportes, *Dogs, Dead Game, and Fruit,* The Wallace Collection, London

26

was commented upon by Dézallier d'Argenville: "Les études que Desportes a faites d'après nature sont coloriées, parce qu'il ne croyoit pas moins nécessaire d'étudier la vraie couleur des objets, que leur forme" (A.-J. Dézallier d'Argenville, *Abrégé de la vie des plus fameux peintres,* 1748).

This remarkably vivid oil sketch is the artist's preparation for the painting *Dogs, Dead Game, and Fruit,* now in the Wallace Collection, London (cf. Ingamells 1985–92, III, P594, p. 138f., repr.), a work signed and dated by the artist 1715 (Fig. 1). A barking spaniel is seen at the left of the painting, while the pointer appears at the right, apparently guarding and enjoying the sight of a set piece of dead game and fruit in the center. The painting is one of a pair of works by the artist that Richard Wallace bought in 1857 at the sale of Théodore Paureau of Brussels. The other piece, of the same name, is similar in size and subject. At the time of their purchase Lord Hertford described them as "a little rubbish for the country . . . beautiful of the sort and perfect for my shooting place" (Ingamells 1985–92, III, P623, p. 141f., repr.).

CDD

GIOVANNI PAOLO PANINI

Piacenza 1691/92–1765 Rome

12 *Piazza San Pietro and the Vatican Palace from the Colonnade of St. Peter's*

Pen and brown ink, brush and brown wash, watercolor, and white gouache, over traces of black chalk. 9⅝ x 6 9/16 in. (245 x 166 mm). Watermark: None visible through lining. Inscribed in pen and brown ink on eighteenth-century mount, *J. P. Pannini,* and in pen and black ink, *Sub porticibus S." Petri plateam amplectentibus.*

PROVENANCE: Pierre-Jean Mariette (Lugt 1852 or 2097 and 2859 without cartouche); sale, Monte Carlo, Christie's Monaco, 20 June 1994, no. 4, repr.

EXHIBITIONS: New York 1994, not in catalogue; London 1996–97, no. 32, repr. in color.

The foremost Roman painter of real and imaginary architectural views, Panini produced numerous depictions of St. Peter's and of Piazza San Pietro, located just in front of the basilica. These include various views of the interior of the building (Arisi 1986, nos. 188, 200, 212, 217, 280–81, 309, 407, 447–50, 473, repr.) and its atrium (Arisi 1986, nos. 399, 406, repr.) as well as a number of paintings of the piazza and its vast colonnade by Gianlorenzo Bernini, with the facade of St. Peter's, designed by Carlo Maderno at the beginning of the seventeenth century, in the background (Arisi 1986, nos. 308, 443, 445, 472, 476, repr.). Other very similar views of Piazza San Pietro and the facade of St. Peter's appear in both versions of the artist's celebrated *Vedute di Roma moderna,* in the Museum of Fine Arts, Boston, and the Metropolitan Museum of Art, New York (Arisi 1986, nos. 471, 475, repr.). The present watercolor, which exhibits numerous pentimenti, differs from Panini's other known depictions of the piazza in that the view is taken from beneath the colonnade, looking toward the Vatican Palace, rather than toward the facade of the basilica.

Although the blue mount would appear to be that of the great eighteenth-century amateur Pierre-Jean Mariette, the drawing does not seem to have been among the thirty-five sheets attributed to Panini and described in some detail in the catalogue of the 1775 sale of Mariette's legendary collection (nos. 548–74). Two other drawings by Panini from Mariette's collection—a pair of imaginary views of Roman ruins with figures standing amid well-known pieces of antique sculpture, both of which similarly retain their original eighteenth-century mounts—also are in the collection of the Morgan Library (acc. nos. 1982.18.1–2; New York 1995a, nos. 43a–b, repr.; the drawings are fully described under lot 567 in the Mariette sale catalogue).

WMG

J.P. Pannini.

JEAN-ÉTIENNE LIOTARD

Geneva 1702–1789 Geneva

13 *Portrait of Maria Josepha, Fürstin von Clary und Aldringen*

Red and black chalk, heightened with white chalk. 11 ^{11}/16 x 9⅝ in. (297 x 245 mm). Watermark: None.

PROVENANCE: Sale, New York, Sotheby's, 9 January 1996, lot 51, repr.; Bob P. Haboldt & Co., New York and Paris, 1996.

Gifted as a portraitist, Liotard was known as "le peintre de vérité." His pastel portraits were in great demand throughout Europe, and he traveled extensively, most notably to Constantinople, where he lived for four years. During that time he made many pastel portraits of the members of the British colony, acquired a taste for Turkish dress, and grew a long beard. Twice he visited the imperial court in Vienna, where he produced a series of portraits of the empress Maria Theresa and her children. This portrait of the Fürstin von Clary und Aldringen was made during his second stay in Vienna, in the early 1760s. His sitter, by birth the Gräfin von Hohenzollern-Hechingen (1728–1801), then in her mid-thirties, was serving as lady-in-waiting to the empress. She had married Franz Wenzel, Fürst von Clary und Aldringen, in 1747. As this work demonstrates, Liotard's flawless technique is matched by the ability to portray his sitters realistically while conveying a sense of refinement and charm.

In a number of Liotard's portraits, the sitter is depicted half length, enabling the artist to study the countenance and character as well as the costume of his subject. Liotard's subjects are often depicted seated at a table; see, for example, the study of Liotard's elder son, Jean-Étienne, now in a private collection, Geneva, in which the young man is depicted in profile taking some butter for his bread (repr. Geneva and Paris 1992, no. 135). Many of these drawings are executed in a rather firm outline of red or black chalk, sometimes in a combination of both, such as the portrait of the celebrated dancer Mlle Camargo, now in the Albertina, Vienna, or the portrait of a young woman from Utrecht (Geneva and Paris 1992, nos. 95, p. 172, repr. in color and no. 99, p. 180, repr.).

Here, the Fürstin von Clary und Aldringen has just set her fan on the table before her. The artist used a warm cream-colored paper to suggest the sitter's flesh tones. This is heightened by the use of white chalk for her cap and gown as well as the cloth covering the table. Liotard's use of the *trois-crayons* method is unique to his touch. The red chalk outlines the sitter's face and gown. Black is used for the ribbon around her neck, the lace of her gown, the outline of her coiffure, the edge of her cap, her eyes and eyebrows, and the fan on the table. White was applied heavily for her powdered hair, the chair back and tablecloth; it was applied lightly to her face and throat to suggest the face powder she undoubtedly used.

CDD

30

ÉTIENNE-LOUIS BOULLÉE

Paris 1728–1799 Paris

14 *Interior of a Library*

Pen and black and some brown ink, gray wash, over faint traces of black chalk; compass point at center; ruled borders in pen and black ink at outer margin and framing design area. Full sheet: 15⅞ x 25⅝ in. (420 x 653 mm); design area: 15½ x 25 5/16 in. (394 x 644 mm). Watermark: *D & C Blauw / IV* (cf. Heawood 3268).

PROVENANCE: Possibly bequeathed to P. N. Bernard; sale, Paris, Hôtel Drouot, 20 December 1982; private collection, Paris; sale, Paris, Drouot-Richelieu, 15 December 1993, lot 31, repr.; Bob P. Haboldt & Co., New York and Paris.

LITERATURE: Aaron 1985, p. 95, no. 98 (as private collection), repr. in color; Lévêque 1987, p. 274 (as private collection), repr. in color; Pérouse de Montclos 1994, p. 258; *Morgan Library Annual Report* 1995, repr. on cover.

EXHIBITIONS: New York 1994, exhibition only; London 1996–97, no. 25, repr.

Since most of his commissioned architectural works are no longer extant, the architect Boullée is best known for a group of a hundred imaginative and rather grandiose designs that he left to the Bibliothèque nationale, Paris. Most of these drawings are very large, and the group includes Boullée's designs for the expansion of the royal library. Although he was commissioned in 1780, his rather startling and highly innovative plans for the project were never realized. He set forth his ideas in 1785 in a short treatise, "Mémoire sur les moyens de procurer à la Bibliothèque du roi les avantages que ce monument exige," in which he explained:

> My design would transform a courtyard, 300 feet long and 90 feet wide, into an immense basilica lighted from above. . . . For it seems that nothing could be more grand, more noble, more magnificent in appearance than a vast amphitheater of books. Imagine, in this vast amphitheater, disposed in tiers, attendants spread about so that they could pass the books, from hand to hand. Service would be quick as the request, not to mention that this would avoid the dangers that often result from the use of ladders.

Also quite large, the present drawing—a variant of the design in the Bibliothèque nationale—is about two thirds the size of the other, which measures 24⅞ x 38 9/16 in. (630 x 980 mm). Although at first glance it appears to be an exact replica, a number of variations may be observed. For example, while most of the attendants situated on the many levels of the library appear in both drawings, the present one includes two additional figures under the arch at the lower right corner. The skylight is different, and the books are neatly arranged in two rows; for the most part they lean at odd angles in the Bibliothèque nationale drawing. To accentuate the deep vaultlike space, Boullée used subtle gradations of gray wash, casting the lefthand side of the chamber into shadow, while light, apparently emanating from the skylight, throws the righthand side into vivid, almost hyperreal, relief.

Given the grand scale of Boullée's late projects, it is not surprising that his designs were never executed. In fact he never intended them to be more than theoretical illustrations for his "Essai sur l'art," the manuscript of which is also in the Bibliothèque nationale (Fonds français no. 9153; for the published edition, see Pérouse de Montclos 1968). From 1775

to 1777, Boullée, a pupil of J. F. Blondel (1705–1774) as well as of J. L. Legeay (ca. 1710–after 1786), served as architect to the comte d'Artois, a brother of Louis XV. He designed a number of townhouses in Paris between 1761 and 1768. His first recorded work includes altars for St. Roch, Paris, between 1752 and 1754. A defender of the Louis XIV architectural style, he preferred the work of François Mansart (1598–1666), Claude Perrault (1613–1688), and J. F. Blondel to the excesses of the rococo as practiced by Juste-Aurèle Meissonnier (1695–1750) and other eighteenth-century architects. By the 1770s, however, when he designed the Hôtel de Brunoy in Paris, he had radically changed his style and was more directly influenced by the antique. In brilliant, large-scale designs, such as the present example, Boullée went beyond neoclassicism to the visionary—even futuristic—clarity for which his work is now so admired.

CDD

JOHN ROBERT COZENS

London 1752–1797 London

15   *Rome from the Villa Mellini*

Watercolor over preliminary drawing in graphite. 20⅞ x 29¾ in. (531 x 757 mm). Watermark: None visible through lining. Signed (?) in pen and black ink along lower edge, *Jn. Cozens* [abraded]. Inscribed on original mount, in pen and black ink, *JNO COZENS 1791 | ROME, FROM NEAR THE VILLA MADAMA;* on verso, in pen and black ink at center of original mount, *Rome, from ᶰᵉᵃʳ the Villa Madama;* in pen and brown ink at upper left, *Mʳ Annesley's*. Other illegible inscriptions in blue ink.

PROVENANCE: Mr. Annesley (Alexander [?], d. 1813); Christopher Wood Gallery, London, 1995.

EXHIBITIONS: London 1996–97, no. 42, repr. in color; New York 1998b, no. 52.

Cozens was the son and pupil of Alexander Cozens (1717–1786), author of an influential treatise on landscape composition and a member of the first generation of British artists to execute finished landscapes in watercolor. Among the younger Cozens's earliest works was a suite of eight topographical views of Bath, which he published in 1773. Three years later, to much acclaim, he exhibited his first oil painting at the Royal Academy, *Landscape with Hannibal in His March over the Alps* (untraced).

Cozens made two trips to Italy. The first, through Switzerland, took place in 1776–78 with the antiquarian and connoisseur Richard Payne Knight (1750–1824), for whom Cozens produced mainly views of the Swiss mountain landscape. The second trip, in 1782–83, was undertaken with the wealthy young eccentric William Beckford (1759–1844), for whom Cozens filled several sketchbooks recording the classical sites popular with travelers on the grand tour. After returning to England, he used the studies to produce highly finished watercolors such as the present sheet.

This drawing is the largest of three known versions of the subject. The other two are in the Fitzwilliam Museum, Cambridge (Fig. 1), and the British Museum, London (Bell and Girtin 1935, no. 122 I). Once thought to depict the view from the Villa Madama, which Cozens recorded in at least two drawings (Huntington Library, San Marino, California; Whitworth Art Gallery, Manchester), the present drawing is now known to represent the view from the Villa Mellini. Located on the Monte Mario, the Villa Mellini, built in

FIG. 1. John Robert Cozens, *Rome from the Villa Mellini*, Fitzwilliam Museum, Cambridge

the sixteenth century, was a popular vantage point from which artists sketched the picturesque landscape of the Tiber River valley; see, for example, a drawing in watercolor by Giovanni Battista Lusieri (1755–1821), *Rome from the Gardens of the Villa Mellini on Monte Mario*, dated 1793 (Gemäldegalerie der Akademie der bildenden Künste, Vienna; Paris and Mantua 2001, no. 45, repr.).

The existence of two watercolor views by Cozens dated 1790 and 1791 in which the compositions are very close to that of the Thaw

sheet—*The Bay of Naples from Capodimonte* and *London from Greenwich Hill,* both in the Yale Center for British Art, New Haven (New Haven 1980, nos. 136 and 137)—lends support to the suggestion by Stephanie Wiles that the Thaw drawing dates to the 1790s (New York 1998b, under no. 52).

Cozens's work was highly influential on the next generation of British landscape watercolorists, notably J. M. W. Turner (1775–1851) and Thomas Girtin (1775–1802). In the mid-1790s, in the home of the collector and patron Dr. Thomas Monro (1759–1833), Turner and Girtin made copies of Cozens's drawings, which the doctor had acquired while treating Cozens for the nervous disorder that caused his death in 1797 (New York 1992, p. 14).

KS

JACQUES-LAURENT AGASSE

Geneva 1767–1849 London

16 *A White Horse*

Oil on millboard. 11⅝ x 13⅞ in. (294 x 352 mm). Printed label, partially removed, on reverse: *AD V | 103. HIGH HOLBORNE.*

PROVENANCE: William Drummond, London.

Agasse studied for three years in David's Paris studio before he returned to Geneva, where he became especially interested in animals from copying animal sculptures and decided to further his studies of animal anatomy as well as veterinary medicine at the natural history museum. Lord Rivers, who was traveling in Switzerland in 1790, met Agasse in Geneva and persuaded him to go back to London with him. Although Agasse did not stay long on this occasion, he returned to London in the fall of 1800 and spent the rest of his life there. He painted portraits and genre subjects as well, but he considered himself a painter of horses and enjoyed some success painting sporting subjects in the manner of George Stubbs (1724–1806), such as the fine portrait *Lord Rivers and His Friends,* 1818 (now in the Musée d'art et d'histoire, Geneva; repr. Lapaire 1991, fig. 112). Agasse also was well known for his depictions of exotic animals, such as the series of ten paintings commissioned by the Royal College of Surgeons in 1821. As was the present work, they were executed on millboard and are of a similar size, which may suggest a date close to that of the present work. Although the artist kept a record book, it is not possible to identify the white, or, perhaps more correctly, the gray horse from his notes for that year. The Royal College of Surgeons series mainly consists of exotic animals that the artist probably saw in one of the London menageries, such as Polito's on the Strand. Indeed the only horse-like animals in the series are a white mule and a quagga (an extinct, zebralike animal). But perhaps the most famous exotic animal in London at this time was the Nubian giraffe whose portrait Agasse was commissioned to paint by George IV. The portrait is still in the royal collection (Collection of H. M. Queen Elizabeth II; repr. Detroit and Philadelphia ca. 1968, no. 103). It was one of a pair of giraffes sent as diplomatic gifts, one to George IV and the other to Charles X of France.

Despite its execution on a piece of millboard, this portrait of a horse, in contrast to oil sketches, is really a small painting, very complete in its finish. The gray horse stands in a landscape, facing right. This is a familiar formula for Agasse's many horse portraits, such as his portrait of an Arabian stallion posed (looking to the left) in an Alpine landscape, but that picture is much larger, and the Arabian horse's tail is not cropped as is that of this horse (repr. New York 1992, no. 10).

CDD

JOHANN CHRISTIAN REINHART

Hof (Bavaria) 1761–1847 Rome

17 *Two Young Gentlemen Outdoors, One Sketching*

Pen and brown ink, brush and brown wash, over graphite, laid down. 12 $^{15}/_{16}$ x 16 $^{11}/_{16}$ in. (324 x 421 mm). Watermark: None visible. Inscribed in graphite at lower left, *par J. C. Reinhart, environs de Rome, albano.*

PROVENANCE: Private collection, France (part of a lot of six large drawings by Reinhart, according to Bruno de Bayser); Galerie de Bayser, Paris.

EXHIBITION: New York 1997–98.

After briefly studying theology, Reinhart trained as a painter in Leipzig and Dresden. In 1789 he moved to Rome, where he associated with the painters Jakob Asmus Carstens (1754–1798) and Joseph Anton Koch (Nos. 18–19) and their circle and, having married, settled permanently. From 1825 he received an annual pension from King Ludwig I of Bavaria, for whom he painted four views of Rome (1829–35) now in the Neue Pinakothek, Munich.

Reinhart specifically rejected the aims of the Nazarene painters, claiming that they valued the earliest masters above sound draftsmanship. Detailed observation and a freshness of approach, especially in his drawings, characterize his oeuvre. He primarily produced landscapes; many were drawings of Rome and the Campagna, though some were freely invented. He was strongly influenced by the work of Claude Lorrain (No. 10) and Nicolas Poussin, and the *repoussoir* motif of the tree in the foreground of this drawing clearly derives from this classical tradition. Together with Koch, Reinhart represents the heroic tradition of German Romantic landscape painting in Rome.

The French inscription on the drawing probably refers to the town of Albano Laziale, a popular destination twenty-five kilometers south of Rome on the Via Appia. In 1792 Reinhart and two other German painters, Albert Christoph Dies (1755–1822) and Jakob Wilhelm Mechau (1745–1808), embarked on a series of seventy-two etchings with views of Rome and its surroundings, entitled *Painterly Etchings with Views of Italy* (see Schmid 1998, pp. 161–90). These include three views of sites near Albano: Reinhart provided the designs for *Remains of the Roman Theater at Albano,* 1792 (Feuchtmayr 1975, fig. 370) and *Antique Tomb Known as the Tomb of the Horatii and Curiatii at Albano,* 1795 (Feuchtmayr 1975, fig. 386), while the *Hermitage at Albano* of 1795 is by Mechau.

This drawing may have been made on the spot in the early 1790s as the artists gathered material for the *Views of Italy.* It depicts two young men, one seated and apparently sketching the panoramic view, the other standing and supporting the umbrella that shades his companion. According to F. Carlo Schmid (correspondence, September 2001), an etching by Dies from this series, entitled *Cascade and Bridge at Tivoli,* also depicts an artist at work, seated beneath an umbrella. An album of sixty-four drawings by Reinhart, signed, inscribed, and dated *Roma 1790,* in the collection of Georg Schäfer in Schweinfurt, includes two studies of an artist, similar to the seated figure at left (Feuchtmayr 1975, figs. 213 and 214). He sits on a collapsible stool and moves his pen over a large sheet of paper that rests on a portfolio, a pot of ink by his side.

REP

JOSEPH ANTON KOCH

Obergibeln, Tyrol, 1768–1839 Rome

18 *Farm Scene in the Hasli Valley near Meiringen in the Bernese Oberland*

Graphite, pen and dark brown ink, brush and brown wash, heightened with white bodycolor, on light brown paper, laid down on board; framing line by the artist in graphite. 8¼ x 11⅛ in. (209 x 283 mm). Watermark: None visible through backing.

PROVENANCE: Edward His, Bern, early nineteenth century; by descent to his great-great-grandchild, San Antonio; art market, San Antonio, 1997 (all previous provenance according to Fred R. Kline); Fred R. Kline Gallery, Santa Fe, 1997.

Among the most important landscape painters of the early nineteenth century, Koch attended the Karlsschule in Stuttgart from 1785 to 1791, studying with Philipp Friedrich von Hetsch (1758–1838), a pupil of Jacques-Louis David. Trained in the classical tradition of the idealized, heroic landscapes of Nicolas Poussin and Claude Lorrain (No. 10), Koch also was keenly interested in the natural sciences, especially geology, and he made studies from life in the countryside around Stuttgart. Following a sketching trip to Switzerland in the spring of 1791, he left the Karlsschule to begin a three-year sojourn in Bern.

Christian von Holst dates this drawing to Koch's sojourn in Switzerland in 1792–94 (collector's files, correspondence, 16 November 1998). As von Holst has observed, the drawing was composed by combining two different studies: the foreground scene, which may represent the village of Reuti above Meiringen, and the background view, which depicts the region above the Aare River, with the Reichenbach falls in the middle distance and the cliffs of the Rosenlaui and the peaks of the Wellhorn and Wetterhorn mountains behind. Meiringen and the Haslital—the valley of the Aare River—are located east of Bern and directly north of the Italian border. Von Holst has pointed out that the background landscape of waterfalls, cliffs, and mountains is depicted from a site too near the viewer to accommodate the foreground scene as it is represented.

FIG. 1. Joseph Anton Koch, *The Haslital near Meiringen,* Tiroler Landesmuseum Ferdinandeum, Innsbruck

In a rough sketch of 1792/94 (formerly private collection, Basel; Stuttgart 1989, p. 41, fig. 18), probably made on site, Koch recorded a view in the Haslital in which the valley recedes naturalistically into depth, and the Reichenbach falls—so near the picture plane in the present drawing—are in the deep background. Likewise, the distances implied in the sketch between falls, cliffs, and mountains more closely conform to those in nature than do those in the Thaw drawing.

40

The Swiss Alpine landscape around Bern continued to figure in Koch's paintings long after he moved to Italy in 1795, where he remained for most of the rest of his life. In a painting of 1817, *The Haslital near Meiringen* (Fig. 1), he once again depicted the landscape in the Haslital above Meiringen represented in the present drawing.

KS

JOSEPH ANTON KOCH

Obergibeln, Tyrol, 1768–1839 Rome

19 *River Landscape Along the Tiber near the Acqua Acetosa,*

1814

Watercolor with touches of gum arabic over graphite, on wove paper; ruled border in black ink. 8 x 10 $^{15}/_{16}$ in. (202 x 278 mm). Signed and dated on original support, folded under, in graphite at lower left, *Joseph Koch 1814;* inscribed on original support, folded under, at lower center, *Acqua Cetosa / bei Rom.*

PROVENANCE: Sale, Berlin, Amsler & Ruthardt, 92, 5 June 1912, lot 765, repr. (according to C. G. Boerner Inc.); Dr. Hans Boerner, Leipzig; by descent; C. G. Boerner Inc., New York.

LITERATURE: Lutterotti 1940, p. 268, no. 538; Lutterotti 1985, p. 327, no. Z 538.

After a three-year sojourn in Bern (No. 18), Koch left for Rome in 1795, traveling on a scholarship from an English patron he had met in Switzerland. He remained in Italy for most of the rest of his life, becoming an important member of the expatriate colony of Northern artists promoting a classical revival.

This drawing, which represents a stretch of the Tiber River north of Rome, with Mount Soracte in the distance, was made while Koch was in Vienna, where he lived from 1812 to 1815, during the French occupation of Rome. The Acqua Acetosa, a mineral spring, was a popular destination for Northern artists of the period. C. W. Eckersberg (No. 28) depicted the same view in a painting, *The Fountain of Acqua Acetosa* (Statens Museum for Kunst, Copenhagen; Paris and Mantua 2001, no. 195, repr.), done the same year as this drawing. Koch represented the site in numerous works over a period of several years, beginning with a pen and ink drawing of 1805 (formerly Kupferstich-Kabinett, Dresden; Lutterotti 1985, no. Z 282). This was followed by a print of 1810 that was included in his Roman views (Lutterotti 1985, fig. 243). In 1812 he executed his most elaborate depiction of the site in a painting formerly in the Nationalgalerie, Berlin (Lutterotti 1985, no. G 19, fig. 21). Two years later, on a commission from the French diplomat and writer François-Gabriel Count de Bray, he made a copy in a smaller format of the painting formerly in Berlin (private collection; Lutterotti 1985, no. G 28a, fig. 22). Other works on paper include two drawings in the Kupferstichkabinett, Berlin (Lutterotti 1985, no. Z 87, fig. 181, and Z 86), and two drawings each made in the preparation of a print (Staatsgalerie Stuttgart, Lutterotti 1985, no. Z 635; and Kunstmuseum, Bern, Lutterotti 1985, no. Z 670).

KS

43

PHILIPP OTTO RUNGE

Wolgast (Pomerania) 1777–1810 Hamburg

20 *The Child*

Pen and black ink over black chalk; framing lines in black chalk and pen and brown ink; on wove paper; vertical crease at center. 5 ¹³/₁₆ x 8 ¹/₁₆ in. (147 x 205 mm). Inscribed on verso in pen and light brown ink at right edge (possibly by the artist's brother, Daniel?), *Original von Philipp Otto Runge 1809.*

PROVENANCE: Estate of the artist; by descent to his son Otto Sigismund Runge; given by the son to the Hamburg Künstlerverein, Hamburg; sale, Leipzig, C. G. Boerner Inc., 19 June 1937, lot 183, pl. III; sale, Munich, Sotheby's, 27 June 1995, lot 60, repr.

LITERATURE: Isermeyer 1940, p. 131; Waetzoldt 1951, pp. 127, 142, fig. 46 (cited in Traeger and auction entry); Krafft and Schümann 1969, p. 285; Traeger 1975, p. 424, no. 392, repr.

EXHIBITIONS: Hamburg 1935, no. 112 (according to sale catalogue, Munich, Sotheby's, 27 June 1995, p. 23); London 1996–97, no. 50, repr.; New York 1997–98.

Runge's northern German pietism and love of nature had been nurtured by the pastor and poet Ludwig Theobul Kosegarten, who was his teacher in Wolgast from 1789 to 1792. This religious view of nature was the principle behind Runge's best-known theme, the Times of Day cycle, which the artist began in 1802. The initial four compositions—*Morning, Evening, Day,* and *Night*—were symmetrical designs in which flowers, children, and light were used to symbolize the artist's religious philosophy of landscape. The arabesque, linear quality of these early drawings was influenced by his exposure to engravings of scenes from Homer, Aeschylus, and Dante by the English artist John Flaxman (1755–1826), which had been sent to him by his brother Daniel in 1801. The fluid, neoclassical, linear style of these engravings transformed the scenes into their "hieroglyphic" form; this symbolic approach to subjects appealed to the artist. Runge produced engravings for his Times of Day drawings in 1805 and 1807, a set of which is in the Morgan Library (acc. no. P1985.70:1–4).

FIG. 1. Philipp Otto Runge, *Small Morning,* Hamburg Kunsthalle

In 1807 he began making further studies for a painted version of the series. He would, however, complete only two oils before he died—one sketch known as the *Small Morning* (Fig. 1) in 1807 and in 1808, the *Large Morning* version, which was cut up some time after his death and reassembled in 1927. Both paintings are now in the Hamburg Kunsthalle.

This sheet is a preparatory sketch for the baby who appears in the *Small Morning* oil. As Traeger points out, here the child lies on his back, feet raised and together, hands apart. The sheet is devoid of indications of the vegetation that is included in the subsequent painted sketch. The child appears in additional studies

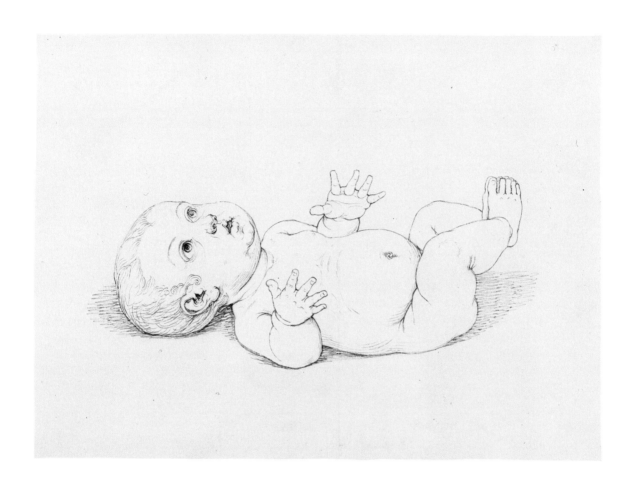

in the Hamburg Kunsthalle, including a compositional study for the middle section of the oil. There are slight variations in the placement of the baby's feet and hands, but the basic pose remains the same. Runge's artistic theories encompass many levels of interpretation of his work. According to the pantheistic reading, the baby both witnesses and represents the new day; within the tradition of Runge's northern German Protestant heritage, the child symbolizes the Christ Child, or Redeemer.

EJP

JOSEF REBELL

Vienna 1787–1828 Dresden

21 *View of the Falls of Schaffhausen on the Rhine,* 1810

Watercolor over graphite, laid down on canvas. 10¾ x 16 in. (272 x 405 mm). Watermark: None. Signed and dated in black ink at lower right, *J. Rebell, 1810.*

PROVENANCE: Sale, London, Sotheby's, 26 November 1970, lot 100, repr.; Julius Böhler, Munich, 1972; Walter Feilchenfeldt, Zurich, 1972.

Rebell studied landscape painting with Michael Wutky (1739–1822) at the Academy of Fine Arts in Vienna before traveling to Switzerland in 1809. He continued to northern Italy in 1810 and was employed as court painter by Eugène Beauharnais in Milan for two years. This was followed by sojourns in Naples, where he worked for Joachim Murat from 1813 to 1815, and finally in Rome, where he resided until 1824. Upon his return to Austria, he was appointed director of the Belvedere Gallery in Vienna. He is best known for his oil paintings and watercolors of luminous landscapes, romantic scenes, and views of Naples, which were to prove a major influence on subsequent Viennese landscape painting.

Starting in the eighteenth century, the falls at Schaffhausen—the largest in Europe—began to attract artists and travelers, such as the two gentlemen (accompanied by a local, barefooted guide) and the elegant couple depicted by Rebell. They would have come to admire the sublime spectacle of the foaming and thundering masses of water, which an 1819 traveler's guide describes as follows:

> A league below Schaffhausen is the famous fall of the Rhine, near two places called Laufen; one of which, consisting of a castle and a village, is situated on the Swiss bank; and the other, an old decayed castle, on an island opposite the first. About five hundred paces above the fall the river is intersected by enormous masses of rock, rising above the surface of the water. It begins to foam, and the slope becoming more and more steep, it falls from rock to rock, dividing into a number of small branches, till it reaches the edge of an enormous rock, over an abyss nearly eighty feet deep. In falling from this mass, it forms three different cascades: the most impetuous is that on the south side, which rushes across two rocks resembling two pillars. The noise made by this fall may be heard, in the night, at two leagues distance (Schreiber 1819, pp. 38–39).

Much of the vista, such as Laufen Castle, visible at the upper right in the drawing, and the viewing platform, very lightly sketched in below it, remains largely unchanged today.

Rebell must have traveled to the site on his way south in early 1810 since the Thaw drawing appears to have been executed just previous to, and *en serie* with, a group of watercolors of Lake Como on similar paper and of similar dimensions, dated 1810 and 1811 (sale, London, Christie's, 23 June 1981, lots 108, 109, both repr.; sale, London, Sotheby's, 26 November 1970, lots 98, 99, both repr.; lot 98 again sale, London, Christie's, 24 June 1982, lot 136, repr.).

REP

GERHARDT WILHELM VON REUTERN

Rösthof, near Walk (Livonia, on the Baltic), 1794–1865 Frankfurt

22 *Portrait of George Hinrich*

Pen and black ink on paper. 8 x 5¾ in. (203 x 143 mm). Watermark: None. Inscribed in pen and black ink at lower left, *d 24ten J.,* and at lower center, *sein jüngster Sohn George Hinrich* (?).

PROVENANCE: Hazlitt, Gooden & Fox, London, 1978; Marianne Feilchenfeldt, Zurich, ca. 1996.

EXHIBITION: London 1978, no. 16, repr.

Scion of an aristocratic German family living in the Baltic, Reutern studied military sciences at Dorpat University, where he also learned the rudiments of painting and drawing from Carl August Senff (1770–1838). He began a career in the Russian army but lost his right arm in October 1813, at the age of nineteen, after being wounded in the Battle of Leipzig, fighting the French. While convalescing in Germany in 1814, he was introduced to Johann Wolfgang von Goethe. The poet later befriended the young man, encouraging him to draw with his left hand and to pursue a career as an artist.

In August 1814 Reutern traveled for the first time to the village of Willingshausen in the Schwalm region of Hesse, in order to visit the von Schwertzell family, parents-in-law of his elder brother Carl. There he met Charlotte von Schwertzell, whom he was to marry six years later. Having come into a family estate that provided him an income, Reutern resigned from the army in December 1819. He lived in Switzerland before settling in Willingshausen in 1824, where he remained until 1831. The painter and draftsman Ludwig Emil Grimm (1790–1863), younger brother of Jacob and Wilhelm, the compilers of *Grimm's Fairy Tales,* proved to be a decisive influence on the artist during the Willingshausen years. Together the two artists roamed the countryside, drawing animal and landscape studies as well as numerous portraits of the villagers in colorful local costume (Bantzer et al. 1994, passim). From the mid-1830s, Reutern increasingly turned to painting in oils; in 1837 he was appointed court painter to the Russian imperial family.

This drawing belongs to a series of half-length portrait studies in pen and ink executed by the artist in the period from 1825 to 1831 in Willingshausen. Often dated and inscribed with the names and professions of the sitters, the drawings include likenesses of such characters as the blacksmith Johannes Daum, the horse breaker Hans Heinrich Stamm, the hunter Johann Christian Kellner, and the night watchman (London 1978, nos. 15, 17, 20, 21, all repr.). The studies combine the precise linear style of late neoclassicism with an interest in the beauty of simple rural life, characteristic of early realism. Though the subject of the Thaw drawing has not been identified, the inscription, which translates as "his youngest son George Hinrich," suggests that it once accompanied a likeness of the father. The boy wears a double-breasted jacket with upright collar and a loose necktie over a shirt with a folded-down collar, also seen in many of the other portrait drawings. According to Dr. Karin Mayer-Pasinski (verbal communication, September 2001), the boy's clothes are typical of the Schwalm region's costume, which derives from the courtly dress of the eighteenth century. Thus his—to modern eyes—elegant appearance probably belies humble origins. The boy may well have been the son of a local farmer.

REP

1724 ætat J.

sein jüngster Sohn George Hinrich.

JOHANN SCHEFFER VON LEONHARDSHOFF

Vienna 1795–1822 Vienna

23   *Agnus Dei (The Virgin and Child with S. Agnes, Genevieve [?], and John the Baptist, and the Archangel Gabriel)*

Pen and gray ink on paper. 12⅝ x 16⅜ in. (320 x 415 mm). Inscribed on the scroll at the head of the reed cross, *Agnus Dei.*

PROVENANCE: Private collection, Germany; sale, Amsterdam, Christie's, 24 March 1999, lot 522 (as circle of Philipp Otto Runge); Fred R. Kline Gallery, Santa Fe; private collection, Santa Fe.

This highly accomplished drawing, quintessentially Nazarene in subject and spirit, is one of a small group of compositions on New Testament and other Christian themes from the earlier period of Scheffer's all too brief career. It is one of his most Italianate drawings, in which late quattrocento Florentine compositional types are combined with Northern, mainly German, traditions derived from Stephan Lochner through to Albrecht Dürer (1471–1528).

Iconographically, especially in the choice of the secondary female protagonists, it is unusual. In the center of the composition is the Virgin, depicted kneeling as a token of her humility and supporting Christ as he attempts to stand. To the right kneels the infant John the Baptist wearing a short animal-hair tunic. In his right hand he holds the traditional baptismal cup, while his left hand is raised above the simple reed cross lying on the ground beside him. Curled around the top of the cross is a scroll on which the words *Agnus Dei* are clearly legible. This inscription refers to John's own words, recorded in the fourth gospel (1:36), "Behold the Lamb of God" (Ecce Agnus Dei). As an attribute of John the Baptist, the recumbent lamb on the right forms a visual link with the kneeling female figure behind it, who is almost certainly intended to represent St. Agnes. A virgin martyr (*Agnes* derives from the Greek word for "chaste"), her attribute is invariably also a white lamb, usually curled up at her feet, an emblem erroneously given to her because of the similarity between her name and the Latin *agnus.* She holds the crown that was given to her by an angel at her martyrdom. The identification of the person standing behind her is more problematic. The lily in her right hand is associated with the virgin saints, though the doe at her side suggests that she is perhaps the saintly Genevieve, a figure popularized in Germany at this time by the writer Ludwig Tieck. On the left of the composition, the winged figure with his hands in an attitude of prayer is probably the archangel Gabriel. In front of him a kneeling youth plays the lute.

The group is surrounded by a rose-covered trellis, a version of the *hortus conclusus* (enclosed garden) commonly employed in late medieval German art as a symbol of Marian virginity. The plants in the foreground include the strawberry, a symbol of humility, and various bitter herbs associated with Passover and thus with the time in the Jewish calendar when Christ was crucified. Among these, the plantain symbolizes the difficult path of Christianity. The birds on the trellis supporting the roses (the Virgin is called "the rose without thorns") might signify the Christian soul or, in the case of the finches, Christ's Passion.

Insofar as it is possible to establish a clear chronology for the drawings of such a short-lived artist, the present composition can be most plausibly placed among the drawings he executed between around 1815 and 1818.

In its conflation of Florentine Renaissance and late medieval German symbols and motifs, its dependence on Florentine quattrocento compositional formulas, and its pious treatment of a sacred subject in a self-consciously historicizing manner (the German equivalent of Pre-Raphaelitism), the present work not only typifies the artist but also embodies what was central to the Nazarene aesthetic, directed to what they themselves described as a "new religious and patriotic form of art."

CJB

CARL PHILIPP FOHR

Heidelberg 1795–1818 Rome

24   *The Ruins of Hohenbaden*

Watercolor and bodycolor over preliminary indications in graphite, on wove paper; ruled border in black ink, partially laid down on original green paper album folio. $7^{11}/_{16}$ x $8^{11}/_{16}$ in. (195 x 220 mm). Inscribed by the artist in pen and black ink at lower center of original green paper mount, *Die Trümmer eines Stammes der Zähringer ehemalige Wohnung;* numbered at upper right corner of original mount, *5.;* printed label on reverse of original green paper mount, *Carl Philipp Fohr (1795–1818). Umstehendes Blatt ist eine Originalarbeit von Carl Philipp Fohr und zwar No. 5 aus dem badischen Skizzenbuch, gewidmet der Erbgrossherzogin Wilhelmine von Hessen. Dies wird hiermit bestätigt. München, den 1. Februar 1927. Die Direktion der Graphischen Sammlung,* [signature of Otto Weigmann, surprinted with the institution's stamp].

PROVENANCE: Grand Duchess Wilhelmina of Hesse; by descent to her grandson Prince Henry of Hesse; Princess Emily of Hesse; her sale, Munich, Ludwigsgalerie, 1927; sale, Munich, Hartnung & Hartnung, 13 November 1998, lot 4047, repr. in color on inside back cover.

LITERATURE: Heidelberg 1925, under no. 5.

EXHIBITIONS: Munich 1927, no. 35; Heidelberg 1968, no. 35, repr. (as "whereabouts unknown").

Fohr began drawing lessons at age thirteen in Heidelberg as the pupil of Friedrich Rottmann (1768–1816), father of Carl Rottmann (No. 94). He continued his training, largely on his own, while living in Darmstadt from 1811 to 1813, and in 1815–16 he studied landscape painting at the Kunstakademie in Munich.

From 1813 until the end of his life, Fohr received commissions from Grand Duchess Wilhelmina of Hesse (1774–1837). Two were for sketchbooks of watercolor views in southwestern Germany—one of the Neckar River valley, dated 1813–14, the other of the former state of Baden, dated 1814–15. The sketchbooks have been dismembered, and many of the folios and preparatory studies are today in the Hessisches Landesmuseum, Darmstadt (Darmstadt and Munich 1995–97, nos. 100–131, repr.).

The present drawing was folio 5 of the Baden sketchbook. It is partially laid down on the original green paper mount, which bears the artist's inscription identifying the subject as the ruins of Hohenbaden, a twelfth-century castle situated on a promontory above the Rhine on the outskirts of Baden-Baden. The castle, which is still standing, served as the residence of the margraves of Baden until the late fifteenth century.

Among the other subjects represented in the Baden sketchbook are a distant view of Baden-Baden (fol. 2; Darmstadt and Munich 1995–97, no. 103, repr.), a streetscape in the city with the house of one Dr. Meyer (fol. 4; Darmstadt and Munich 1995–97, no. 105, repr.), and a view of the thirteenth-century Lichtenthal Abbey outside Baden-Baden (fol. 6; Darmstadt and Munich 1995–97, no. 107, repr.), all in the Hessisches Landesmuseum, Darmstadt.

Although the preparatory study for the present sheet has not been identified, the preliminary study for folio 25 of the Baden sketchbook, *Christ on the Cross near Weissenbach,* is known and provides insight into the artist's working method (sale, Munich, Hartnung & Hartnung, 13 November 1998, lot 4048, repr.). The study, executed in pen and gray-black ink over graphite on brown paper ruled in gold, is very close in size to the finished draw-

Die Trümmer eines Stammes der Zäringer ehmalige Wohnung.

ing and corresponds to it in composition and details of weather and topography, even to the placement of clouds and of rocks in the stream (Hessisches Landesmuseum, Darmstadt; Darmstadt and Munich 1995–97, no. 120, repr.). The artist added to the finished drawing a few staffage figures and grazing cows as well as plants and flowers in the foreground as *repoussoir* elements.

The present drawing is characteristic of the artist's style of the period, which features a sharply detailed, crystalline quality. Individual strokes of pale green, gray, and terra-cotta provide textural interest in the walls of the castle, and tiny dots of pigment and delicate strokes of an extremely fine brush describe the foliage in the foreground. The castle seems to emerge from the rocks and surrounding landscape, an impression enhanced by a palette of closely chromatic tones.

KS

CARL PHILIPP FOHR

Heidelberg 1795–1818 Rome

25 *Studies of a Greyhound and a Mastiff*

Pen and black ink and watercolor. 4⅜ x 5¾ in. (112 x 147 mm). Watermark: None. Inscribed in ink at lower right in a later hand, *Hunde von dem Vater des Karl Rottmann aus Heidelberg*, and numbered in ink at upper right, *76*.

PROVENANCE: Collection of Artaria brothers (according to Dorotheum entry); sale, Vienna, Palais Dorotheum, 3 October 2000, lot III, repr. in color on cover.

These delightful drawings (the watercolor study of the greyhound is particularly exquisite) are among the most charming of the many studies of dogs that were made by Fohr before his premature death from drowning in the Tiber. In the Dorotheum catalogue, it is claimed that the dog on the right is Fohr's faithful canine companion Grimsel, who accompanied the artist on his journey across the Alps to Rome in 1816. Fohr and Grimsel were often depicted together. There is, for example, a lively pen and wash drawing by Fohr of *The Artist with Two Friends and His Dog Grimsel* in the Hessisches Landesmuseum in Darmstadt and a pen and ink drawing, also by Fohr, in the manner of a caricature, in a private collection in Munich depicting *Fohr with His Dog Grimsel on the Way to Italy*. The dog in all these drawings, however, is not the one recorded on the present sheet. Besides, Grimsel was a Saint Bernard, not a mastiff. Thus it seems likely that the old inscription on this sheet is accurate and the two dogs depicted belonged not to Fohr but to his drawing master in Heidelberg, Friedrich Rottmann, father of the great landscape painter Carl Rottmann (No. 94), the protégé of Ludwig I of Bavaria.

Fohr evidently was very fond of animals, especially dogs, throughout his life. The drawings previously cited were patently autobiographical, but most of his studies of dogs were made with the clear intention of incorporating them in more ambitious compositions, such as his oil paintings. Superb canine specimens, worthy of Stubbs or Landseer, are depicted in his early paintings *The Lost Knight* in the Nationalgalerie, Berlin, and *The Castle and Town of Zwingenberg on the Neckar* in a German private collection. The hound at the lower right of the latter has exactly the same stance as that of the dog in the present study: head raised, both pairs of feet close together, and the tail hanging low between the legs. Also very similar is the drawing of a greyhound sniffing the air in a pen and ink composition, now in Darmstadt, by Fohr depicting *The Count of Habsburg and the Priest*, datable to around 1815/16. The two breeds of dog most frequently recorded in Fohr's drawings are precisely those depicted on the present sheet, the greyhound and the mastiff. Of his mastiff studies, arguably the finest are those included on a sheet with *Studies of Seven Dogs*, in Darmstadt, executed in pen with gray and brown wash, on which two of the dogs are identified by name. In type and pose, the mastiff of the present work is closest in appearance to the dog on the right of Fohr's pen and ink drawing *Three Knights Accompanied by a Dog*, which is in Darmstadt and is signed and dated 1815.

Stylistically, and on the basis of the inscription identifying the dogs as those of Fohr's teacher, the present study might reasonably be dated around 1816, prior to the artist's departure for Italy. As anatomical studies they demonstrate not only Fohr's precocious gifts as a draftsman but also his burgeoning talent as a sophisticated watercolorist.

CJB

54

Hunde von dem Werkund des
Karl Rottmann und Heidelberg. †

FRIEDRICH PRELLER THE ELDER

Eisenach 1804–1878 Weimar

26   *Hawks on a Mountain*

Point of brush and brown wash and watercolor, over graphite, on wove paper. 10^1/₁₆ x 6¾ in. (256 x 172 mm).

PROVENANCE: Sale, Leipzig, C. G. Boerner Inc., 25 May 1938, lot 306, repr.; sale, Stuttgart, Stuttgarter Kunstkabinett, 24 May 1955, lot 601; sale, Munich, Ketterer Kunst, 25 November 1986, lot 1573, repr.; Galerie Biedermann, Munich, 1986.

LITERATURE: Gensel 1904, pp. 86, 90, fig. 92; Weinrautner 1997, under no. 247, p. 331.

EXHIBITIONS: Leipzig 1938, no. 306, pl. 23; New York 1994, not in catalogue; New York 1997–98.

Preller began his studies at the Freies Zeichen-Institut in Weimar in 1818, under Heinrich Meyer (1760–1832). In 1821 he moved to Dresden, where for two years, at the suggestion of Goethe, he copied after the works of Nicolas Poussin and Jacob van Ruisdael (No. 9). From 1824 to 1826 he studied with Mathieu Ignace Van Brée (1773–1839) in Antwerp. In 1828, on a scholarship to Rome, he began a three-year sojourn in Italy, becoming the friend and pupil of Joseph Anton Koch (Nos. 18–19), whose landscape style influenced his own. Between 1837 and 1847 he traveled often to Norway, the North Sea island of Rügen, the Sudeten Mountains, and the Alps, rugged landscapes that changed his style and gave him a taste for the wild and romantic in nature.

The present drawing belongs to the period following these travels and may plausibly be dated to the mid-1850s because of its close connection to works signed and dated 1856. In one such work, *Mountain Landscape,* a drawing executed in pen and brown ink and brush and brown and gray wash (Fig. 1), Preller depicted a view very similar to this one. Sharply angled boulders and the trunks of dying trees define a triangular area in the foreground of both compositions. In each drawing a trio of pine trees, loosely brushed to suggest the shaggy manner of the Danube school, is set before a distant mountain landscape. In the present drawing a pair of hawks enlivens the scene, while in the Stuttgart sheet a rush-ing stream flows through the center of the composition.

FIG. 1. Friedrich Preller the Elder, *Mountain Landscape,* Staatsgalerie, Stuttgart

In another work of 1856, *Vultures at Felsen,* a painting at the Kunstsammlungen zu Weimar (Weinrautner 1997, no. 247), close parallels with the present drawing suggest that the two are variants of the same theme. Where Preller repre-sented two hawks in the Thaw drawing, one of them in flight, in the Weimar painting he substi-tuted a pair of vultures, one of which broods atop a rock at the center of the composition, establish-ing both the tone and focal point of the work. In contrast to the somber palette of the Weimar painting, the Thaw drawing is light-filled, the white of the paper describing light on the fore-

56

57

ground rocks, the upper surface of the eagle's wings, the distant slope of the mountain in the background, and areas of white cloud. In contrast to the trio of pine trees in the Thaw drawing, the only trees depicted in the Weimar painting are bare branches that erupt from the rocky terrain in the foreground.

The subject of hawks—and presumably vultures—absorbed Preller over a period of several years. He executed his earliest study in 1849 and continued to make them throughout the mid-1850s. In preparation for the Weimar painting, for example, he made meticulous studies of the birds from life in the zoological gardens in Antwerp, even writing several letters to his correspondent Marie Soest about the pleasures his Antwerp sketching trip afforded him (Weinrautner 1997, p. 331).

The precise location of the present landscape is not known. The author of an early monograph on the artist suggests a generic "high mountain landscape" for the Weimar painting (Gensel 1904, p. 134). More recently Weinrautner has situated the painting in Felsen, in a hilly region east of Düsseldorf (Weinrautner 1997, no. 247). The Stuttgart drawing is inscribed by the artist *Weimar,* which is located east of Felsen. It is possible that in all three works Preller combined observed details with elements of recollected terrain.

KS

MORITZ VON SCHWIND

Vienna 1804–1871 Munich

27 *The Elfin King*

VERSO: *Two Studies of a Standing Woman with Hand Raised to Her Chin*

Graphite. 13½ x 17½ in. (344 x 445 mm). Watermark: None. Inscribed in graphite at lower right, *MvSchwind.*

PROVENANCE: Sale, Hamburg, Ernst Hauswedell, ca. 1971–73; Eugene V. Thaw, New York, ca. 1971–73; Janos Scholz, New York, 1973.

EXHIBITION: New York 1997–98a.

Best known for his pictures, prints, and book illustrations depicting scenes from folklore and medieval history, Schwind was one of the most acclaimed artists of his generation in Germany and Austria. He began his artistic training in Vienna in 1821 and soon became a close friend and admirer of the Austrian composer Franz Schubert (1797–1828), frequently attending domestic musical performances, later known as "Schubertiads."

This drawing was inspired by Schubert's song of 1815, *The Elfin King* (Der Erlkönig), which set to music the famous ballad by Johann Wolfgang von Goethe (1749–1832):

> Who rides by night in the wind so wild?
> It is the father, with his child. . . .
>
> "My son, what is it, why cover your face?"
> "Father, you see him, there in that place,
> The elfin king with his cloak and crown? . . . "
>
> "Father, his fingers grip me, O
> The elfin king has hurt me so!"
>
> Now struck with horror the father rides fast,
> His gasping child in his arm to the last,
> Home through thick and thin he sped:
> Locked in his arm, the child was dead.

(Taken from Middleton 1983, p. 87).

FIG. 1. Moritz von Schwind, *The Elfin King*, Österreichische Galerie Belvedere, Vienna

From 1835 until 1866, and possibly even earlier, the artist repeatedly treated the subject of the elfin king. In a letter from Rome dated 25 July 1835, Schwind mentioned his mural designs for a music room dedicated to Schubert; one of the walls was to illustrate Schubert songs after poems by Goethe (Weigmann 1925, pp. 201–26). Unfortunately Schwind's inability to find a patron for such a commission forced him to abandon the project. The subject lived on, however, in two almost identical panel paint-

ings of the elfin king, produced around 1850 and now in the Belvedere at Vienna (Fig. 1; Weigmann 1906, repr. p. 76) and in the Schack Gallery in Munich (Ruhmer et al. 1969, pp. 372–75, fig. 45). Later, in 1865–66, he incorporated the subject into a lunette in the foyer of the Vienna Opera (Weigmann 1906, repr. p. 473).

Besides the present study, four additional versions on paper are known. A drawing in graphite in the Staatliche Graphische Sammlung, Munich, is probably an early design for the original mural (acc. no. 1922:291; Weigmann 1925, repr. p. 221; dated 1828 on verso though Weigmann and subsequently Ruhmer argue that this does not hold true for the recto). There also exists in the National Gallery, Prague, a signed and dated watercolor of 1849, formerly in the collection of Count Thun and Hohenstein (acc. no. K 17899; Weigmann 1906, repr. p. 277). A pen and wash study was sold at auction (sale, Hamburg,

Hauswedell, 6 June 1974, lot 476, repr.), and a further pencil drawing, differing from the present sheet, is mentioned by Ruhmer (location unknown; Ruhmer et al. 1969, p. 374; Kalkschmidt 1943, fig. 123).

The dog, visible here in the foreground at right, and the position of the elfin king—hovering beside the horse and rider, reaching for the terrified child—are unique to the present drawing. The other versions show the king, followed by his daughters, above and behind the galloping horse.

REP

C(HRISTOFFER) W(ILHELM) ECKERSBERG

Bläckrog, southern Jutland, 1783–1853 Copenhagen

28   *A Man-of-War at Sea, Flanked by Three Smaller Vessels*

Pen and black ink, with brush and gray wash. 11⅝ x 18¼ in. (295 x 465 mm). Inscribed in pen and black ink at lower left in a box, *Afstanden fra agterste Pr. . . . 300 Alen | Diametralplanets afvigelse . . . 60 Gr | Kraengning . . . 5 Gr | Nedduvning . . . 2½ Gr | Oiets hoide over vandlinien 5 Alen |* [illegible] *340 Alen* (in graphite, erased); in graphite at lower right (above boat), *Nord* [ost?] *land.*

PROVENANCE: Jørgen Hansen Koch; by descent; Thomas Le Claire Kunsthandel, Hamburg.

One of the most influential artists of the Danish golden age, Eckersberg began his formal artistic training at the age of twenty, under Nicolai Abildgaard at the Kunstakademi, Copenhagen, before traveling to Paris in 1810 to study with Jacques-Louis David (1748–1825). After a brief stay in Rome, from 1813 to 1816, the artist returned to Denmark and earned his living by painting portraits. The following year he was made professor at the Kunstakademi and took up residence at Charlottenberg Palace. Eckersberg's precise and luminous depictions of Copenhagen and the surrounding countryside gave new direction to Danish painting. His style inspired and was imitated by his students, including Constantin Hansen (No. 100), Christen Købke, and Wilhelm Marstrand.

Eckersberg began painting marine subjects seriously in 1821, with *Moonlit Scene Near the Island of Saltholm* (Nivaagaard Collection), and continued to produce scenes of ships at sea until shortly before his death, when encroaching blindness forced him to stop painting. The artist's depictions of seagoing vessels transcended the conventions of traditional ship portraiture and helped to establish the seascape genre in Danish art.

Eckersberg's memoirs document his long-standing interest in maritime subjects and fascination with ships. According to Emil Hannover, the artist's enthusiasm for the art of navigation combined with his passionate interest in perspective and mechanics led him to embrace marine subjects (Hannover 1898, p. 212). During the 1830s Eckersberg recorded in his diaries numerous sea voyages, although his experience was largely derived from daily visits to Copenhagen's harbors and shipyards.

This sheet is typical of Eckersberg's drawings that were preparatory for paintings, in which he created geometrically structured compositions based on careful, precise measurements. In this study related to a painting in the Hirschprungske Samling, Copenhagen (Hannover 1898a, no. 493, detail repr. p. 248), the man-of-war at center with its elaborate rigging is drawn in exact, clean strokes of pen and black ink; a thin gray wash was applied to shade the sails and hull. Eckersberg employed a brush and various strengths of wash augmented by swirling strokes of pen and ink to represent the undulating surface of the water, deftly using the reserve of the paper to depict the crest of the waves and the ship's wake. In the distance there are two smaller vessels at the left and a third at the right. At first glance the ships seem to be sailing on the open sea, but upon closer inspection a faint indication in graphite of a coastline with the partially legible inscription *Nord* [ost?] *land* is visible just beyond the small vessel at right. At the lower left of the sheet, the artist included a key relating vital measurements pertaining to the position

of the ship. Two vertical marks at the top and bottom of the sheet, joined by a faint pencil stroke, reveal the artist's plumb line. Many of his preparatory drawings, including his final study of *Thorvaldsen's Arrival in Copenhagen,* 1838 (Royal Museum of Fine Arts, Copenhagen), contain such markings and notes on perspective.

It is difficult to assign a date to the present work, which must have been executed after the mid-1820s, when the artist began to depict marine subjects, and before 1843, when his eyesight began to fail. This sheet was once owned by the architect Jørgen Hansen Koch, a close friend of Eckersberg and director of the Royal Academy, Copenhagen. In technique and subject it is closely comparable to the artist's preparatory drawing for *Meeting at Sea,* 1841 (Kunstforeningen, Copenhagen).

JT

DAVID ROBERTS

Stockbridge (near Edinburgh) 1796–1864 London

29 *Entrance to the Third Pyramid*

Watercolor on paper. 8½ x 6¼ in. (216 x 159 mm). Watermark: *J. Whatman / Turkey Mill* (partially visible; cropped along lower edge). Signed in brown ink at lower right, *David Roberts*. Inscribed by the artist on verso in graphite at center, *Entrance to the third pyramid*.

PROVENANCE: Christopher Gibbs, London; sale, New York, Christie's East, 21 May 1991, lot 98, repr. (b.i.); Christopher Gibbs, London.

The son of a Scottish cobbler, Roberts apprenticed with a house painter before beginning a successful career designing and painting stage sets. One of his commissions, from Covent Garden in 1827, was for the first performance in London of Mozart's *Abduction from the Seraglio*. In 1830, after fourteen years in the theater, he left to devote himself full-time to his own painting. In 1832–33 he traveled in Spain and Morocco, one of the first British artists to do so, and in 1838–39 he was among the first British artists to visit Egypt and the Near East. From the latter trip he produced the work for which he is best known, *The Holy Land, Idumea, Arabia, Egypt and Nubia,* six volumes of lithographs after his drawings, published in London between 1842 and 1849. The most elaborate of such illustrated books of the 1830s and 1840s, the series was also the first to present extensive views of the region.

Roberts published eight views of the pyramids in *The Holy Land . . .,* all large panoramas seen from a great distance, for example, *Great Sphinx—Pyramids of Gizeh,* a frontal view of the half-buried Sphinx, with the pyramids in the far background. Although preparatory drawings for these prints have not been identified, studies for other prints in the volumes devoted to Egypt and Nubia are known. These include two watercolor views of Karnak signed and dated 1838, one in the Morgan Library (acc. no. 1977.25; New York 1992a, p. 45, fig. 24), and one in the Yale Center for British Art, New Haven (New York and elsewhere 1972, no. 134, repr.). The sheets on which these studies are made all measure approximately 12 x 19 inches, as do other sketches Roberts made while touring Egypt and the Near East (see, for example, New York 1968, nos. 1–7, 10, 12, repr.), suggesting that he carried a sketchbook of this size.

The present drawing, likely made during one of the artist's two visits to the site (October 1838 and January 1839), stands in contrast to these large-format studies. It depicts the entrance to the third pyramid in a dramatic close-up, viewed at eye level with the tiny, robed figures huddled at the base of the colossal structure next to its darkened opening. A close-up view of the entrance to the second pyramid, with a single figure about to enter the tomb, is depicted in a drawing formerly on the art market in Boston (sale, James R. Bakker, 15 September 1996, lot 133, repr.). The Boston drawing, executed in watercolor and signed by the artist, is drawn on a sheet with dimensions very close to those of the present work. The dimensions correspond closely to those of an additional group of compositional sketches in graphite or pen and ink formerly in the collection of Rodney G. Searight, London. The existence of these small-format drawings suggests that Roberts made sketches on site, some likely for his own interest. *Back View of the Giant Sphinx,* an unconventional view of the monument (formerly Searight collection, London; Frick

Art Reference Library, New York, photographic archive), is perhaps an example of the latter. Likewise, Roberts may have made the present drawing as a personal souvenir, a reminder of the human element not usually portrayed in the sweeping vistas that appealed to subscribers of his published volumes.

KS

SIR EDWIN HENRY LANDSEER

London 1802–1873 London

30 *Head of a Stag*

Oil on gessoed millboard. 16½ x 14¾ in. (418 x 373 mm). Signed with initials at lower left.
PROVENANCE: Ronald A. Lee, London.

Landseer, a prodigiously talented painter of animals, was the best-known member of a family of accomplished artists and one of the most highly esteemed and popular British painters of the nineteenth century. For Queen Victoria, his most important patron, he executed genre scenes and family portraits that featured favored pets. The British royal collection is among the greatest repositories of his works.

Landseer trained first with his father and then with Benjamin Robert Haydon (1786–1846) and at the Royal Academy Schools in London. From an early age he seems to have been absorbed by the study of animals. He made frequent visits to sketch and paint at the menagerie in Exeter Change in the Strand, London, and he was encouraged by Haydon to study animal anatomy through dissection. His first exhibition pieces, in 1815 at the Royal Academy, were drawings of a mule and the heads of dogs.

Although dogs became Landseer's favorite subject, he devoted himself as well to deer and hunting scenes following his first trip to Scotland, in 1824, in the company of the artist C. R. Leslie (1794–1859). Landseer studied deer assiduously, recording their likenesses not only in oil, such as in this work, but also in pen and ink (for example, *Stags and a Deer;* sale, Winchester, Dreweatt Neate, 8 October 1997, lot 35, repr.). He often depicted them in atmospheric highland landscape settings, which themselves occasionally became the artist's subject; see, for example, *View in the Highlands,* an oil sketch recently on the art market (sale, London, Christie's, 15 April 1994, lot 53, repr.). But his primary interest was the animals, whose muscular bodies and great horned heads dominated the compositions; see, for example, a painting of 1857, *Scene in Braemar—Highland Deer* (private collection; sale, London, Christie's, 25 March 1994, lot 85, repr.). Occasionally he anthropomorphized his animal subjects, as in *The Deer Family,* a painting of 1838 recently on the art market (sale, London, Sotheby's, 3 June 1994, lot 164, repr.), in which a stag, standing between two young deer who face the landscape around them, gazes directly at the viewer as though in identification with the role of the male human parent, the bulk of the stag's head and neck emphasizing its strength and protective role in relation to its young.

Landseer's art is characterized by an illusionism that approaches photographic realism. In the present work, the artist began by sketching the outlines of his subject with a dry brush as though it were chalk. Through scrupulous modeling of form and modulation of stroke, he convincingly suggested the contours of the animal's skull beneath the skin and conveyed the range of textures in his subject—the lapidary sheen of the antlers, the thickly matted fur above the snout, and the spongy thickness of the ears. Closely observed studies of the heads of animals have a long tradition, and this work bears comparison with *Head of a Roebuck* by Albrecht Dürer, a drawing in watercolor of about 1503 (Musée Bonnat, Bayonne; Talbot 1971, p. 48, fig. 11a).

KS

SAMUEL PALMER

Newington 1805–1881 Redhill

31 *Oak Tree and Beech, Lullingstone Park*

Graphite, watercolor, white gouache, and gum arabic, on gray paper. 11⅝ x 18 ⁷/₁₆ in. (296 x 468 mm). Watermark: None. Signed in graphite at lower left, *S Palmer fecᵗ–.* Inscribed on verso in pen and black ink at lower right, *Shoreham.*

PROVENANCE: John Linnell; by descent to his grandson Herbert Linnell; Mrs. E. A. C. Druce; Mrs. Hilda Pryor; private collection, England; sale, London, Christie's, 8 June 2000, lot 111, repr. in color pp. 108, 110 (detail), and on front cover (detail).

LITERATURE: Palmer 1892, p. 46; Binyon 1925, pl. 21; Grigson 1947, pp. 89, 169–70, no. 60, pl. 25; *Letters* 1974, pp. 36, 47–48; Sellars 1974, pl. 51; New Haven 1977, under no. 217; Lister 1988, pp. 4, 64, no. 86, repr.

EXHIBITIONS: Liverpool 1937, no. 87; New York and elsewhere 1956–57, no. 73; Cambridge 1984, p. 14, no. 16, repr.

Palmer is considered one of the most innovative landscape artists of the nineteenth century. The son of a London bookseller, he was introduced to poetry at an early age, and it remained an inspiration throughout his career. He briefly studied drawing with William Wate (d. 1832), which constituted his only formal artistic training. Through the artist John Linnell, whom Palmer met in 1822, he was exposed to the work of Albrecht Dürer and Lucas van Leyden (1494–1533), for which he developed a passion. In 1824 Linnell introduced Palmer to William Blake (1757–1827), who became a friend and mentor.

The decade following Palmer's introduction to Blake is known as his Shoreham period for the village in Kent where he lived from 1826 until 1832. The work he did at Shoreham, visionary landscapes without precedent in British art, is his most famous. The present drawing belongs to this period. It represents a view in Lullingstone Park, near Shoreham. The park was the location of Lullingstone Castle, since 1500 the seat of the Hart Dyke family. The drawing is one of three commissioned by John Linnell depicting Lullingstone Park (Lister 1988, nos. 87–88, repr.).

This drawing traditionally has been dated 1828 because of two letters Palmer wrote that year. In the first, written in September to his friend George Richmond, Palmer stated, "Mr Linnell tells me that by making studies of the Shoreham scenery I could get a thousand a year directly. Tho' I am making studies for Mr Linnell, I will, God help me, never be a naturalist by profession" (*Letters* 1974, p. 36, cited in Lister 1988, p. 64). In the second, written in December to John Linnell, Palmer alluded to his having been "trying to draw a large [oak] in Lullingstone" (*Letters* 1974, pp. 47–48, cited in Lister 1988, p. 64). However, a letter from Palmer to Linnell written in 1824, in which the artist tells his friend that he has "begun two studies for you on grey paper at Lullingstone," may indicate that the Lullingstone drawings were executed or at least begun that year (*Letters* 1974, p. 8, cited in Lister 1988, p. 64).

Palmer characteristically focused his descriptive attention on one section of a work—in this case the range of textures in the giant oak in the foreground, whose "lichened, knotted and fissured boles and branches" (Lister 1988, p. 64) are represented by a skein of dots and circles and tiny scribbled strokes. The unevenness and controlled chaos of these strokes are a modern restatement of the careful cross-hatching of the Renaissance masters.

Equally modern is Palmer's representation of light. He used a complex media to describe the rising or setting sun along the horizon and left edge of the giant oak in the foreground: white gouache overpainted with yellow watercolor to which gum arabic, imparting shine, has been applied, with occasional dots of red watercolor applied to the yellow. The effect is startling, and seems to express pictorially his idea of the Kentish countryside as a "Valley of Vision" (Lister 1988, p. 4).

It has been observed that Palmer's striking modernity in this drawing and others of the Shoreham period anticipates the work of such twentieth-century artists as Graham Sutherland (Lister 1988, p. 4).

KS

RICHARD DOYLE

London 1824–1883 London

32   *Fairy Subject: Dame Julianna Berners Teaching Her Young Pupils the Art of Fishing*

Watercolor and bodycolor over graphite. 8¼ x 17¹⁵/₁₆ in. (209 x 454 mm). Signed with monogram in pen and brown ink at lower right, *ЯD*.

PROVENANCE: E. Joseph, London.

LITERATURE: Engen 1983, pp. 153–54, repr.

EXHIBITIONS: London 1883; London 1983–84, p. 53, no. 153, repr. in color, endpaper and inside back cover.

This picture, one of the last exhibited by Richard Doyle at the Grosvenor Gallery in 1883, depicts the legendary Dame Julianna Berners, said to be the prioress of the nunnery of Sopwell, Hertfordshire, who wrote the first treatise on fishing in English, published at St. Albans in 1486. Since both Richard and his brother Charles Altamount Doyle were keen anglers, the subject intrigued Richard, and he created his own unpublished version of the treatise. Dame Julianna's interest in field and stream included hawking and hunting, and she wrote treatises on these activities as well. It is typical of Doyle to treat Dame Julianna as a quasifairy subject; here she is depicted serenely sitting on a bank reading from the treatise and keeping an eye on her charges, pixies who sit on the riverbank casting their rods with considerable success, judging from the basket at the left, which brims with fish. It is not surprising that Doyle, who was famous for his fairy illustrations, made a fairy subject out of this, replacing children with pixies or elves. He got off to an early start working as an illustrator for *Punch.* His father and brother were illustrators, but doubtless the most famous member of the family was his nephew, Sir Arthur Conan Doyle, author of the Sherlock Holmes stories. Doyle had a fondness for English history subjects, and he responded to the Gothic Revival with a series of illustrations entitled *Manners and Customs of ye Englyshe.* He was strongly attracted to fantasy and legends and was immensely popular in Victorian England.

CDD

FRANÇOIS-MARIUS GRANET

Aix-en-Provence 1775–1849 Malvalat

33 *Portal of Nôtre Dame de Marsat, near Riom, Auvergne*

Watercolor and point of brush over graphite on cream paper. 8½ x 7 ⁵/₁₆ in. (215 x 186 mm). Watermark: None.

PROVENANCE: Zangrilli, Brady & Co., Ltd., New York.

EXHIBITIONS: New York 1986, no. 28, repr. in color; Paris and New York 1993–94, no. 101, repr.; Moscow and St. Petersburg 1998, no. 97, repr.

Granet's Catholicism and interest in medieval architecture (he was the son of a master mason) was shared by some of his colleagues in Jacques-Louis David's studio, notably Fleury-François Richard (1777–1852) and Pierre-Henri Révoil (1776–1842). Étienne Jean Delécluze related that shortly after leaving David's atelier, Granet took a studio in a Capuchin monastery on the rue de la Paix, alongside Gros, Ingres, and Girodet. According to Delécluze, [Granet] "qui devait se rendre célèbre en imitant des intérieurs de couvent, commença a en effet par peindre les longs corridors de celui des Capucines . . . chaque jour Granet . . . était établi dans le cloître avec son chevalet et sa toile . . . " (Delécluze 1855, p. 298). The artist earned a great deal of popular praise for his mysterious views of dimly lit church interiors peopled with monks performing religious rituals. He first presented such a subject, *Le Cloître des Feuillants,* at the Salon of 1799 and thereafter continued to produce and exhibit these popular scenes throughout his career. Having departed for Rome in 1802, in 1814 Granet achieved overwhelming success with *Choir of the Capuchin Church in Rome,* which earned the artist wide public and official acclaim and warranted the production of no less than thirteen variants.

This watercolor is preparatory for a lithograph in the *Voyages pittoresques et romantiques dans l'Ancienne France,* a seventeen-volume work assembled by Charles Nodier, Baron Justin Taylor, and Alphonse de Cailleux and published by A. Firmin Didot in 1829–33 (pl. 14). The large number of reproductions—mostly of picturesque landscapes or architectural studies—resulted in commissions for many French artists during the first half of the nineteenth century. The lithograph after the present drawing was executed by Jean-Baptiste Arnoult (or Arnout or Arnould; b. Dijon 1788) and is inscribed *Granet del. 1831;* it is titled *Vue de la porte de l'église de Marsel* [sic] *près de Riom, Auvergne,* and represents Nôtre Dame de Marsat in the Auvergne. The lithograph closely corresponds to Granet's drawing, although Arnoult clarified the figures significantly, rendering the seated one at left as a mother with child. A second plate for the *Voyages pittoresques,* titled *Vue de la nef de l'église de Cebazat,* was produced by Adrien Dauzats (1804–1868) based on a drawing by Granet, which Isabelle Néto-Daguerre dates to 1820 (pl. 32). Granet may have executed the present sheet on one of his trips between Aix-en-Provence and Paris in 1831, according to the date inscribed on the print.

The rich, subtle washes of color in this sheet reveal Granet's talent as a watercolorist. Throughout his career he executed thousands of drawings and watercolors, a number of which he left to the Musée du Louvre, Paris, and the majority of which reside with the

bulk of his oeuvre of works on paper at the Musée Granet, in his native Aix-en-Provence. The artist recorded sites throughout Paris, Rome, Aix, and the French countryside, including depictions of architecture and landscape as well as a number of domestic scenes. His use of wash was fluid, often with soft-edged strokes of colors bleeding into each other on the damp paper.

JT

JEAN AUGUSTE DOMINIQUE INGRES

Montauban 1780–1867 Paris

34 *Frau Reinhold and Her Daughters,* 1815

Graphite on fine wove paper cut from prepared tablet in such a way as to result in an irregular edge made up on all sides with Japanese paper. 11 ^{15}/$_{16}$ x 8 ^{13}/$_{16}$ in. (303 x 225 mm). Watermark: None. Signed and dated at lower right, *Ingres Del. Rome 1815.*

PROVENANCE: Johann Gotthard Reinhold, Hamburg, until 1838; his widow, Hamburg, until 1846; their daughter, Frau Louis Köster, Hamburg, until 1873; probably her husband, Louis Köster, Hamburg, until 1880; Martin Birnbaum, New York; Mrs. John D. Rockefeller II, New York, 1931; John D. Rockefeller II; by descent to David Rockefeller, New York.

LITERATURE: Varnhagen von Ense 1865, vol. 7, p. 220 (entry for 17 June 1850); Naef 1956, pp. 649–54 (identified); *Rheinische Merkur* 1956 (V.), p. 8; Naef 1958 ("Meisterwerk"), p. 9; Birnbaum 1960, p. 188; Naef 1967, p. 6, n. 1; Mongan 1969, p. 144, fig. 18, p. 153; Naef 1977–80, vol. 4 (1977), pp. 274–75, no. 149, repr.; Potter 1984, pp. 100–101, no. 15, repr.

EXHIBITIONS: New York 1953; Cambridge 1967, no. 34, repr.; London and elsewhere 1999, no. 56, repr. in color (as in private collection).

In his book on portrait drawings by Ingres, Hans Naef wrote extensively about Johann Gottfried Reinhold and his family (Naef 1956, pp. 649–54). When Reinhold was the Dutch ambassador to Rome from 1814 to 1827, he commissioned at least three portraits from Ingres, including this one of his wife and daughters. Born in Germany, Reinhold was brought up in the Netherlands and served as a Dutch diplomat, first in Hamburg, where he met and married Sophie Amalie Dorothea Whilhelmine (called Minna) Ritter. Their daughter Susette was born in Hamburg in 1808, and a second daughter Marie was born in Berlin in 1810. Susette is on her mother's left in the family portrait, Marie on the right. After Napoleon's demise in 1814, Reinhold was appointed ambassador to Rome and Florence, an office he retained for thirteen years. In 1838 his obituary described him as "more scholar than soldier, more man of the world than scholar, but in truth more poet than man of the world and scholar."

It is evident that Ingres spent even more time on this very complete portrait drawing than he customarily did. His usual approach was to visit with the subject in the morning, study his or her mannerisms during lunch, and then make the drawing after lunch, usually completing it around four. He worked on specially prepared tablets made up with layers of paper wrapped around a cardboard center and finished with a finely surfaced white English paper. The cushioning protected the fine white paper on which the drawing was executed as well as provided him with a taut and resilient surface not unlike that of a stretched canvas on which his finely pointed pencil could be applied with dazzling virtuosity and differentiation of stroke.

This portrait is one of the artist's most memorable, made especially enchanting, as Gary Tinterow and Philip Conisbee have noted, by the graceful arabesque of Frau Reinhold holding the hands of her children (London and elsewhere 1999, no. 56).

CDD

FERDINAND VICTOR EUGÈNE DELACROIX

Charenton-Saint-Maurice 1798–1863 Paris

35 *Arab Chieftain with a Musket* (Chef Arabe tenant un fusil)

Watercolor and gouache. 8⅞ x 6⅝ in. (226 x 170 mm). Signed in pen and brown ink at lower right, *E. Delacroix.*

PROVENANCE: Private collection, France; sale, Paris, Hôtel Drouot, 5 May 1986, lot 29, repr.; Walter Goetz, London.

EXHIBITIONS: Paris 1994–95, no. 72, repr. in color; London 1996–97, not in catalogue.

In 1832 Delacroix accompanied the comte Charles de Mornay on a diplomatic mission to Morocco. Sent by Louis Philippe, de Mornay was to visit the sultan of Morocco at Meknès and try to settle certain disputes arising from France's occupation of Morocco. As Delacroix was not there in an official capacity, he was obliged to pay his own expenses beyond passage. An elegant, interesting man, he was invited to keep de Mornay company but he also went along to satisfy his own curiosity about north Africa. It was not a short trip: the journey from Paris to Tangiers by carriage and ship took more than three weeks, thirteen days of which were spent on the open sea. The party left on New Year's day and did not return to Paris until the following summer. Two years later Delacroix executed several studies like this portrait of an Arab chieftain, resorting to the hundreds of sketches he made on the spot during his six-month stay in Morocco. Exotic Arab subjects had a lifetime appeal for the artist, both before and after his Moroccan sojourn.

Remarkable for its fresh color, this sheet is a variant of a small painting mentioned in the posthumous sale, in 1864, of the contents of Delacroix's studio. It is oriented a little differently and is somewhat smaller than the painting but is unmistakably the same composition as that formerly in the Spaeth collection (repr. Johnson 1986, no. 363, p. 174, pl. 179). There is also another watercolor of the same subject, signed and dated 1834 (repr. sale, Paris, Hôtel Drouot, 2 June 1950, lot 2).

CDD

FERDINAND VICTOR EUGÈNE DELACROIX
Charenton-Saint-Maurice 1798–1863 Paris

36 *Landscape with a Carriage*

Brush and brown ink on paper. 6 ⁹/₁₆ x 10⅛ in. (168 x 257 mm). Delacroix estate stamp at lower right.

PROVENANCE: Lucien Guiraud, Paris; their sale, Paris, Hôtel Drouot, 14 June 1956, lot 25, repr.; Marianne Feilchenfeldt, 1958; Dr. and Mrs. Alfred Scharf, London; sale, London, Sotheby's, 27 November 1991, lot 219, repr.

EXHIBITIONS: London 1964a, no. 108, repr. pl. 53; New York 1998, no. 18, repr. in color.

This small but highly evocative work seems to suggest a story in progress. Much of its romantic appeal is attributable to Delacroix's rapid and varied brushwork. Using a wet brush, the artist indicated a dense forest in an undulating, hilly landscape with the ruins of Valmont Abbey on the horizon. He left the foreground of the sheet almost blank except for a few summary strokes to suggest the road leading away from the forest, toward which the seemingly tiny horse and carriage, just emerging from the forest in the middle ground, are headed. Delacroix picked out this important but minutely rendered feature of the composition, along with some of the tree trunks and bushes in the forest, with the point of his brush.

This view is near the château de Valmont, near Fécamp in Normandy, where Delacroix often spent holidays with his cousins, the Batailles, who owned a country house that had the remains of the ancient Gothic abbey on its grounds, which fascinated the artist. These ruins were so powerfully appealing to Delacroix that he is said to have discovered the emotional power of Gothic architecture there. He also made a watercolor study of the interior of the abbey with tombs and stained glass (present location unknown; sale, Versailles, Palais des Capri, 2 June 1971, lot 74bis).

CDD

VICTOR HUGO

Besançon 1802–1885 Paris

37 *Fantastic Castle at Twilight,* 1857

Pen, brush, brown and black ink, and stump, with touches of white gouache on cream paper, partly rubbed. 12⁵/₁₆ x 9⁵/₁₆ in. (310 x 460 mm). Watermark: None. Signed and dated in white gouache at lower center, *VICTOR HUGO—Guernsey. 1857.*

PROVENANCE: Galerie Jan Krugier, Ditesheim, et Cie, Geneva; private collection, France; Galerie Berès, Paris.

EXHIBITIONS: New York 1998a, no. 74, repr. in color; Brussels 1999, no. 31, repr. in color on cover and in catalogue.

After delivering an impassioned speech against Louis Bonaparte and publishing *Quatorze discours,* a volume of political writings in 1851, Hugo found his position in France precarious. Participating in the coup d'etat of 2 December 1852, at the end of the year he fled Paris for Brussels, from where he was later expelled by Bonaparte. Hugo then moved to Jersey, which his acts of political agitation forced him to leave in 1855. The remainder of his exile was spent in Guernsey, although he traveled frequently to Brussels and abroad. The day following the founding of the Third Republic, 5 September 1870, he returned to France with his family.

During his first few years in Guernsey, occupied with the decoration of his new home, Hauteville House, Hugo was more active as a draftsman than as a writer. The rough, extreme setting of the Channel Islands fostered dramatic and violent imagery in his work as well as the author's meditations on nature, death, and the sublime. He wrote to his friend, the literary critic Abel-François Villemain (1790–1870), from Hauteville House on 17 November 1859, "I need these periods of rest sometimes in my solitude, in face of the ocean, amid this sombre scenery which has a supreme attraction for me and which draws me toward the dazzling apparitions of the infinite. Sometimes I spend the whole night meditating on my fate, before the great deep, and at times all I can do is exclaim: 'Stars! Stars! Stars!'" (Meurice 1898, p. 152).

Hugo began drawing in 1831; however, it was not until 1848 that he developed the rich wash technique, incorporating stencils and other media, that characterizes his mature style. The castle motif is found throughout his texts and drawings; although many of his drawings are reminiscent of castles he visited during his travels to the Continent, these structures are fundamentally works of the imagination, having assumed their final form only during the process of creation. In this large, dramatic sheet he masterfully utilized many of the techniques with which he began experimenting in Jersey. Hugo used a stencil to mask the silhouette of the château; the white reserves of paper provide a luminous contrast to the rich, fluid ink taches. After broadly applying the wash, he dipped his pen in the pools of ink to quickly draw out delicate architectural details, causing forms to coalesce from the chiaroscuro of the inky background. There are a number of sheets representing similar structures, also dated *Guernsey 1857,* that reveal Hugo's experimentation with the castle motif at that time (see Villequier and Paris 1971–72, nos. 106–8, 126). In his commentary on the Salon of 1859, Baudelaire noted, "la magnifique imagination qui coule dans les dessins de Victor Hugo [was found in] ses dessins à l'encre de Chine, car il est trop évident qu'en poésie notre poète est le roi des paysagistes."

JT

THÉODORE ROUSSEAU

Paris 1812–1867 Barbizon (Seine-et-Marne)

38 *The Près-Bois, Franche-Comté, with the Mountains of Doubs in the Background,* 1863

Pen and brown ink, over graphite, on cream paper, laid down on light brown paper. 5¼ x 8⅛ in. (133 x 206 mm). Watermark: None. Estate stamp at lower left, *TH.R.* (Lugt 2436).

PROVENANCE: Estate of the artist; sale, Paris, Hôtel Drouot, 27 April–2 May 1868, lot 226; Alfred Sensier, Paris; Émile Joseph-Rignault, Paris (Lugt 2218); Georges Aubry, Paris; private collection, Paris; Mr. and Mrs. John Rewald, New York, by 1953; Rewald sale, London, Sotheby's, 7 July 1960, lot 107 (as *Paysage avec champs lavourés*); sale, New York, Christie's, 22 May 1996, lot 124, repr.

LITERATURE: Terrasse 1976, repr.; Schulman 1997, no. 667, repr.

EXHIBITIONS: Rotterdam 1958, no. 147, p. 131; Paris 1958–59, no. 147, pl. 143; Los Angeles 1959, no. 119; New York 1959, no. 147, p. 131.

Among Rousseau's earliest drawings, found in a sketchbook now in the Minneapolis Institute of Arts, are a number of sketches made in 1825 during his first trip to the Jura, in the Franche-Comté region of northwestern France, when he was twelve years old. His talent led his cousin, the landscape painter Alexandre Pau de Saint-Martin (1782–1850), to encourage the young artist. After a trip to the forest of Compiègne with Pau, Rousseau entered the atelier of Joseph Rémond in 1826. Shortly thereafter he transferred to the studio of Guillaume Guillon Lethière, before abandoning his academic training in favor of working directly from nature. In 1830 Rousseau began to travel France, an activity that shaped his career as a landscape painter. He made his professional debut at the Salon the following year.

In 1834, at the age of twenty-two, Rousseau returned to Franche-Comté. Along with his traveling companion Lorenz, the artist explored the mountains in Jura and Doubs, the western range of which forms the border with Switzerland. After traveling for about four months in the Jura, the two journeyed to the Swiss Alps. This trip preceded by two years Rousseau's first extended stay at Barbizon and his initial rejection by the Salon. His travels revived his work, and in 1835 he used sketches from his trip the previous year as the basis for *Les Vaches dans le Jura* (Mesdag Museum, The Hague), which was one of the last paintings by the artist to be accepted at the Salon.

In 1862, five years before his death, Rousseau traveled through the Franche-Comté for the last time, visiting his wife's family and returning to Barbizon via the Col de la Faucille, the main pass of the Jura mountains on the French-Swiss border, with a remarkable view of Mont Blanc and Lake Geneva. This study, dated by Michel Schulman to 1863, represents a view executed during these travels. The mountains of Doubs are to the northeast of the Jura and form a rugged backdrop to the wooded setting depicted here. The choice of pen and brown ink, in concert with the delicate technique composed of dots and short strokes of the pen, reflects Rousseau's interest in and study of Dutch seventeenth-century drawing. Here he made the initial sketch in graphite, probably en plein air, and then more carefully executed the final drawing in pen and ink, perhaps in his studio. This sheet was purchased from the artist's estate by Alfred Sensier, a lifelong friend of the artist and the author of an 1872 monograph, *Souvenirs sur Th. Rousseau.*

JT

JEAN-FRANÇOIS MILLET

Gruchy, near Greville, 1814–1875 Barbizon

39   *Woman Churning Butter* (La Baratteuse), 1855–58

VERSO: *Study of a Shepherd Tending Goats on a Hillside*

Conté crayon on buff paper; verso: Conté crayon. 18⅞ x 15⅝ in. (479 x 397 mm). Signed in Conté crayon at lower right, *J. F. Millet.*

PROVENANCE: Quincy Adams Shaw, Boston, by 1907; Wildenstein & Co., London and New York, 1969; Henry Moore, Hoglands, Hertfordshire; by descent to his daughter, Mary Moore; sale, New York, Sotheby's, 13–14 May 1997, lot 6, repr.

LITERATURE: Gaunt 1969, p. 9, repr.; Boston 1984, p. 38 (as location unknown).

EXHIBITIONS: Boston 1919–20; London 1969, no. 31, repr.; Tokyo and elsewhere 1970, no. 30, repr.; Buenos Aires 1971, no. 16, repr.; Paris 1991–92, repr. in color p. 23; Tokyo and elsewhere 1992–93, repr. in color; Williamstown 1999, no. 46, repr. in color.

Millet's choice of subject matter—the everyday activities of the rural peasant class around Barbizon—challenged the traditional hierarchy of genres established at the Salon and inspired heated political discussion. In the wake of the 1848 revolution, the agricultural economy of the French countryside underwent a crisis as commercial farms were established and many displaced workers fled small towns to find menial jobs in the cities. The continued tradition of agricultural labor in the towns outside Paris formed the subject matter for much of Millet's mature work, and the artist often used a single figure at work as a symbol of *la condition humaine.*

The artist's representation of genre subjects began on a modest scale while he worked as a portraitist in Le Havre, producing his earliest mature genre paintings about 1847, shortly before he and his family relocated to Barbizon. About 1850 he began to make independent, finished drawings, probably for sale or reproduction and publication. Millet first depicted a woman churning butter in a painting of the mid-1840s (formerly Musée des Beaux-Arts, Montréal) and continued to do so in drawings, etchings, pastels, and paintings, until his last large canvas of 1870 (Malden Public Library, Massachusetts), which was one of two paintings the artist sent to the Salon of 1870 (the other being *Novembre,* destroyed in Berlin, 1945), the last in which he participated. Alexandra Murphy attributes Millet's fondness for the subject to the crucial role of the production of butter in his native Normandy, which is one of the principal provincial exporters of *beurres de luxe* to Paris. Encouraged by Alfred Sensier to produce etchings for commercial publication, Millet replicated his compositions, including an earlier one of a woman churning butter, in a number of etchings from the 1850s and 1860s. Murphy noted that this sheet was likely executed shortly after the artist's 1855/56 etching of the subject (Delteil 1906, no. 10) and reveals a shift in the artist's representation of the subject to a more refined and monumental format.

In this highly finished sheet, a woman, her form softly molded by light and shadow, stands in a dairy barn lined with shelves. A cat rubs against her legs as she manipulates a butter churn. She wears a *marmotte,* or head scarf, commonly worn by Barbizon peasants.

86

Millet paid great attention to capturing the physical aspects of labor, the stresses and movements of a particular task; his formal vocabulary viscerally evokes the exertion and repetition of routine chores. In the present drawing, the repeated rounded lines and curvilinear forms suggest the repetitive motion of churning.

The verso of this sheet contains a rapidly executed study in Conté crayon representing a shepherd seated on a hillside and leaning on his staff as his small flock of goats grazes and rests. Millet began making drawings of shepherds and their flocks in and around Fontainebleau shortly after arriving at Barbizon with his family in 1849. The rapid, fluid strokes of Conté crayon in this drawing suggest that the sheet dates to the mid-1850s, when Millet's sketches became more broadly executed and less composed than his earlier work.

By 1907 this drawing had entered the collection of Quincy Adams Shaw (1825–1908), a Boston collector who began buying works by Millet during the early 1870s. Shaw amassed the largest collection of paintings, pastels, and etchings by the artist in America. In 1917 the majority of the collection was given by his heirs to the Museum of Fine Arts, Boston. *Woman Churning Butter* subsequently was purchased by the sculptor Henry Moore for his extensive private collection of drawings.

JT

JEAN-FRANÇOIS MILLET

Gruchy, near Greville, 1814–1875 Barbizon

40 *Landscape,* ca. 1866–68

Pen and brown ink over graphite, with touches of green, gray, and brown ink on cream paper. 4⅛ x 5⅞ in. (105 x 149 mm). Watermark: None. Stamped at lower right, *J. F. M.;* variously inscribed in graphite, *vert, bleu* [illegible] *brises, vert* [illegible].

PROVENANCE: Faith Stern, New York.

LITERATURE: Lepoittevin 1973, pp. 146–47.

During the latter half of the 1860s—in 1866, 1867, and 1868—Millet made three month-long sojourns to the mineral spas at Vichy with his ailing wife. While the first two trips were extraordinarily productive, the artist's own poor health made the third notably less fruitful. Among Millet's approximately two hundred drawings of the countryside surrounding Vichy are a number of studies in graphite or pen and ink, accented with watercolor. Many of the sketches were executed en plein air in small notebooks and colored later by the artist in his hotel room; watercolors from this period were made at evening in Vichy or following the artist's return to Barbizon.

This drawing was executed on a leaf taken from a book; the verso contains a faint offset impression of a printed page. Millet often carried sketchbooks on carriage rides into the countryside in order to record his observations of the landscape. In lieu of a sketchbook, he may have used a page from a book he had at hand. Initially sketched in graphite and inscribed with color notations, the sheet was rapidly executed in pen and ink, with touches of wash accenting the roofs of the houses at center. Informal sketches such as this served the artist as aide-mémoire in the preparation of his watercolors and more finished drawings.

JT

ADOLPHE VON MENZEL

Breslau 1815–1905 Berlin

41 *Sleeping Youth, His Head and Arms Resting on the Back of a Sofa*

Graphite, with light brown wash (in background). 5⅛ x 7⅛ in. (132 x 182 mm). Artist's stamp on verso, *AM;* below, in another direction, *MAC* [illegible].

PROVENANCE: Estate of the artist; B. Grönvold collection; Prentzel collection; sale, Berlin, H. W. Lange, 1942, lot 89; C. G. Boerner Inc., Düsseldorf, 1959.

LITERATURE: Ebertshäuser 1976, repr. p. 952; *Artemis Annual Report* 1995–96, no. 10, repr.; New York 2001, under no. 102.

EXHIBITIONS: London 1996–97, not in catalogue; New York 1997–98.

The sleeping young man portrayed here is Carl Johann Arnold (1829–1916), whose parents had been friends with Menzel since 1833. Menzel's pupil, Arnold spent October to December of 1846 with the artist in Berlin. His father, Carl Heinrich Arnold (1793–1874), was a tapestry designer and lithographer. Young Arnold worked tirelessly with Menzel, who wrote to his parents in praise of the young man's perseverance, "He keeps painting and drawing from morning until night." In this sensitive study, Menzel caught the young man asleep, still wearing his printmaker's apron, and managed to convey his serious demeanor while placing a certain emphasis on his right hand. This is one of several studies Menzel made of his seventeen-year-old pupil. Another sketch, which must date to the same moment, depicts the youth awake on the same sofa (Wirth 1965, p. 64, repr.). One, now in the collection of Charles Ryskamp (New York 2001, no. 102, repr.), probably executed some time later, to judge from the subject's appearance, depicts him standing with his right hand in his pocket. Menzel's pastel drawing in the Kupferstichkabinett, Berlin, depicts the pensive youth turned to the left in three-quarter profile (Berlin 1955, no. 161, repr.). Later Arnold was known as a genre and animal painter as well as court painter at Weimar.

CDD

LOUIS EUGÈNE BOUDIN

Honfleur 1824–1898 Deauville

42   *Women on the Beach,* 1865

Watercolor over graphite. 5⅞ x 8⅝ in. (148 x 218 mm). Watermark: None. Dated in graphite at lower right, *1865;* studio stamp at lower right, *E. B.* (Lugt 828).

PROVENANCE: Estate of the artist; private collection, France; Emmanuel Moatti, New York and Paris.

EXHIBITION: New York 2001a, no. 42, repr. in color.

The son of a sailor, Boudin began his professional life in Le Havre as a stationer's clerk before opening his own paper and art supply shop with a partner. Occasionally exhibiting artwork in the shop window, Boudin came into contact with a number of artists, including Eugène Isabey, Thomas Couture, Constant Troyon, and Jean-François Millet (Nos. 39–40). In 1846, after the partnership dissolved, Boudin began making a modest living selling the drawings he had made of picturesque sites at Le Havre. After traveling to Paris and Normandy, the artist returned to his native Honfleur in 1854 and began painting the marine scenes that would attract the attention of Gustave Courbet, and consequently the critic Baudelaire, who became one of Boudin's most avid admirers.

First exhibiting at the Salon of 1859, Boudin was urged to move to Paris by his friends, including the young Claude Monet. He returned to the seaside the following year, when he regularly began to spend his summers painting and drawing at the neighboring resort towns of Le Havre, Trouville, and Deauville. His depictions of fashionable men and women at the beach were well received and helped to establish his reputation as a painter. These works responded to Baudelaire's call for artists to represent the "beauty of the contemporary" and capture the manners, fashion, and activities of the bourgeoisie at popular beach resorts. Boudin continued to paint scenes of elegant vacationers throughout his career; the latest such work is dated 1896, two years before the artist's death at age seventy-four.

This drawing is related to a number of beach scenes executed by Boudin during the summer of 1865, which he spent at the seaside along with James McNeill Whistler and Courbet. Boudin produced many studies of women at the beach, which served as aide-mémoire for the many groups of fashionably dressed figures in his paintings. He would make a lively drawing in graphite to which he would then apply brilliant touches of watercolor. This extraordinarily fresh sheet is similar to a larger study of five seated women, which was executed that summer and is now in the St. Louis Art Museum (St. Louis Art Museum 1975, p. 155, repr.). The artist did not reproduce the figures in his rapid watercolor sketches exactly but rather repeated the poses with slight variations of costume. The two seated women engaged in conversation depicted in the present study are similar to figures in Boudin's *L'Heure du bain sur la plage de Deauville,* 1865 (Mr. and Mrs. Paul Mellon), and *Scène de plage au soleil couchant,* 1865 (National Gallery of Art, Washington, D.C.).

JT

CAMILLE PISSARRO

Charlotte Amalie, St. Thomas, Danish Virgin Islands, 1830–1903 Paris

43 *Two Peasant Women, Study for* Les Mendiantes, ca. 1890

Black crayon on paper, laid down on board. 18 x 15 in. (457 x 381 mm). Watermark: None. Stamped with the artist's initials in black ink at lower left, *C.P.* (Lugt S. 613a); inscribed in black crayon along left margin, *Caraco gris vert bleu / orangé rouge fond / bleu vert / bleu foncé / orangé jaune / vert jaune gris / tabliers bleu outremer / jupe bleu outremer / foncé outremer;* numbered in blue pencil at upper left, *2/4.*

PROVENANCE: Henry Hyde, New York; Liza Hyde, New York; Artemis Fine Arts, New York.

EXHIBITION: New York 1998, no. 22, repr. in color.

An avid draftsman, Pissarro rarely left his studio without a sketchbook to record his observations. The catalogue of the over three hundred drawings by Pissarro in the Ashmolean Museum, Oxford, provides an excellent summary of the artist's work as a draftsman (Brettell and Lloyd 1980). In 1879 his career reached a turning point with a series of peasant images that marked the shift in his interest from urban and rural landscapes to genre scenes, largely under the influence of Degas, with whom Pissarro began to work on prints. Regarding figure studies, he wrote to his son Lucien on 5 July 1883: "Don't strive for skillful line, strive for simplicity, for the essential lines which give the physiognomy. . . . Rather incline toward caricature than toward prettiness" (Bailly-Herzberg 1980, p. 166). This simple, strong sense of line and concentration on salient detail is evident in many of Pissarro's later drawings, including this sheet. The later works are on a larger scale and are more boldly executed than his earlier drawings.

This study of two young peasant girls is preliminary to a sheet drawn in black chalk, watercolor, and gouache, dated *Eragny 1890* (private collection, Toronto; Pissarro and Venturi 1939, no. 1445, repr.), which was used by the artist four years later as the basis for an etching printed in color, *Young Beggar Girls* (Fig. 1; Delteil 1923, no. 110). Pissarro depicted two young women in peasant dress seen from behind and inscribed color notations

FIG. 1. Camille Pissarro, *Young Beggar Girls,* Ashmolean Museum, Oxford

along the left margin of the sheet. The notations confirm that he intended the drawing to serve as a basis for the watercolor. As with many of his late drawings, Pissarro studied the figures in isolation on the page with little or no suggestion of a setting. In the watercolor and print the figures of the two girls overlap as they stand close to one another on a path in front of a gate.

This work, one of the artist's rare depictions of the rural poor, was executed late in his career in his studio at Eragny par Gisors, Eure, northwest of Paris. Although known for his landscape paintings, during the 1880s Pissarro developed an interest in representing the human figure. He produced a large number of figure drawings, albeit few paintings with figures, between 1880 and 1903. Conversely he made few landscape drawings, although the subject dominates his painted oeuvre from this period. Over the course of the decade he developed an elaborate preparatory process for his compositions and produced numerous studies from life of peasants at work. Like the present drawing, many of these studies represent young women and were made from costumed models who posed in the studio. This sheet may have belonged to a sketchbook from about 1890 that remained in Pissarro's studio at the time of his death. It, along with a sheet in the Louvre, *Étude pour La Causette* (RF 29 534) bears a number in the upper left corner as well as the atelier stamp with the artist's initials.

JT

ÉDOUARD MANET

Paris 1832–1883 Paris

44 Autograph letter to Marguerite Guillemet, illustrated with two daisies and a bee, [1880]

Graphite with brush and gray, green, ocher, and blue watercolor; letter in pen and brown ink. 7⅞ x 4 ¹³/₁₆ in. (198 x 123 mm).

PROVENANCE: Konrad Kellen.

Purchased as the gift of Eugene V. and Clare Thaw, 1991; Acc. no. 1991.98

On the advice of his doctor, Manet spent some five months—the summer and fall of 1880—convalescing at Bellevue, outside Paris. He amused himself by writing to his friends and family, illustrating about forty of the letters with watercolor sketches. Many of the letters he wrote at this time were sent to Mlle Isabelle Lemonnier or to Mme Jules Guillemet, the wife of a well-to-do merchant, but he also wrote at least two—both of which are now in the Morgan Library—to Mlle Marguerite, the younger sister of his friend Mme Guillemet. The letters are illustrated with charming sketches of a flower and a bee. In one Manet invited Mlle Marguerite to the country, suggesting that she bring "the light-colored summer dress you told me about, and if you have a pretty garden hat don't leave it behind" (Fig. 1). Mlle Marguerite accepted his invitation, and during her visit the artist painted her in the garden at Bellevue. The painting is now in the collection of the E. G. Bührle Foundation in Zurich. The flower illustrated here is a daisy or marguerite, an obvious play on Mlle Marguerite's name. The letter reads, *Je t'aime | on vous le dira surement, | Marguerite—, je t'aime | un peu beaucoup passionement.*

While this letter is the briefer of the two, the sentiment is charming and the flowers, which provide the focal point, fill the page nicely. A full, long-stemmed daisy extends along the left margin, while another, partially opened daisy with a bee—whether approaching or departing cannot be determined—is brushed in at the bottom left. In his illness Manet would increasingly turn to flower painting to occupy himself. Every year until his death in 1883, he would spend his summers in some suburb of Paris; in 1881 it was Versailles, and in 1882 he stayed at Rueil.

It has been observed that Manet's letters are some of the most lyrical examples of a nineteenth-century artistic sensibility. An exhibition at the Musée d'Orsay, Paris, and the Walters Art Gallery, Baltimore, included more than twenty of these letters (repr. Paris and Baltimore 2000, pp. 45–64, pls. 699–776).

The other letter was acquired at the same time (MA 4716). Although the Library's collection already included five hundred letters by Manet, acquired with the help of Mrs. Charles Engelhard in 1974, and an additional thirty were given by Mrs. Mina Curtiss, none was illustrated.

CDD

FIG. 1. Édouard Manet, Autograph letter to Mlle Guillemet, ca. July 1880, The Pierpont Morgan Library, New York

96

HILAIRE GERMAIN EDGAR DEGAS

Paris 1834–1917 Paris

45 *Three Studies of a Dancer*

Black chalk, Conté crayon (?), and pink chalk, heightened with white chalk, on blue paper faded to light brown. 18¾ x 24¾ in. (475 x 628 mm). Signed in black chalk at upper right, *Degas.*

PROVENANCE: Degas atelier (Lugt 586bis); Jacques Doucet, Paris; his sale, Paris, Galerie Georges Petit, 28 December 1917, lot 79, repr.; André Wormser, Paris; Walter Feilchenfeldt, Zurich.

LITERATURE: Lafond 1918, p. 117, repr.; Meier-Graefe 1920, pl. 53; Rewald 1944, repr. p. 62; Lemoisne 1946, no. 586bis, repr.; Shackelford 1984, fig. 3.2, p. 71, repr.; Gordon and Forge 1988, repr. p. 205; Kendall 1998, pp. 15, 38, 42, 175, no. 41, repr.

EXHIBITIONS: Paris 1937, no. 92; Paris 1939, no. 18; Paris 1960, no. 28; Omaha and elsewhere 1998, no. 41, repr.

Gift of a foundation in honor of Eugene and Clare Thaw; Acc. no. 2001.12

This handsome, large-scale work is one of the artist's studies made over a two-year period, between 1878 and 1880, for the celebrated sculpture in wax *Petite Danseuse de quatorze ans* (Little Dancer), which he exhibited at the Salon in 1881 (Fig. 1). Degas had been fascinated by the ballet for a decade, sometimes accompanying his friend, the librettist Ludovic Halévy to the Paris Opéra at the Palais Garnier. Ballet was even more of universal art form then and caught the public imagination, both highborn and popular. It was an exciting world seen from different aspects—the dedication of the dancers and the high cultural value of the work on the one hand, while on the other, it provided the opportunity to view lightly clad female figures. As Richard Kendall has observed, this world, with its exaltations and scandals, was well described by the realist novelist Émile Zola in such novels as *Nana,* and when Degas's *Little Dancer* first appeared, it caused quite an uproar (Kendall 1998, p. 47). Far from the present-day perception of her as an earnest and charming dancer at the beginning of her career, in 1881 she was seen as ugly.

There are about ten known drawings for this sculpture, which is two thirds life size. One, in the Musée d'Orsay, Paris (Kendall 1998, no. 43), identifies the model as Marie de Gouthem, one of three Belgian sisters who were at an early age apprenticed to the ballet. As they lived just a few streets away from Degas's Montmartre studio, it would have been

FIG. 1. Hilaire Germain Edgar Degas, *Petite Danseuse de quatorze ans,* Musée d'Orsay, Paris

relatively easy for Marie to come to the studio and pose for the artist. Marie was fourteen in 1878, and it is apparent that the artist took a relatively long time to complete the sculpture. Another study in the Art Institute of Chicago (Kendall 1998, no. 40, repr. in color) is very close in size and presentation to the present sheet. Other studies are in the Metropolitan Museum of Art, New York, and Nasjonalgalleriet, Oslo; several are in private collections in London (Kendall 1998, nos. 35, 36, 38, 42). While the drawing in Chicago shows the same three studies of the girl turned to another angle, one in an English private collection depicts her from the same angle as that of the present sheet, only the figures are nude. The Thaw sheet is impressive for its size, the beauty and mastery of its execution, and because it is a true working drawing for one of the most famous sculptures of the nineteenth century.

99

IGNACE-HENRI-JEAN-THÉODORE FANTIN-LATOUR

Grenoble 1836–1904 Buré

46   *Portrait of Arthur Rimbaud* *(1854–1891)*, 1872

Brown and gray wash, with white bodycolor mixed with the wash in some places and used as heightening in others, on light brown paper. Sheet: 5⅜ x 4⅝ in. (138 x 115 mm). Lined with a heavier board on which frame is drawn with wash; full sheet: 7¹/₁₆ x 5⅝ in. (177 x 143 mm). Signed in pen and black ink at upper left, *Fantin. 72,* and below framed area and partially effaced by wash at lower right, *F. Latour | F. Latour.*

PROVENANCE: Louis Barthou; Léon Barthou; by whom presented to Georges Duhamel in 1936 (according to old autograph inscriptions in pen and black ink on label on back of frame, *A Georges Duhamel, qui a dit | de Rimbaud: "exception héroïque | et inquietant" le portrait que | lui offre un admirateur et | ami | Léon Barthou | 19 déc. 1936.*); M. Viardot; Alain Clairet, Paris.

LITERATURE: Carré 1939; *Labyrinthe* 1945, no. 2 (according to Ruchau 1946, q.v.); Ruchau 1946, no. 12 (as in Georges Duhamel collection), pl. 12; *Rimbaud* 1955, repr. on cover.

EXHIBITIONS: Paris 1991, repr. in color; London 1996–97, no. 76, repr. in color.

In 1872 Fantin-Latour exhibited his now famous painting *Coin de table* at the Salon (Fig. 1). This work was a continuation of the series the artist had begun in 1864 with *Hommage à Delacroix;* both are now at the Musée d'Orsay, Paris. Before executing *Coin de table,* Fantin had conceived and carried out a number of preparations for yet another painting—*Le Repas,* or *Le Toast*—a sort of allegorical work depicting painters he admired. The artist, however, was dissatisfied with the finished work and destroyed it. *Coin de table* also may be considered an homage, since Fantin assembled a number of writers he admired, including Verlaine and Rimbaud, in this group portrait. His original conception of this work was an homage to Baudelaire, who died in 1867. There are numerous sketches in which a portrait of Baudelaire is prominent at the center of the work, but it seems that eventually Fantin's focus shifted: both Verlaine and Rimbaud, seated together, are isolated from the rest of the group. It is rather fascinating that Rimbaud occupies about the same place that Fantin (who depicted himself) does in *Hommage à Delacroix,* since they occupy approximately the same position in the paintings. In *Coin de table* Rimbaud gazes dreamily into the middle distance, his right elbow leaning on the edge of the table, his face cupped in his right hand, while in *Hommage à Delacroix* Fantin is conspicuous as the only member of the group not properly attired—he appears in his shirtsleeves holding a palette. Both Fantin and Rimbaud are bathed in a misty half light as if to convey the isolation of young,

FIG. 1. Ignace-Henri-Jean-Théodore Fantin-Latour, *Coin de table,* Musée d'Orsay, Paris

creative people from their elders. While Fantin was twenty-seven or twenty-eight in 1864, Rimbaud would have been only seventeen in 1872. Verlaine wrote (on the corrected galley of his *Hommes d'Aujourd'hui,* dedicated to Rimbaud) of Fantin-Latour's depiction that Rimbaud had "Une sorte de douceur luisant et souriant dans ces cruels yeux bleu clairs et sur cette forte bouche rouge au pli amer; mysticisme et sensualité, et quels!" When Verlaine read Rimbaud's *Illu-*

minations in 1871, he invited the youthful poet to come to Paris; it is well known that the two quickly entered into a passionate relationship. The present drawing is dated 1872, the same year as the painting depicting Rimbaud in an identical pose. The close connection between the painting and drawing makes it highly likely that Fantin executed this sensitive portrait after Rimbaud's painted image, a hypothesis put forth by the authors of the Paris 1991 exhibition catalogue. Reduced on all four sides, the image probably was made for a book illustration, as the presence of brown and gray wash—a combination often used at the time in preparatory designs for prints—suggests.

CDD

ODILON REDON

Bordeaux 1840–1916 Paris

47 *Self-Portrait*

Conté crayon. 12¾ x 9⅞ in. (322 x 250 mm) folded down to 8⁹/₁₆ x 6⅜ in. (217 x 163 mm). Signed at lower center, *Od. R.*

PROVENANCE: Gift of the artist to Ary Leblond (possibly to be identified as Aimé Merlot, 1880–1958), Paris (?); Mme Ary Leblond, Paris (?); private collection (according to Wildenstein 1992); Galerie Waring-Hopkins, Paris.

LITERATURE: Wildenstein 1992, no. 4, repr.

Redon was to portray his own features a number of times during his lifetime. Wildenstein lists and reproduces twelve self-portraits, including five paintings and seven drawings, ranging in date from 1867 to 1904. The present example dates to 1880 and may be compared with a photograph of the artist taken that year (Wildenstein 1992, p. 2, repr.). The year 1880 was important for Redon: on 1 May he married Camille Falte. Redon and Camille had met in the home of Mme Berthe de Rayssac, who was well known for her literary and musical salons. In 1881, shortly after his marriage, he exhibited his charcoals for the first time at the office of *La Vie moderne,* with a second exhibition the next year at the office of yet another newspaper, *Le Gaulois.* Although the public did not understand his art, it was at these exhibitions that he became acquainted with Émile Hennequin and J.-K. Huysmans, who were to become his friends as well as his champions and critics. Hennequin equated Redon with Baudelaire and remarked that he had given the world a new "frisson." As in all of his self-portraits, Redon has a serious countenance, a frown line is visible between his eyes, which are narrowly focused as if to carefully appraise his own features. Unlike some of the painted portraits and the mysterious worked portrait in charcoal, the portraits of the 1880s are spare—and relatively small—and consist of simple head studies, with no indication of a neck or shoulders. In these studies he apparently always examined his reflection from the same angle, his head turned to the left with his gaze toward the spectator. The charcoal (now in The Hague, Netherlands), dated 1888, is the exception. In this richly worked likeness, his head turned to the right, Redon achieved a mysterious intensity.

The present drawing was folded down from a larger sheet of paper to a more attractive size, perhaps at the time it was presented to Ary Leblond. It also must have been at this time that Redon signed it. The larger sheet would have accommodated a number of other studies, including the start of another self-portrait, to the left and just above the present study. Not visible in the existing folded configuration of the sheet, it is simply a study of the nose and eyes, which the artist struck out with a series of diagonal strokes of Conté crayon.

Among the portraits of Redon by other artists is the drawing by Emile Schuffenecker for *Men of Today* (1890), the portrait by Maurice in *Hommage à Cézanne* (1900), and the 1901 portrait by Vuillard (Wildenstein 1992, no. 206).

CDD

ODILON REDON

Bordeaux 1840–1916 Paris

48 *Lady Macbeth* (Prêtesse d'Egypte)

Charcoal and some black chalk, erased or gone over in areas with stump, on pink paper. 19 $^7/_{16}$ x 12⅛ in. (495 x 307 mm). Signed at lower left, *ODILON REDON.*

PROVENANCE: Baron Robert de Domècy, Château de Domècy, Sermicelles, near Vézlay, April 1896 (according to Redon's account book as "Un dessin prêtesse égyptien, rigide avec un flambeau devant elle [elle fut exposé sous le titre Lady Macbeth]"); The Artemis Group, London.

LITERATURE: Chicago and elsewhere 1994–95, fig. 94, p. 182, repr. in color; MRC, no. 46.

EXHIBITIONS: New York 1994, not in catalogue; London 1996–97, no. 84, repr.

In this highly charged work, the subject is dramatically illuminated by candlelight, her features schematized into a mask and her face reduced nearly to cubist forms. While her costume is brightly lit, her face—especially her expressive eyes, staring upward, away from the viewer—provides the true focus of the work. Redon simplified all forms here and contrasted the tones of the rich charcoal with the warm but pale tones of the pink paper to create a powerful chiaroscuro effect. He also added some black chalk to the charcoal and sharpened some of the outlines with a finely pointed eraser.

There is no strict textual illustration here. Indeed, as Redon's title indicates, he interpreted the subject alternatively as Lady Macbeth or as an Egyptian priestess. For Lady Macbeth, he effectively suggested the moment after the murder of Duncan rendered in the lines "Out, out brief candle. Life's but a walking shadow . . . " (act 5, verse 17). Redon may have considered a series inspired by the works of Shakespeare, judging from a number of the artist's other works, including Bottom from *A Midsummer Night's Dream,* another charcoal in the Thaw Collection (New York and elsewhere 1975–76, no. 102, repr.), and Caliban from *The Tempest,* now in the Louvre (Département des Arts Graphiques, fonds du Musée d'Orsay, Paris).

The artist later produced a pastel of the same subject, which he sold to Ambroise Vollard in 1899 (Wildenstein 1992, no. 408, repr.). Although it lacks something of the intensity of the Thaw original, Redon's choice of dark rich color—reddish brown, dark red, and sulphurous ochers—is very evocative and helps to underscore the dark, violent mood of this work.

While the present work follows a large series of mysterious frontal portraits by Redon, the subject bears some resemblance in both type and mood to the woman depicted in *La Voile,* an oil on paper (Wildenstein 1992, no. 409, repr.).

CDD

ODILON REDON
Bordeaux 1840–1916 Paris

49 *Young Girl in an Interior* (La Fillete au noeud)

Black pastel and brown and black charcoal. 19⅝ x 14⅛ in. (500 x 360 mm). Signed at lower right, *ODILON REDON.*

PROVENANCE: Ambroise Vollard, Paris; Jacques Seligmann, New York; John S. Newberry, Detroit; Museum of Modern Art, New York; Eugene V. Thaw, New York; Robert A. Rowen, California; Tucker Collection, St. Louis; Allan Frumkin Gallery, New York; Leslie Hindman and Associates, Chicago; Eugene Chesrow, Chicago, 1991.

LITERATURE: *The Art Quarterly* 1961, repr. on cover; Wildenstein 1992, no. 111, repr. p. 56; Chicago and elsewhere 1994–95, p. 366, p. 267, repr.

EXHIBITIONS: Paris 1948, no. 18; Syracuse 1949, no. 17; New York 1951, no. 30; New York 1959a, no. 132, repr.; New York 1960–61, no. 86; New York and Chicago 1961–62, no. 117; New York 1962–63, no. 37.

This is one of two portraits of Jeanne Roberte, granddaughter of Robert de Domècy, that Redon executed in 1905—at the same time, to judge from her hair and costume. The identity of the little girl in this portrait was unknown for some years until the appearance of the other one, which is inscribed and dated (Wildenstein 1992, no. 725, p. 286, repr.), made it apparent that this is the same child. If an artist like Redon can ever be considered conventional, the Thaw portrait is much less orthodox than the one acquired by Robert de Domècy in 1905. In that portrait the subject is posed frontally (in a dark space lit by a mysterious light to the left) and there is no other detail to distract from her image. In the present work she emerges from the dark at the right of a gathering of decorative elements, so mysterious and amorphous as to make identification almost impossible. They might be construed as a curtain next to a sculptural column or arch, illuminated from overhead by a lamp or decorated skylight of some sort. This image bears comparison with plate 3 of Redon's illustrations to Flaubert's *La Tentation de Saint Antoine* (Fig. 1), in which the artist illustrated the passage about basalt columns and a light that shines down from the ceiling ("Et partout se sont des colonnes de basalte. . . . La lumière tombes des voûtes"; Mellerio 1913, pl. 136, opp. p. 114, repr.).

FIG. 1. Odilon Redon, plate 3 of *La Tentation de Saint Antoine,* Museum of Modern Art, New York

It is almost as if Redon was making various studies of the child to catch something of her mood and character before moving on to the frontal portrait. He probably made a number of sketches at the same time, because at least one of these still exists (Wildenstein 1992, no. 112, repr.). It is a quick study of her head and shoulders only, in which she gazes upward with a somewhat anxious expression. In the present work, she looks uncertain and even intimidated by the ornately carved and draped decorative feature to her left. Earlier, in 1901–2, M. de Domècy had commissioned Redon to decorate his dining room at the château de Domècy. The artist also completed a portrait of de Domècy's wife in 1902.

CDD

HENRI EDMOND CROSS (HENRI-EDMOND-JOSEPH DELACROIX)

Douai 1856–1910 Saint-Clair

50 *Portrait of Georges Seurat Seated*

Graphite. 12½ x 10½ in. (315 x 240 mm). Atelier stamp in red ink at lower right, *H. E. C.* in an oval (Lugt S. 1305a). Watermark: *A. Lepage Aîné. Tochon Lepage Succ'.*

PROVENANCE: Estate of the artist; Félix Fénéon, Paris; sale, Paris, Hôtel Drouot, 15 October 1980, lot 43.

During the founding of the Société des Artistes Indépendants in 1884, Cross came into close contact with the Neo-Impressionists Seurat, Charles Angrand (1854–1926), Paul Signac (1863–1935), and Albert Dubois-Pillet (1846–1890). The conservative Cross did not adopt the avant-garde divisionist style until after departing Paris for the Mediterranean coast in 1891, where he took a house at Cabasson. His first such canvases were exhibited at the Salon des Indépendants of 1892, by which time both Dubois-Pillet and Seurat had died.

In this deft study, Cross depicted Seurat seated with his head turned to the right; his hands are held in front of him, gesturing to the left. A faintly indicated figure stands behind him with his head inclined as if speaking. Cross repeatedly reworked the position of Seurat's hands, leaving visible pentimenti. Like the portrait of Seurat by Ernest Laurent (1859–1929) dated 1883, the present sheet seems to depict the artist as a young man, during the mid-1880s (Musée d'Orsay, Paris; see Paris and New York 1991–92, p. 401, repr.). Seurat and fellow painter Alphonse Osbert (1857–1939) posed for Laurent's lost painting *Le Concert Colonne* in 1883; it is not surprising that he may have sat for Cross shortly thereafter as well.

Little is known of Cross's work before 1884. As Isabelle Compin observed, a small number of portraits, roughly datable 1880–83, are among his earliest known subjects. These portraits remained in the hands of Cross's heirs, and include two self-portraits, one of the artist's mother, and another of his cousin Dr. Soins (Compin 1964, pp. 23–24). It is likely that the present depiction of Seurat dates shortly after 1884, when the two artists became involved in the founding of the Société des Artistes Indépendants; it is not known, however, if the work was intended as a true portrait or if Seurat was serving as a model for Cross. The latter explanation seems more feasible, considering the presence of a second figure in the composition and the unusual informal pose of the sitter.

The drawing was first owned by the critic Félix Fénéon, one of Seurat's most ardent supporters (No. 51).

JT

GEORGES SEURAT

Paris 1859–1891 Paris

51 *Approach to the Bridge at Courbevoie*, 1886

Conté crayon. 9⅛ x 11¾ in. (232 x 298 mm).

PROVENANCE: Félix Fénéon, Paris; sale, London, Sotheby's, 10 July 1957, no. 43; Jacques Seligmann and Co., New York; Margaret H. Drey, London; Samuel Courtauld, London; Arthur Kaufmann, London; Heinz Berggruen.

LITERATURE: Seligman 1947, pp. 32, 56, pl. 14; De Hauke 1961, no. 650, p. 227, repr.; Madeleine-Perdrillat 1990, p. 105, repr.; *Artemis Annual Report* 1997–98, no. 15, repr. in color.

EXHIBITIONS: Chicago 1935; New York 1947; Bielefield and elsewhere 1983–84, no. 77, p. 193, repr.; Geneva 1988, no. 23, p. 69, repr.; London 1991, no. 13, repr. in color.

This masterful drawing depicts the Pont Bineau at Courbevoie, the subject of the painting *Bridge at Courbevoie*, now in the Courtauld Institute Galleries, London. Completed in 1886—the same year as the artist's masterpiece *Sunday Afternoon on the Island of La Grande Jatte* (Art Institute of Chicago)—the *Bridge at Courbevoie* was exhibited in the third Salon des Indépendants in March 1887. A later, finished study preparatory for the painting is in a private collection (Paris and New York 1991–92, no. 172, repr.).

In the early 1880s, Seurat began exploring the villages along the banks of the Seine northwest of Paris, which were frequented by the Impressionists. In 1883 he painted *Une Baignade, Asnières* (National Gallery, London), which depicts working class men at leisure on an embankment of the Seine at Asnières, opposite the tip of the island of La Grand Jatte, with a view of a railroad bridge and the factories at Clichy in the background. In the following years, he made a number of studies in the immediate area around La Grand Jatte. The Pont Bineau joins Courbevoie to the island approximately at its middle. Seurat depicted the bridge and its environs in a small oil sketch from 1884 (Nationalmuseum, Stockholm) and in a small canvas and an oil sketch on wood from the following year (private collection; Berggruen collection; see Paris and New York 1991–92, nos. 153, 154) before he began the present study.

Executed in the artist's preferred technique of Conté crayon on textured paper, this study of the bridge may have been made en plein air at Courbevoie: it is more vibrant than many of the artist's studies done in the studio. The composition achieves a balance between the vertical buildings in dramatic perspective along the quay at left, the horizontal thrust of the bridge bisecting the background, and the diagonal slope of the riverbank. The tollhouse on the bridge and the ambiguous vertical forms of what are perhaps smokestacks to the left stabilize the composition and contribute to its rhythmic tension.

Richard Kendall has described Seurat's mature drawing style, evident in the present sheet, as composed of "a meandering, almost arbitrary line that curves and weaves over the surface of the paper" (London 1991, p. 44). The tonal range varies from the radiant spots of untouched paper that form a halo around the buildings and bridge to the hazy gray of the sky achieved through a web of loose strokes, to the rich, black areas of Conté that nearly fill the creamy interstices of the paper. The energetic, staccato strokes in the foreground create a sense of movement that is contained by the static forms of the buildings and bridge.

JT

III

HENRI-MARIE-RAYMOND DE TOULOUSE-LAUTREC

Albi 1864–1901 Château de Malromé

52 *Au Café*, 1886

Brush and brown ink, over graphite, with blue pencil on a thin translucent paper, mounted to card. 26 x 20⅞ in. (660 x 530 mm). Signed in graphite at lower left, *T Lautrec.*

PROVENANCE: Caressa, Paris; Georges Bernheim, Paris; John Nicholas Brown, Providence; Knoedler and Co., New York; Stanley S. Snellenburg, Philadelphia; sale, New York, Christie's, 7 November 1979, lot 14; Cowen family; by descent to Judy Cowen, New York; sale, New York, Sotheby's, 10 November 2000, lot 140, repr. in color.

LITERATURE: Brook 1923, repr. p. 153; Joyant 1927, p. 189, repr. p. 11; Dortu 1971, no. D.2.968, repr. p. 483.

EXHIBITIONS: Cambridge 1929; Chicago 1930–31, no. 40; New York 1931, no. 36; Providence 1937; Omaha 1941; New York 1946, no. 40; San Francisco 1947, no. 122; New York 1956, no. 49; New York 1964, no. 63.

Shortly after Toulouse-Lautrec arrived in Paris with his mother in 1882, he began his professional career by assisting Fernand Cormon (1845–1924) with commissions for book illustrations. His work had its first public appearance in 1886, with illustrations depicting the Montmartre nightlife published in *Le Courrier français* and *Le Mirliton*. Although his work was recognized, it was not until 1891 that Toulouse-Lautrec achieved fame with his poster *Moulin Rouge—La Goulue* and became known for depicting the Parisian demimonde.

This large-scale sheet is preparatory for the painting *Femme au café*, executed when the artist was only twenty-two (Fig. 1). The painting depicts a solitary woman reading a journal in a Parisian café. In the drawing a fashionably dressed woman sits back from the table, with a journal propped on her knees, a glass with a stirrer and a saucer are on the table in front of her. In the painting the artist omitted the glass and retained the saucer; the background is formed by curtains illuminated from behind by sunlight.

In this preliminary drawing, the dimensions of which are slightly larger than those of the painting, Toulouse-Lautrec first indicated the composition lightly in pencil, with an irregular, intermittent line. He then used a brush dipped in brown ink to delineate the composition. This initial drawing was supplemented by broad strokes of blue pencil to distinguish the material of the woman's dress from the fur trim, to render the different textures of her elaborate millinery, and to describe and embellish the background of the scene. The artist's economical use of line, laid down quickly with a wet brush, marks a new direction in his graphic work and presages his mature style as a draftsman and illustrator. In his drawings of about 1885–86, Toulouse-Lautrec often employed blue pencil in his sketches drawn rapidly from life, in which he indicated the outline of figures with a fluid line, capturing gestures with undulating strokes of the crayon.

FIG. 1. Henri de Toulouse-Lautrec, *Femme au café*

112

The café-concert and unaccompanied young women at Parisian cafés were subjects first popularized by Manet in the late 1870s. Such themes also were taken up by the Impressionists as well as by writers such as Zola and Huysmans. Rather than depicting a dejected working-class woman, Toulouse-Lautrec represented a well-dressed lady reading a journal, similar to the subject of *A Woman Reading in a Café* by Manet (1879; Art Institute of Chicago). Anterior to the depictions of the lurid dance halls of Paris with which Toulouse-Lautrec is commonly associated, this composition reflects the affinity of the artist's style and subject matter to Impressionism at the outset of his career.

The same year he executed the present composition, Toulouse-Lautrec made *At Grenelle: The Absinthe Drinker* (Joseph Hazen, New York), a slightly smaller painting (21¾ x 19¼ in.; 552 x 489 mm) also depicting a solitary woman in a café. Over the next four years he would repeat this type of composition depicting a young woman drinking alone. Many of these canvases, named after popular drinking songs, were hung in *Le Mirliton,* the cabaret owned by Aristide Bruant.

JT

FÉLIX (-EMILE-JEAN) VALLOTTON

Lausanne 1865–1925 Paris

Le Poker, 1896

Brush and black ink, over graphite and blue pencil. 9⅝ x 12¾ in. (244 x 324 mm). Watermark: None. Inscribed in blue pencil at lower left, *Le Poker;* signed with initials in blue pencil at lower right, *FV.*

PROVENANCE: Estate of the artist; by descent through the artist's family to Paul Vallotton, Lausanne; August Laube, Zurich.

LITERATURE: Vallotton and Goerg 1972, p. 184, repr.

EXHIBITIONS: Ottawa and elsewhere 1976–77, p. 31; Lugano 1980; Rome 1980; Zurich 2001, no. 8, repr.

In February 1882, at the age of seventeen, the Swiss-born Vallotton moved to Paris, where he enrolled at the Académie Julian and settled for the rest of his career. He had already begun working in drypoint the previous year; however, it was not until 1892 that he first explored the graphic possibilities of woodcuts. Vallotton's career coincided with a dramatically heightened media presence in Paris. Producing illustrations for periodicals helped support the artist and establish his reputation, although he continued to paint throughout his career. During the 1890s his woodcut illustrations appeared in literary and political journals such as *Le Rire, La Revue Blanche,* and *Le Mercure de France.* In 1892 the artist joined the Nabis and developed close relationships with Édouard Vuillard, Pierre Bonnard, and the critic Félix Fénéon. That year his woodcuts were displayed in the first Salon de la Rose + Croix held at the Paris gallery of Paul Durand-Ruel.

Representing scenes from contemporary urban life, Vallotton's woodcuts are composed of flat black and white forms, stripped of detail and often bordering on caricature. The artist frequently used the reserve of the paper to create a fine outline of white around the silhouette of a form, or as form against a dark background. The uneven saturation of the paper with thick strokes of brush and ink along with the evident traces of the underdrawing in graphite and blue pencil directly contrast with the flat, pure areas of rich black and pristine white that dominate his woodcuts.

Although there is little detail in the scene, the intimate atmosphere of the card game is evoked by the closed circle of men and their expressions of concentration. This sheet was executed in 1896 when Vallotton and his wife returned to Paris after spending the summer in Normandy. Vallotton's wife, Gabrielle Rodrigues-Henriques, was the daughter of Alexandre Bernheim, a successful art dealer who promoted the Impressionists and Post-Impressionists through the Bernheim-Jeune Gallery. Along with a drawing titled *Le Billard, Le Poker* is indicative of the amusements at the Bernheim family residence.

The composition of this sheet was retained in the woodcut, although Vallotton added some details to the stark purity of the forms in the drawing (179 x 224 mm; repr. in Lausanne 1985, fig. 6). In the woodcut, the candelabra at left—awkwardly placed between the two figures in the drawing—has been placed closer to the near edge of the table, on the opposite side of the man seated at left. The glow of the candles is indicated by delicate rays radiating from the flames. The second figure from the left, seated at the far side of the table, appears older, with a white (rather than black) beard and a heavily creased forehead. The figures emerge from the dark background in their crisp evening dress; the foreground figure, seen from the back, is indicated by the outline of his figure against the white table and a finely reserved white outline around the contour of his head.

There is a second version of this composition in the private collection of Phillippe Vallotton, Lausanne. Slightly smaller than the present drawing (230 x 190 mm; repr. in Paris 1966, no. 141), the sheet is preparatory for the cover illustration to the *Cri de Paris* of 19 December 1897 (no. 47). The drawing was executed in 1897 and is closer to the woodcut than to the present sheet; the clean contours and precise shapes of the Vallotton collection drawing render it almost indistinguishable from the illustration. *Cri de Paris* was a weekly magazine published by Alexandre Natanson, one of the three brothers who founded *La Revue Blanche,* a distinguished literary and artistic review. The periodical was originally intended as a forum for discussion of the Dreyfus affair; Natanson and Vallotton were both staunch Dreyfusards.

JT

VINCENT (WILLEM) VAN GOGH

Zundert 1853–1890 Auvers-sur-Oise

54 Autograph letter, to Paul Gauguin, with a sketch of *Bedroom at Arles,* [17 October 1888]

Pen and dark brown ink on two sheets of graph paper, joined vertically. 8¼ x 10⅜ in. (210 x 264 mm). Inscribed in graphite at upper left, *1890,* at upper right, *22,* at lower right, *22;* inscribed on verso, at lower right, *9766* and *1000;* in graphite below image, *le dessin seulement;* marked at upper left in blue crayon, *x.*

PROVENANCE: Baroness Goldschmidt-Rothschild, Paris; private collection, New York.

LITERATURE: Bernard 1911, no. 22, pl. 29; New York 1984, p. 160; Amsterdam and Otterlo 1990, pp. 172–76, fig. 69b.

No nineteenth-century painter has left as much correspondence as Vincent van Gogh, and no artist's thoughts and sentiments framing his works of art are as accessible. The great majority of van Gogh's letters—only a few written to him survive—are preserved in the museum dedicated to the artist in Amsterdam. A new compilation of his letters is being prepared.

Like so many of van Gogh's letters, the present one to Paul Gauguin expresses a mood (see Appendix B for a transcription). He had come to know Gauguin in Paris when he was living with his brother, Theo, from 1886 until he left for Arles in February 1888. A few months after his arrival, he wrote to Theo that he had found a studio for rent, which he dubbed the "yellow house." Seeing a kindred spirit in Gauguin, van Gogh imagined that working with him would be a mutually fruitful and revealing experience. He repeatedly urged Gauguin to come to Arles. In the present letter he conveyed his gratitude to Gauguin for having decided to come to Arles by the twentieth of October (1888). He extolled the attraction of Arles, the intensity of the sunlight, and minimized the unpleasant and depressing effects of the cold, biting *mistral* of the season. Looking forward to working with Gauguin, he installed gas lighting so they could work through the winter, and made light of the financial hazards they undoubtedly were to face. His efforts were premature, however. Gauguin did arrive before the end of the month, but by late December they had already parted ways: After repeated episodes of insanity, van Gogh was admitted to the asylum of Saint-Rémy-de-Provence, and Gauguin left Arles.

The letter also chronicles van Gogh's work on one of his masterpieces from the period, the *Bedroom at Arles,* and contains a sketch of the

FIG. 1. Vincent van Gogh, *Bedroom at Arles,* Van Gogh Museum, Amsterdam

composition. The original canvas is now in the Van Gogh Museum, Amsterdam (Fig. 1), a second version is in the Art Institute of Chicago, and a third, smaller version, made for his mother and sister later that month, is in the Musée d'Orsay, Paris. The whereabouts of this letter, crucial to understanding the artist's intentions for this seminal canvas, were unknown for many years, and Ambroise Vollard erroneously grouped it with the artist's letters to Émile Bernard, published in 1911.

Van Gogh developed the idea for *Bedroom at Arles* in a few days. Having begun by 16 October, he finished the canvas two days later. In a letter to Theo of 16 October 1888, Vincent wrote:

> At last I can send you a little sketch to give you at least an idea of the way the work is shaping up. For today I am all right again. My eyes are still tired, but then I had a new idea in my head and here is the sketch of it. . . . This time it is simply my bedroom, only here color is to do everything, and giving by its simplification a grander style to things, is to be suggestive here of rest or of sleep in general. In a word, looking at the picture ought to rest the brain, or rather the imagination (*Van Gogh* 1978, p. 86).

The following day, the artist wrote the present letter to Gauguin—whose arrival in Arles had been postponed because of illness—describing the painting and providing a sketch of the composition that more closely reflected the final painting than did the drawing contained in his letter to Theo.

> I have done, still for my decoration, a size 30 canvas of my bedroom with the white deal furniture that you know. Well, I enormously enjoyed doing this interior of nothing at all, of a Seurat-like simplicity, with flat tints, but brushed on roughly, with a thick impasto, the walls pale lilac, the ground a faded broken red, the chairs and the bed chrome yellow, the pillows and the sheet a very pale green-citron, the counterpane blood-red, the washstand orange, the washbasin blue, the window green. By means of all these very diverse tones I have wanted to express an absolute restfulness, you see. . . (New York 1984, p. 191).

This letter, and the sketch contained therein, identify the Van Gogh Museum canvas as the original version of the composition.

On 18 October 1888, van Gogh again wrote to Theo, adding as a postscript, "I am adding a line to tell you that this afternoon I finished the canvas representing the bedroom . . . " (*Van Gogh* 1978, p. 89). A few days later, on 23 October, Gauguin finally arrived to share the yellow house with van Gogh.

JT

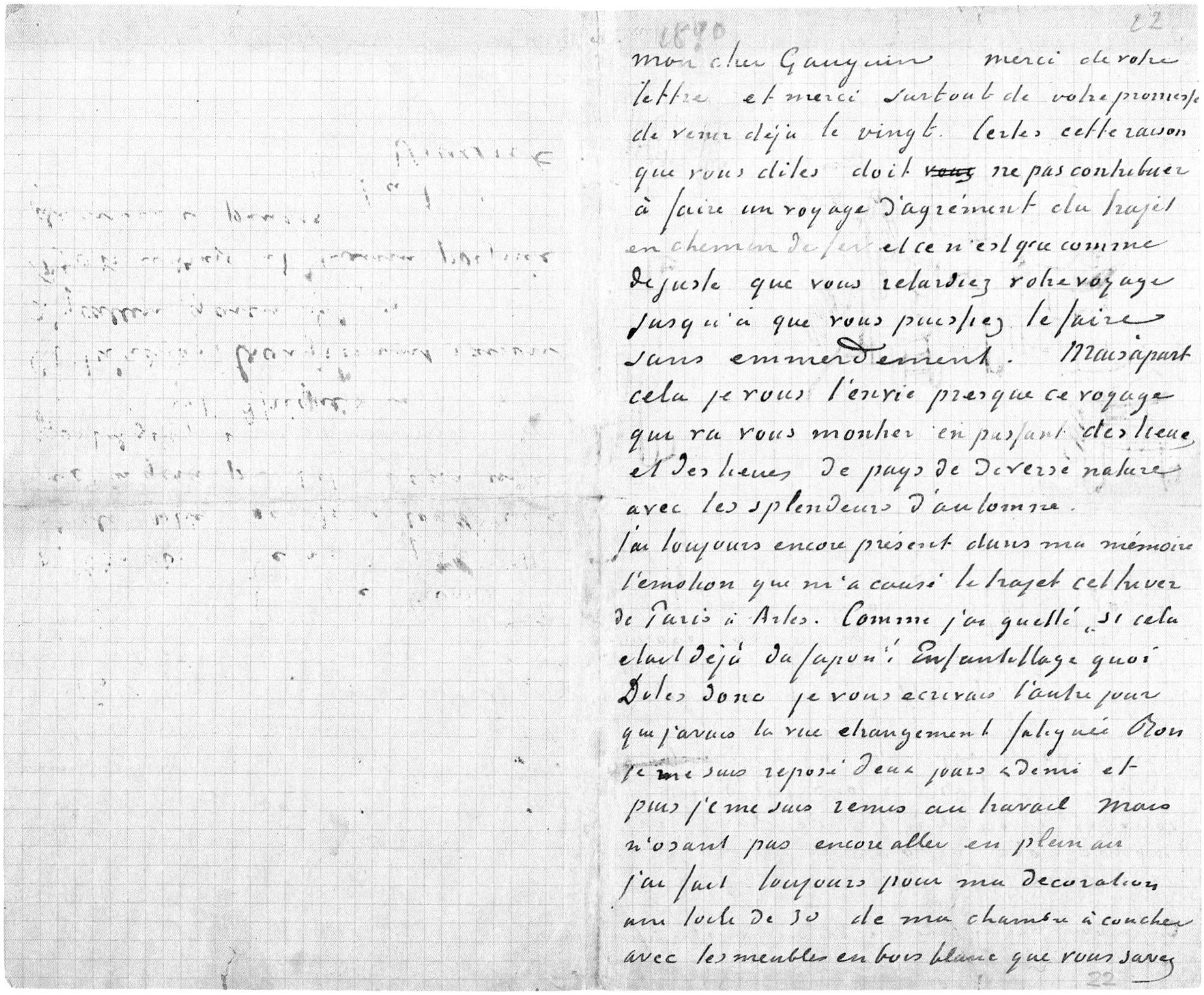

1890

mon cher Gauguin merci de votre lettre et merci surtout de votre promesse de venir déjà le vingt. Certes cette raison que vous dites doit ~~vous~~ ne pas contribuer à faire un voyage d'agrément du trajet en chemin de fer et ce n'est que comme de juste que vous retardiez votre voyage jusqu'à que vous puissiez le faire sans emmerdement. Mais à part cela je vous l'envie presque ce voyage qui va vous montrer en passant des lieues et des lieues de pays de diverse nature avec les splendeurs d'automne.

J'ai toujours encore présent dans ma mémoire l'émotion que m'a causé le trajet cet hiver de Paris à Arles. Comme j'ai guetté si cela était déjà du Japon! Enfantillage quoi. Dites donc je vous écrivais l'autre jour que j'avais la vue changement fatiguée. Bon je me suis reposé deux jours à demi et puis je me suis remis au travail mais n'osant pas encore aller en plein air j'ai fait toujours pour ma décoration une toile de 30 de ma chambre à coucher avec les meubles en bois blanc que vous savez

22

Eh bien cela m'a énormément amusé de faire cet intérieur sans rien. D'une simplicité à la Seurat.

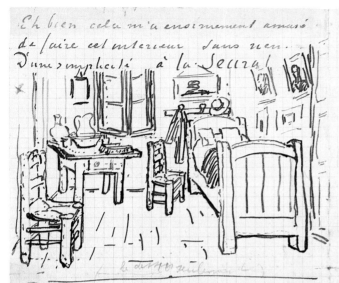

(le dessin seulement)

À teintes plates mais grossièrement brossées en pleine pâte les murs lilas pâle le sol d'un rouge rompu et fané les chaises et le lit jaune de chrome les oreillers et le drap citron vert très pâle la couverture rouge sang la table à toilette orangée la cuvette bleue la fenêtre verte. J'avais voulu exprimer un repos absolu par tous ces tons très divers voyez et où il n'y a de blanc que la petite note que donne le miroir à cadre noir (pour fourrer encore le quatrième paire de complémentaires dedans.)

Enfin vous verrez cela avec les autres et nous en causerons car je ne sais souvent

9766

par ce que je fais travaillant presqu'en somnambule.

Il commence à faire froid surtout les jours de mistral.

J'ai fait mettre le gaz dans l'atelier pour que nous ayons une bonne lumière en hiver.

Peut être serez vous désenchanté d'Arles si vous y venez par un temps de mistral mais attendez... C'est à la longue que la poésie d'ici pénètre

Vous ne trouverez pas encore la maison aussi confortable que peu à peu nous chercherons à la rendre. Il y a tant de dépenses et cela ne peut pas se faire d'une seule haleine. Enfin je crois qu'une fois ici vous allez comme moi être pris d'une rage de peindre dans les intervalles du mistral les effets d'automne. et que vous comprendrez que j'ai insisté pour que vous veniez maintenant qu'il y a de bien beaux jours. Allons au revoir

t à v
Vincent

MARY CASSATT

Allegheny City (now part of Pittsburgh) 1844–1926 Le Mesnil-Théribus

55 ## *Sewing by Lamplight,* ca. 1883

VERSO: Offset of soft-ground

Graphite on wove paper. Miscellaneous traces of red chalk at center. Sheet: 9⅞ x 11⁷/₁₆ in. (250 x 291 mm). Design area: 7⅞ x 5¹⁵/₁₆ in. (202 x 151 mm). Signed with initials at lower left, *M.C.* Inscribed in blue crayon at left edge, *142.*

PROVENANCE: The artist's studio; Ambroise Vollard, Paris, ca. 1904–6; by descent to his heirs; Henri M. Petiet, Paris; by descent to his heirs; private collection, New York; Marc Rosen Fine Art, Ltd., New York.

LITERATURE: Breeskin 1970, no. 768, p. 263, repr.

EXHIBITION: New York 2000a.

This work was part of a large group of the artist's drawings and related prints that she assembled over several decades and kept in her studio until selling it en bloc to Ambroise Vollard about 1904–6. The collection, numbering over one hundred sheets, remained largely intact and was seldom exhibited until the 1990s, when it was acquired by the New York dealer Marc Rosen.

The drawing was executed in the preparation of a soft-ground etching, made in only one state of which only a single impression is known (Fig. 1; Breeskin 1979, no. 71+, p. 51). Recently acquired for the Morgan Library (acc. no. 2001.47), the print shares the provenance of the Thaw drawing.

Despite, or perhaps owing to, her training—at the Pennsylvania Academy of the Fine Arts and, after settling in Paris in 1874, in the studio of the salon painter Jean-Léon Gérôme—Cassatt disdained academic draftsmanship and made very few preparatory drawings for her paintings (Mathews 1994, p. 141). It was not until after accepting the invitation of Edgar Degas to join the Impressionists, in 1877, that she began to execute drawings in significant numbers, and these were made in order to create prints. Cassatt made prints during the day at Degas's studio and drew in the evening to prepare more prints for the

FIG. 1. Mary Cassatt, *Sewing by Lamplight,* The Pierpont Morgan Library, New York

next day's work. These early drawings and the prints made after them record Cassatt's "lamplit homelife," a visual diary of family members knitting, reading, and sewing (Mathews 1994, pp. 142–43). This drawing, which has been dated to about 1883, is such a work.

Cassatt sometimes used a drawing to transfer a design directly to the plate, creating an offset of the soft-ground on the verso of the sheet (Cantor 2000, p. 130). Such is the case here. Once the sheet was applied to the plate, Cassatt redrew the lines that define areas in shadow—especially across the back of the figure at the right and in the outlines of the head and hairline of the figure at the left—causing some of the soft-ground to adhere to the verso.

In works such as this, Cassatt anticipated by almost a

decade the silhouetted figures in domestic interiors painted by Édouard Vuillard (1868–1940); see, for example, *Dressmakers Under the Lamp* of about 1891–92 (Norton Simon Art Foundation, Pasadena; Houston and elsewhere 1989–90, no. 23, repr.).

KS

WALTER RICHARD SICKERT

Munich 1860–1942 Bathampton, Somerset

56 *La Rue Nôtre Dame, Dieppe, with the Quai Duquesne in the Foreground,* 1899

VERSO: *Café des Tribuneaux, Dieppe*

Pen and black ink over graphite, with watercolor and gouache, on blue paper. Verso: pen and black ink. 13¾ x 10 in. (349 x 254 mm). Watermark: None. Inscribed in pen and brown ink at lower left, *La rue Nôtre Dame / Dieppe;* inscribed and signed at lower right, *To Lady Auckland in Exchange / Walter Sickert.*

PROVENANCE: Lady Auckland; The Fine Art Society, London.

LITERATURE: Baron 1973, no. 112.

EXHIBITION: London 1994, no. 32.

Sickert first visited Dieppe on his honeymoon in 1885. During this stay his relationship with Degas, whom he met in Paris in 1883, deepened. In the following years, he routinely summered in Dieppe, and after divorcing his wife, the artist returned to Dieppe in 1898 and remained there until 1905. During this period, he abandoned the Impressionist method—and that of his mentor, James McNeill Whistler—of working on site and painting directly on canvas. Instead, under the influence of Degas, Sickert began working in the studio from drawings and memory. Views of Dieppe comprise the majority of Sickert's landscapes; he was so closely associated with the town that Jacques-Émile Blanche dubbed him "the Canaletto of Dieppe."

This sheet represents a narrow street in Dieppe, the rue Nôtre Dame, running between the quai Duquesne and the place National, site of the church of St. Jacques. The rue Nôtre Dame and its vicinity became the subject of numerous paintings by the artist, several of which date between 1898 and 1900. Wendy Baron records at least twelve canvases related to the present subject (Baron 1973, no. 112). She also identified at least seven other known drawings of the same site (Baron 1973, no. 112). A large oil sketch, *La rue Nôtre Dame and the Quai*

FIG. 1. Walter Richard Sickert, *La Rue Nôtre Dame, Dieppe,* Museum of Fine Arts, Boston

Duquesne, in the National Gallery of Canada, Ottawa, is one of four paintings that was commissioned in 1902 by M. Mantren, the proprietor of a restaurant at the Hôtel de la Plage, Dieppe, as mural decorations (Baron 1973, no. 148). It was derived from Sickert's earlier drawings recording the scene, including the present sheet, which probably dates to about 1898.

Sickert returned to this drawing in 1909; it was the basis for his only print produced that year (Fig. 1). In the print the artist fully explored the potential of the medium. Known in at least sixteen states, most of which exploit the tonal capacity of aquatint, it captures the scene at an angle that is less oblique than that of the drawing and, like the Ottawa painting, eliminates the wooden structure and

La rue Nôtre Dame
Dieppe.

To Lady Auckland in exchange
Walter Sickert

cart at the left. Sickert enlivened the scene with figures, and more of the building at right, including a sign for the Café Marine, is visible.

The verso of this sheet contains a sketch of the Café des Tribuneaux, in the place Le Puits Salé, Dieppe, which was the subject of an 1885 etching by Sickert and that of two canvases he painted about 1890–91 (Tate Gallery, London; National Gallery of Canada, Ottawa). This quick pen and ink study depicts the café, from a more acutely inclined vantage and slightly greater distance than does the painting, with the buildings and an awning on the rue de la Barre obscuring the view. Sickert later produced another series of drawings and paintings, from a more distant viewpoint of Le Puits Salé, which Baron dates about 1898–1900 (listed under Baron 1973, no. 128).

The sheet is enigmatically inscribed *To Lady Auckland in Exchange*. Lady Auckland (Lady Sybil Eden) was the wife of Sir William Eden, Baron Auckland (1819–1915), who commissioned a portrait of his wife from Whistler. Unhappy with the payment, Whistler kept the portrait and the money, which he eventually was forced to return when Eden filed suit. This conflict sparked the 1899 publication of Whistler's account of the incident, *The Baronet and the Butterfly*. The rift between Sickert and Whistler deepened when Sickert sided with Eden following the trial. The nature of the exchange between Lady Auckland and Sickert is not known, but she was also the subject of a portrait by the artist, known through a drawing, now lost (ca. 1894–98; Baron 1973, no. 63).

JT

VILHELM HAMMERSHØI

Copenhagen 1864–1916 Copenhagen

57 *Study for* Interior of San Stefano Rotondo, Rome, 1902

Pencil. 6⅜ x 7 in. (162 x 178 mm). Watermark: *Handgjord Post / Lessebo,* with a hive on a pedestal bearing the date 1719, encircled and surmounted by a crown.

PROVENANCE: Lady Jane Abdy, Bury Street Gallery, London.

LITERATURE: Vad 1992, pp. 247–54, fig. 163; Copenhagen and elsewhere 1997–98, p. 162.

Although Hammershøi's reputation faded after his death, he was considered the most controversial and original Danish artist active around the turn of the century. Having shown promise at an early age, he was well educated in the arts. He began drawing lessons at age eight and attended the Kunstakademi, Copenhagen, at age fifteen before departing four years later for the less conservative Kunstnernes Studieskoler to study with Peder Severin Krøyer (1851–1909). At age twenty-one he exhibited *Portrait of a Young Girl* (Anna Hammershøi, 1885; Den Hirschsprungske Samling, Copenhagen), which was startling in its departure from the conventions of academic portraiture and established his reputation. Despite his travels abroad, Hammershøi was not seduced by the formal vernacular of the avant-garde and maintained a consistent style throughout his career, focusing on interior scenes in which the emphasis on form and light led critics to compare his work to that of Johannes Vermeer and Pieter Saenredam.

Unable to secure a fellowship for travel from the Kunstakademi, Hammershøi made his second trip to Italy in 1902 supported by funds collected by a group of artist friends. On 7 October 1902 he and his wife arrived in Rome, where they took rooms overlooking the Forum, before traveling to Naples. While in Rome, the artist and his wife remained aloof from the Scandinavian community and explored the city on their own. It is not surprising that while searching for a subject Hammershøi settled on the interior of the seldom visited San Stefano Rotondo, a rare Byzantine circular plan church built on Monte Celio between 468 and 483 that at the time was believed to be an antique structure.

This luminous, highly finished pencil study is preparatory for Hammershøi's painting *Interior of San Stefano Rotondo, Rome,* now in the Fyns Kunstmuseum, Odense. Hammershøi began the painting in December 1902 and finished it the following month. Happy to have discovered a "new" subject in Rome, the artist later was dismayed to find that the church's interior had been reproduced on a postcard. He wrote to his brother Svend on 20 December 1902: "Yesterday I discovered by chance a postcard with the interior of San Stefano Rotondo, which I am herewith sending you so that you can get an idea of what it looks like. I don't otherwise much like seeing it on a postcard, I thought it had escaped" (Vad 1992, p. 250).

Hammershøi depicted the circular interior with its inner ring of elegant granite columns with white marble ionic capitals surrounding the octagonal altar rail, which is flanked by two columns with Corinthian capitals, also in white marble. The structure had a roof with an oculus, which allowed for direct illumination by the sun, and the lower register of windows punctuating the drum are visible along the upper edge of the

sheet. Hammershøi exploited the tonal range of graphite to capture the effects of light, which creates the sense of vast interior space. The serene, austere interior undoubtedly appealed to the artist, although in its original state the interior probably was covered in marble *revetments*. The rigid geometric forms of the columns juxtaposed with the curvilinear forms of the base of the drum and lunettes on the outer walls creates a dynamic tension that enlivens the composition.

JT

PIET MONDRIAN

Amersfoort 1872–1944 New York

58 *Dahlia,* ca. 1920

Graphite and watercolor on wove paper. 9⅝ x 8¾ in. (244 x 222 mm). Signed in graphite at lower center, *P. MONDRIAAN.*

PROVENANCE: Sale, Amsterdam, Christie's, 26 May 1988, lot 68, repr. in color p. 69 (as *Mauve Chrysanthemum Against a Blue Background*).

LITERATURE: Shapiro 1991, p. 41, repr. in color; Joosten and Welsh 1998, no. C103, repr.

EXHIBITION: New York 1991, no. 36.

Mondrian, who began as a naturalistic painter, depicted flowers throughout his career. His earliest such drawings date to the late 1890s and early 1900s. He seems to have put aside flower studies in 1903 and returned to the subject in 1908/9 while living in Amsterdam. In fact flower studies from the period 1908/9 to 1911 comprise nearly half his output. These studies were frequently exhibited, most prominently at the spring 1910 exhibition at the Society of St. Lucas, Amsterdam, which included five of the artist's large-scale flower studies. A year later, following the Moderne Kunst Kring's exhibition that marked the debut of French cubist works in the Netherlands, Mondrian decided to move to Paris.

Mondrian's mandatory residence in the Netherlands during World War I put him in desperate financial straits, as his radically abstract paintings had not yet found buyers. He resorted to producing copies of other works, accepting portrait commissions, and offering private drawing lessons. In about 1917, at the urging of friends, he began making a number of flower studies, many based on earlier works, for commercial sale. In 1921, despite a prolific period of painting, the nearly destitute artist was compelled to intensify the production of such works in order to earn a living. In an undated letter from spring 1922, Mondrian wrote to Antony Kok, "For a couple of months I have been busy making flowers—drawings in watercolor, *naturalistic,* the way I used to, without any pretensions of 'newness' in them! I see them as temporary craftsmanship because I can sell these things. For a low price of course. In this way I will be able to return to my own work after a while. A great many things are half finished" (Joosten and Welsh 1998, vol. 2, 461).

The artist's frustration may have derived from the lack of opportunity to render deeper meaning in the forms, as he had during his earlier period. In February 1915, he wrote to Augusta de Meester-Obreen, "and as to what you say about the appearance of a flower: you are surprised that I wish to dissect the delicate beauty and transform it into vertical and horizontal lines. I very readily admit your wonder, but it is not my intention to depict the delicate beauty. That which in the flower affects us as beauty and does not arise from the deepest part of its being, is beautiful but not the deepest beauty. I, too, find the flower beautiful in its physical appearance; but there is hidden in it a deeper beauty" (*Elsevier's Maandschrift* 25, 1915, pp. 394 n. 24, 396–99).

Mondrian's later flower studies are in many cases indistinguishable from those of his earlier Amsterdam period. Reinforcing the similarity of style and technique, the artist often returned to these works during his later career in New York, ca. 1940–44, where-

P. MONDRIAAN

upon he added his signature and an earlier date. The Morgan Library has a watercolor of a dahlia, which likely dates to the 1920s but was subsequently dated 1907 by the artist. Sometime after 1920 the artist signed the present sheet with the form of his name he had used before he changed the spelling in 1912.

Although the subject of this sheet repeatedly has been identified as a chrysanthemum, Joosten and Welsh classify it among the several studies made by the artist of dahlias. Indeed the cactus (or pompon) dahlia is easily confused with the Japanese-style chrysanthemum, which the artist also depicted frequently.

JT

PAUL KLEE

Münchenbuchsee/Bern 1879–1940 Muralto-Locarno

59 *Big Ones and Little Ones* (Grosse und Kleine), 1923

Oil transfer drawing. 12⅜ x 8⅞ in. (314 x 225 mm). Signed in brown ink at upper right, *Klee;* dated, numbered, and titled by the artist in pen and brown ink at lower center on mount, *1923 / 81 Grosse und Kleine.*

PROVENANCE: Nierendorf Gallery, New York; Girard collection, Santa Fe.

LITERATURE: Grohmann 1934, no. 12, repr.; Dover Art Library 1982, pl. 6.

EXHIBITION: New York 1999, no. 76, repr. in color.

At the behest of Walter Gropius (1883–1969) and Johannes Itten (1888–1967), in January 1921 Klee joined the faculty of the Staatliches Bauhaus, Weimar, where he spent his most productive years and developed his artistic theory. Itten drew on the German tradition of art pedagogy for children when devising the Bauhaus curriculum, which stressed the role of creative spontaneity. Klee was the ideal instructor in this capacity. He relocated to Dessau with the Bauhaus in 1925, but by 1931 he severed relations with the school, which was becoming increasingly politicized.

Klee endlessly experimented with unconventional drawing techniques and media. This sheet was produced through the oil transfer method, which the artist devised during the early 1920s; these sheets represent humorous and whimsical subjects, such as the well-known *Twittering Machine,* 1922 (Museum of Modern Art, New York). In the oil transfer process, a drawing is executed on a sheet of tracing paper, laid down on a second sheet, the verso of which has been coated with black ink or oil, simulating carbon paper. A third sheet receives the impression of the tracing in black ink as well as chance marks or smudges made during execution. To make *Big Ones and Little Ones,* Klee traced the drawing onto a sheet, which he then mounted onto another that was dated, numbered, and titled. In other instances, the artist added touches of watercolor and pen and ink to the final drawing. The oil transfer technique was ideally suited to Klee's emphasis upon chance and spontaneity in the creative process, while upholding the quality of his fine, bare line drawings.

The elaborate linear construction of the group and interdependence of parts reveal Klee's interest in the relationship between children and adults. The angular, stiff, and hollow-eyed adults exert control over the children with their curly hair and twirling poses. A metamorphosis is suggested: the children, playful and animated, will eventually become the serious adults whose latent playfulness is suggested by the heart-shaped mouth of the figure at the left as well as his companions' silly hat and curly hair. As Dorothea Dietrich observed, the gap between the children and adults is mediated by a man wearing glasses and a beret who waves at the viewer. This figure may be identified as a representation of the artist at the juncture between child- and adulthood (New York 1999, p. 182). Klee's formal vocabulary during the 1920s both recalled his earlier line drawings from the 1910s and reflected the contemporary interests of the Bauhaus. At Weimar, the artist became increasingly interested in physiognomy, puppet theater, and the expressive potential of masks. The abbreviated facial features depicted in the present sheet reflect such concerns.

JT

1922 81 Grosse und Kleine

FERNAND LÉGER

Argentan, Orne 1881–1955 Gif-sur-Yvette, Seine-et-Oise

60 *Composition,* 1918

Watercolor and brush and black ink over graphite on artist board. 9 x 11 in. (229 x 279 mm).

PROVENANCE: Galerie F. Moeller, Berlin; Lilienfeld Gallery, New York; Walter P. Chrysler, Jr., New York; his sale, New York, Parke-Bernet, 1949–50, lot 29; Philip Johnson; Susan Cable Herter, Santa Fe; Artemis Fine Arts.

EXHIBITION: Salzburg 1990, no. 2, repr. in color.

During the First World War, Léger's artistic activity was limited mostly to drawing. He remained productive, however, while hospitalized for over a year in Villepinte, near Paris, after exposure to mustard gas in Verdun in late 1916. He continued to draw and paint during this period with materials close at hand. Returning to Paris in 1918, the artist moved away from his prewar style toward an aesthetic informed by mechanical forms and bold colors. Of his works from this time, Léger remarked: "On my return from the war, I continued to make use of what I had felt at the front for three years, I used geometrical forms; this will be called the mechanical period" (Cassou and Leymarie 1973, p. 45). His fascination with military equipment became infused with his enthusiasm for visual culture, resulting in a style characterized by flat areas of pure color, letters and words, and geometric shapes. The machine aesthetic was a subject of discussion among many artists active in postwar Paris. In 1920 Le Corbusier wrote in *L'Esprit Nouveau:* "La machine et toute de la géométrie. La géométrie est notre grande création et elle nous ravit. La machine fait luire devant nous des disques, des sphères, des cylindres d'acier poli, d'acier, taillé avec une précision de théorie et une acuité que *jamais la nature* ne nous montra."

Léger's postwar works began as purely mechanist compositions devoid of human presence, constituted of geometrical forms derived from industrial objects. The artist used these elements to construct rhythmic, dynamic compositions that would "introduce us to the contemporary world of speed and technical efficiency, with which Léger totally identified himself" (Cassou and Leymarie 1973, p. 45). His two masterpieces from this period are *The Discs,* 1918 (Musée d'Art Moderne de la Ville de Paris) and *The City,* 1919 (Philadelphia Museum of Art). Eventually, by about 1923, the need to reintroduce a human presence into this universe of geometric shapes brought an end to such purely formal works.

The artist's explorations in watercolor form a vital part of his creative process for oil painting. He often worked in series, by making numerous drawings in graphite, watercolor, and gouache. In works such as this one, the artist refined ideas about form and color in anticipation of the series of paintings titled *The Discs,* which culminated in the Paris canvas. This series is characterized by a combination of circular and semicircular shapes and stripes punctuated by curvilinear forms. The combination of forms and color creates a dynamic pattern that is a metaphor for the vitality and energy of modern urban life. It was from this series that Léger's compositions devoted to man and the machine developed about 1919–20.

JT

ROGER DE LA FRESNAYE

Le Mans 1885–1925 Grasse

61 *Study for* Le Quatorze juillet, 1914

Charcoal. 10¼ x 8½ in. (260 x 216 mm). Stamped with the artist's signature at lower right, *R de la Fresnaye*.

PROVENANCE: Paul Chadourne, Garches; Germain Seligman (1893–1978), New York (stamp at lower right, not in Lugt); Ethlyne Seligman, New York.

LITERATURE: Seligman 1969, no. 146, repr.

EXHIBITIONS: London 1931, no. 15; Baltimore 1964, no. 121, repr.

La Fresnaye joined the informal gatherings of the Puteaux Group following its participation in the 1911 Salon des Indépendants. The group united artists working outside Montmartre in the formal vernacular of Cubism. As a member of the Puteaux Group, La Fresnaye was involved in the historic 1912 Cubist exhibition *Salon de la Section d'Or,* at the Galerie la Boëtie, Paris. This exhibition featured the work of the principal artists in France, aside from Picasso and Braque, associated with Cubism, including Juan Gris, Francis Picabia, Marcel Duchamp, Léger, Robert Delaunay, Albert Gleizes, Louis Marcoussis, and Alfred Dunoyer de Segonzac.

Inspired by his studies of Cézanne, La Fresnaye was attracted to Analytic Cubism in 1910–11, although like Léger, the artist never fully exploited its potential. La Fresnaye's compositions retained an identifiable subject and were characterized by a vocabulary of simplified geometric forms as well as an interest in the possibilities of color. Germain Seligman compared La Fresnaye's search for order, rational composition, and balance to the tradition of French classicism, stemming from Poussin and David, through Seurat.

This study of two figures, a male seated next to a table, and a female standing behind him, is directly related to one of La Fresnaye's most important compositions. A cluster of waving tricolor flags appears in the left background, a direct allusion to the celebration of the last Bastille Day before World War I. A small oil of the subject is now in a private collection in California (see Cogniat and George 1950, no. 145); a second, larger but unfinished, canvas was donated by Seligman to the Musée nationale d'art moderne, Paris (Fig. 1). The artist's work on this painting likely was interrupted by the onset of the war in August 1914

FIG. 1. Roger de la Fresnaye, *Le Quatorze juillet,* Musée nationale d'art moderne, Paris

and his enlistment in the infantry the following month. The male figure seated at a table was a recurring motif in La Fresnaye's work leading up to *Le Quatorze juillet:* a similar figure appears in *La Partie de cartes,* 1912; *La Vie conjugale,* 1912–13; *La Conquête de l'air,* 1913; and particularly *L'Homme assis,* 1913–14. Seligman, who organized the first major monographic exhibition of the artist's work in America in 1945, considered the period from 1910 to 1914 La Fresnaye's "most vital," during which "a complete transformation of the artist's thinking took

place." He turned to brighter colors, simpler forms, and a more rhythmic composition and sought to eliminate all extraneous elements.

As a result of exposure to mustard gas during the war, La Fresnaye was released from the army in 1918 and repeatedly hospitalized for tuberculosis. During and after the war, he completed a number of projects and increasingly turned to portraiture and depictions of the human body. Before he was able to fully explore the potential of figural representation, he succumbed to illness and died at the age of forty.

JT

GIORGIO MORANDI

Bologna 1890–1964 Bologna

62 *Still Life*, 1956

Watercolor over graphite. 7½ x 11 in. (191 x 279 mm). Watermark: None. Signed in graphite at lower center, *Morandi*.

PROVENANCE: Galleria del Milione, Milan; Mr. and Mrs. M. Frank, New York, 1957; by descent to Mrs. Dorrit Sander, New York, 1981; private collection, 1992; sale, London, Christie's, 8 February 2001, lot 489.

LITERATURE: Pasquali (forthcoming).

EXHIBITION: Brooklyn 1957, no. 78.

At the age of seventeen, Morandi entered the Accademia di Belle Arti, Bologna, where he began to explore contemporary French art in books. He traveled to Florence, where he saw the work of Giotto, Masaccio, and Paolo Uccello, and Rome, where he developed his interest in Cézanne. The remainder of his career was spent in Bologna and—briefly during World War II—in the neighboring village of Grizzana. In 1956, despite the protests of his colleagues, Morandi retired from the faculty of the Accademia, where he had taught printmaking for over twenty-six years.

Cézanne's working method served as a model for Morandi, who also repeatedly depicted the same motifs in an effort to explore the essence of form. The most prevalent subject in Morandi's oeuvre, aside from landscapes, are still-life studies of bottles, which he painted and drew almost obsessively from the 1920s, changing only the number and rhythmic arrangement of objects. This singular motif—stripped of narrative possibility—allowed him to focus on the facture of the painting: the physical reality of the paint, and the relationship of form and tone. The simplicity of an empty bottle reduced the number of distractions and extraneous details in a given composition, allowing the artist to focus on a careful analysis of form. The emphasis was upon analytical inquiry, cognitive investigation, and the method of creation. Having settled on depicting bottles early on freed Morandi to the point that the subject of his works became almost irrelevant.

In his later works from the 1950s, the artist increasingly thinned his paint to reduce the density of the surface. For this same reason he embraced the use of watercolor and wash, which enabled him to experiment with form while retaining evidence of the individual brushstroke, allowing the paper or canvas to show through the pigment. The three bottles depicted here were first sketched lightly in graphite and described in a combination of subtle purple and brown washes. The sinuous purple shadows clarify and define the forms, while the reserve of the paper is used as a formal element. The delicate chromatic variation among the objects further emphasizes Morandi's innate understanding of color as a means of defining form and not only as an end in itself.

JT

Minault

OIL SKETCHES

RICHARD WILSON

Penegoes 1713/14–1782 Colomendy

63 *Welsh Landscape with a Ruined Castle by a Lake*

Oil on wood panel. 7⁷/₁₆ x 8¹¹/₁₆ in. (188 x 220 mm). Inscribed on reverse in pen and blue ink on a label at upper right, *B 724*; in pen and black ink on a label at center, in an eighteenth-century hand (?), [illegible] *Landscape. Wilson.*

PROVENANCE: Possibly Samuel J. Day (d. 1806), Hinton Charterhouse, Bath; possibly bequeathed to Mr. Robertson-Glasgow, Hinton House, Hinton Charterhouse, Bath, from 1846; by descent to Robin F. Robertson-Glasgow, Hinton Charterhouse, Bath; his sale, London, Christie's South Kensington, 23 November 1995, lot 22, as circle of Richard Wilson (b.i.); unidentified collector (according to Robin F. Robertson-Glasgow); sale, London, Sotheby's, 3 April 1996, lot 95 (as Richard Wilson), repr. in color; Agnew's, London.

The son of a Welsh clergyman who provided him with an excellent classical education, Wilson trained as a portraitist in London, where he also executed topographical landscapes. He decided to devote himself to landscape about 1752 during a seven-year sojourn in Italy (1750–57), where he was exposed to the work not only of his contemporaries Francesco Zuccarelli (1702–1788) and Jan Frans van Bloemen (1662–1749) but also to that of seventeenth-century masters Salvator Rosa (1615–1673), Claude Lorrain (No. 10), and Gaspard Dughet (1615–1675). He may have been influenced in his decision by Claude-Joseph Vernet (1714–1789), then in Rome, who is also thought to have encouraged him in the practice of painting en plein air. Although it has been suggested that Wilson did not paint in oil en plein air (London 1999, p. 24; Washington and elsewhere 1996–97, p. 110), it has also been noted that he was not unfamiliar with the practice. In the left foreground of a painting of 1752, *Tivoli: The Cascatelli Grandi and the Villa of Maecenas,* he depicted an artist who paints the landscape before him at a portable easel (National Gallery of Ireland, Dublin; Washington and elsewhere 1996–97, no. 1, repr.).

Wilson returned to London in 1758, quickly becoming the principal British painter of the classical landscape. He attracted numerous wealthy patrons for whom he executed large, classicizing paintings, such as *The Destruction of the Children of Niobe,* commissioned by the duke of Cumberland (Yale Center for British Art, New Haven; London 1982–83, no. 87, repr.). From the early 1760s he began to represent the landscape of England, Scotland, and Wales, applying the principles of the arcadian landscape he had absorbed in Italy and thereby legitimizing the British countryside as a subject worthy of depiction in art (Rosenthal 1982, p. 64). His pictures of these regions blend elements of the Claudean ideal landscape with a (somewhat) truthful record of the actual landscape.

The present oil sketch likely belongs to this period. Although the view has not been identified, the suggestion that it represents a location in Wales, put forth when the work was on the art market in 1996, no doubt is based on

FIG. 1. Richard Wilson, *The Keep of Okehampton Castle,* Manchester City Art Galleries

the similarity in terrain between this study and the numerous Welsh landscapes by Wilson featuring a ruined castle perched atop a rugged headland overlooking a lake with a hilly landscape in the distance. Two works with which this sketch has compositional affinities are *Llyn Peris and Dolbadarn Castle* of 1762–64 (Felton Bequest, National Gallery of Victoria, Melbourne; London 1982–83, no. 105, pl. 9) and *The Keep of Okehampton Castle* of 1771–72 (Fig. 1).

KS

THOMAS JONES

Trevonen, Powys, 1742–1803 Pencerrig, Powys

64   *Ponte Loreto near Nettuno*

Oil over traces of graphite on paper, laid down on canvas. 13⅜ x 20⅞ in. (340 x 530 mm). Signed at lower right, *T. Jones | Nº 42*; inscribed by the artist at lower right, PONTE LORETO | *near | Nettuno.*

PROVENANCE: Possibly Capt. John Dale (son-in-law of the artist); possibly by descent through his daughter Rose to the Adams family; Canon J. H. Adams (great-great-grandson of the artist); his sale, London, Sotheby's, 27 November 1975, lot 92, repr.; Colnaghi, London, 1975; Galerie Bruno Meissner, Zollikon, Switzerland, 1976; Pierre Boissonnas, Zurich, 1978; sale, London, Christie's, 10 June 1999, lot 14, repr.; Artemis Fine Arts Ltd., London.

EXHIBITIONS: London 1787, no. 58; Bremen 1977–78, no. 218, repr.; Paris and Mantua 2001, no. 31, repr. in color.

The son of a Welsh landowner, Jones trained for the church at Jesus College, Oxford, before beginning to study painting. In 1761 he enrolled at Shipley's School in London, and in 1763 he entered the studio of Richard Wilson (No. 63), with whom he studied for two years. Between 1765 and 1780 he exhibited at the Society of Arts and later at the Royal Academy. His paintings—landscapes in the Claudean style popularized in England by Wilson—were acquired by collectors at the highest levels of society.

In 1776 Jones set out for Italy, where he remained until 1783, spending his first two years in Rome. Five months after his arrival, while on a sketching trip through the countryside he recorded in his journal for 1 May 1777 a visit to the site depicted in the present oil sketch: "We now descended into the Campania in a direction toward the antient Ostia, and arrived at an antique bridge of One Arch & built of large square blocks of the Peperino Stone, called Ponte Loreto—" (Oppé 1951, p. 59).

The present work is the artist's only known depiction of Ponte Loreto. Although he referred in his journal entry to having made sketches of the bridge, these have not been identified. The Small British Museum Sketchbook, whose cover is inscribed *2 Dec[ember 1776] to 6 May [1777]*, contains dated drawings that Jones made around the time of his visit to Ponte Loreto: one of Lake Nemi dated 30 April (fol. 151); one of Lanuvio, the distant hilltop town depicted at the center of the present work, dated 1 May (fol. 152); and one of Albano dated 2 May (fol. 153; correspondence with Timothy Wilcox, 7 February 2002).

Anna Ottani Cavina (Paris and Mantua 2001, p. 50) has theorized that because of its substantial size and high degree of finish, the present oil sketch could not have been executed on the spot but only sometime later, after drawings made on site. Her further observation that the sketch's fluid, dilute medium would have allowed for rapid application, however, leaves open the possibility that the sketch might have been executed on the spot. Another option, suggested by Wilcox (correspondence, 7 February 2002), is that the artist may have begun the work on site and later finished it in oil. Such may be the case as well with an oil sketch of a site that Jones visited two months after Ponte Loreto, *An Excavation of an Antique Building Discovered in a Cava in the Villa Negroni at Rome* (Tate Gallery, London; Paris and Mantua 2001, no. 60, repr.). Like the present work, the Tate oil sketch is highly finished and executed on a sheet with dimensions very close to those of the Thaw work. Both oil sketches bear numbers inscribed by the artist, suggesting that they once belonged to a sketchbook or portfolio. Both works also show traces of underdrawing, which might have been made on site.

KS

JEAN-JOSEPH-XAVIER BIDAULD

Carpentras 1748–1846 Montmorency

65 *View of the Bridge near La Cava, Kingdom of Naples*

Oil on paper, mounted on canvas. 8½ x 11¾ in. (216 x 298 mm).

PROVENANCE: Sale, Paris, 25–26 March 1847 (?); sale, New York, Sotheby's, 25 January 2001, lot 227.

A pupil in Lyon of his brother Jean-Pierre-Xavier, Jean-Joseph-Xavier Bidauld settled in Paris in 1783. There he made the acquaintance of the landscape painter Joseph Vernet (1714–1789) and of a dealer, Dulac, whose financial support was to enable him to travel to Italy two years later. The period from 1785 to 1790, during which Bidauld visited Rome and Naples, was critical to the formation of his style. While in Italy he painted numerous sketches in oil on paper, their laborious execution remarkably unlike that of the quickly rendered plein-air studies of his near-contemporary Pierre-Henri de Valenciennes (Nos. 66–71). Bidauld's sketches later would serve as the basis for many of the paintings that he exhibited at the Salon between 1791 and 1844. Greatly admired by Jean-Baptiste-Camille Corot (Nos. 90–92), Bidauld was the first landscape painter to be named a member of the Académie des Beaux-Arts, in 1823. Nevertheless, by the time he died, his stubborn defense of an outmoded, neoclassical style, together with his vocal disdain for the realism favored by such young artists as Théodore Rousseau (Nos. 38 and 105), had earned him the contempt of the critics. Only recently has the merit of his work again been recognized.

Bidauld traveled widely during his five-year sojourn in Italy, and a number of his works depict picturesque sites in the Kingdom of Naples. This sketch, typical of Bidauld's style in both delicacy of execution and the opalescent quality of the light, depicts a bridge at Cava de' Tirreni, a town situated in the hills, not far from Salerno. The posthumous sale of the contents of Bidauld's studio included both a *Vue du pont et de l'hôpital de la Cava (royaume de Naples;* no. 22) and a *Vue du pont et d'une partie de la ville de la Cava* (no. 21). It is possible that one of these works is the same as the sketch now in the collection of Eugene and Clare Thaw.

WMG

PIERRE-HENRI DE VALENCIENNES

Toulouse 1750–1819 Paris

66   *View of the Colosseum*

Oil on board. 10¼ x 15⅜ in. (260 x 391 mm).

PROVENANCE: Galerie de Bayser, Paris; Claus Virch, Paris.

EXHIBITION: Paris 1973–74, no. 1.

Although not the inventor of the genre, Valenciennes played a critical role in the development of the plein-air oil sketch, as he did in transmitting the practice of painting outdoors on paper to the succeeding generation of French landscape artists. He studied art in his native Toulouse before becoming a pupil in Paris of the history painter Gabriel François Doyen (1726–1806). Valenciennes's first trips to Italy took place in 1769 and 1777–81, but it was during his third voyage, from 1782 until 1784 or 1785, that he created the remarkable series of oil sketches on paper for which he is most famous. After returning to France, he became the leading practitioner and theorist of the neoclassical landscape, influenced by the work of Nicolas Poussin and Claude Lorrain (No. 10) on the one hand and by an intense study of nature on the other. Having debuted in the Salon of 1787, he was instrumental in the establishment of the historical landscape as a distinct category of the Prix de Rome, and his numerous pupils included Jean-Victor Bertin (1767–1842), Pierre-Athanase Chauvin (1774–1832), and Achille-Etna Michallon (No. 93).

Valenciennes's sketches in oil on paper depict a range of subjects—from meteorological phenomena and ordinary buildings at different times of the day to the most celebrated monuments of ancient Rome. The view in this sketch apparently was taken from the Palatine Hill and includes the Colosseum in the middle ground on the left and the Sabine Hills in the distance. Both the vivacity of the brushwork and the striking composition—dense foliage rises abruptly in a steep diagonal at the right—are characteristic of the artist's finest sketches. An almost identical painting on paper was among the more than one hundred works by Valenciennes that Princess Louis de Croÿ presented to the Musée du Louvre, Paris, in 1930 (Washington and elsewhere 1996–97, no. 14, repr.). The survival of two such spirited versions of the same composition is not unique, however; Valenciennes copied a number of his own plein-air sketches. It is astonishing that, although one or the other of these works presumably was created in the studio, both give the impression of having been painted outdoors, very quickly, in front of the motif. Of the two versions of the present composition, that in the Thaw Collection arguably is the freer and more boldly conceived.

The Colosseum anchors the composition of a number of later oil sketches on paper. There is a similar view by Michallon in a private collection, Paris (Washington and elsewhere 1996–97, no. 63, repr.), and the subject was treated by Michallon's pupil Jean-Baptiste-Camille Corot (Nos. 90–92) in one of his best-known sketches, *The Colosseum Viewed from the Farnese Gardens* (Louvre, Paris; Washington and elsewhere 1996–97, p. 103, fig. 5).

WMG

PIERRE-HENRI DE VALENCIENNES

Toulouse 1750–1819 Paris

67   *Landscape with the Pyramid of Gaius Cestius, Rome*

Oil on paper, mounted on canvas. 10½ x 15 in. (267 x 381 mm).

PROVENANCE: Galerie de Bayser, Paris.

EXHIBITIONS: Paris 1973–74, no. 6; New York 1996a.

Much of Valenciennes's impact upon the development of French landscape painting in the first quarter of the nineteenth century derived from the dissemination among artists of his two-part treatise, *Elémens de perspective pratique à l'usage des artistes . . .* (Paris, 1800; reprint: Geneva, 1973). The book is devoted partly to theory and partly to practice and advises the aspiring landscape painter to study nature en plein air. It advocates the creation of sketches in oil on paper as a means of understanding and depicting the effects of atmosphere and light. According to Valenciennes, such sketches should be made quickly—in two hours or less—in order to "seize Nature as she is" (trans. Galassi 1991, p. 27). The initial purpose of the oil sketch, therefore, was strictly didactic. Finish mattered very little, for none of the paintings that Valenciennes and his pupils executed en plein air was intended for public exhibition.

Of the more than one hundred extant sketches that Valenciennes created in the environs of Rome, a number are of recognizable monuments. Here, the locale is identified by the presence at the lower left of the pyramid of Gaius Cestius, erected in the late first century B.C. The nearby Porta San Paolo is visible just to the left of the pyramid.

The pyramid of Gaius Cestius appears in several of the sketches by Valenciennes that entered the Louvre, Paris, as part of the 1930 donation of the princess Louis de Croÿ. In two of them (RF 2992 [Bruno Mantura, in Spoleto 1996, no. 12, repr.] and 2903), the pyramid of Gaius Cestius and Porta San Paolo also are relegated to the background, and, as is true of the Thaw sketch, humbler buildings constitute the principal subject. Bruno Mantura has posited that the cluster of buildings in the right foreground of one of these paintings (RF 2992) may be the early Christian church of Santa Prisca, located on the Aventine Hill. Although the structure on the right in this work clearly is not Santa Prisca, the fact that the pyramid and Porta San Paolo are depicted from approximately the same angle but at a slightly greater distance suggests that it may have been painted somewhere nearby. The pyramid of Gaius Cestius also may be the subject of a fourth sketch by Valenciennes, *Pyramid with a Rainbow,* in which other compositional elements may, however, be imaginary (Spoleto 1996, no. 13, repr.).

WMG

PIERRE-HENRI DE VALENCIENNES

Toulouse 1750–1819 Paris

68 *City Wall at the Foot of a Mountain*

Oil on paper. 14⅜ x 18⅞ in. (365 x 480 mm).

PROVENANCE: Valenciennes sale, Paris, 26 April 1819 (?); Achille Valenciennes (?); Galerie de Bayser, Paris.

LITERATURE: London 1999, p. 166, under no. 67 (as George Augustus Wallis); Paris and Mantua 2001, p. 95, under no. 61 (George Augustus Wallis).

EXHIBITION: Spoleto 1996, no. 54, repr.

This unusual study offers a view with trees and a distant mountain seen from within an ancient city wall. At first sight, the wall, most likely dating from the Roman period, might seem to be a section of Rome's Aurelian wall. Bruno Mantura has noted (Spoleto 1996, no. 54), however, that there are no mountains on the perimeter of the Aurelian wall, which would preclude such an identification. Another view of the same bit of wall and landscape, taken from a different vantage, was executed by Simon Denis (Nos. 72–74) in 1777, some time after Valenciennes's return to Paris (Paris and Mantua 2001, no. 86, repr.).

CDD

PIERRE-HENRI DE VALENCIENNES

Toulouse 1750–1819 Paris

69 *Stormy Sky*

Oil on paper. 11⅝ x 16¹⁵/₁₆ in. (295 x 430 mm).

PROVENANCE: Valenciennes sale, Paris, 26 April 1819 (?); Achille Valenciennes (?); Galerie de Bayser, Paris.

LITERATURE: London 1999, p. 166, under no. 67 (as George Augustus Wallis); Paris and Mantua 2001, p. 95, under no. 61 (George Augustus Wallis).

EXHIBITION: Spoleto 1996, no. 55, repr.

The real subject of this sheet is the sky and clouds. Although mostly dark and indicative of the storm in progress, white clouds in the background suggest areas of sunlight beyond the immediate picture plane. The rolling hills that define the lower margin of the sketch lack attributes that would allow identification of the site, but it may have been painted somewhere in the Roman Campagna. From the number of sky studies he painted, it is clear that Valenciennes was intensely interested in the changing effects of weather.

CDD

PIERRE-HENRI DE VALENCIENNES

Toulouse 1750–1819 Paris

70 *Sky at Dusk*

Oil on paper. 11⅝ x 16¹⁵⁄₁₆ in. (295 x 430 mm).

PROVENANCE: Valenciennes sale, Paris, 26 April 1819 (?); Achille Valenciennes (?); Galerie de Bayser, Paris.

LITERATURE: London 1999, p. 166, under no. 67 (as George Augustus Wallis); Paris and Mantua 2001, p. 95, under no. 61 (George Augustus Wallis).

EXHIBITION: Spoleto 1996, no. 56, repr.

71 *The Marmore Waterfalls*

Oil on paper. 17½ x 14⅜ in. (445 x 365 mm).

PROVENANCE: Valenciennes sale, Paris, 26 April 1819 (?); Achille Valenciennes (?); Galerie de Bayser, Paris.

LITERATURE: Christopher Riopelle, in London 1999, p. 166, under no. 67 (as George Augustus Wallis); Anna Ottani Cavina, in Paris and Mantua 2001, p. 95, under no. 61 (George Augustus Wallis).

EXHIBITIONS: Paris 1973–74, possibly no. 14; Spoleto 1996, nos. 2–3, 54–59, repr.

Nos. 66–71 belong to a group of nine closely related sketches that Mr. and Mrs. Thaw acquired in Paris in 1995. Two depict views of the spectacular Marmore waterfalls at Terni, about thirty-five miles north of Rome. Another represents an unidentified stretch of medieval wall. Three are cloud studies, executed at different times of the day under various meteorological conditions. Two others are panoramic views of the Roman countryside; and one represents a shadowy patch of dense vegetation.

The entire group was attributed to Valenciennes by Geneviève Lacambre, who posited that they might be the nine sketches acquired by the artist's nephew Achille Valenciennes at the sale of the contents of Valenciennes's studio in April 1819. (The subsequent history of the works purchased by Achille Valenciennes is unclear.) In 1996 eight of the nine sketches in the Thaw Collection were exhibited at Spoleto and Lacambre's opinion was published in the catalogue (Spoleto 1996, no. 3, repr. in color).

All nine paintings undoubtedly are by the same hand, and they are in many respects comparable to the extensive series of works in the Musée du Louvre, Paris, by Valenciennes, the leading figure of the plein-air movement in France. Recently, however, some scholars, including Christopher Riopelle and Anna Ottani Cavina, have queried Valenciennes's authorship of the sketches, proposing that they might instead have been executed by his near contemporary, the peripatetic British painter George Augustus Wallis (1761–1847), who spent most of his life in Italy but also worked in Heidelberg. Their dismissal of Lacambre's attribution of the group to Valenciennes has to do with the appearance on the art market of two additional groups of oil sketches, each of which recently has been ascribed to Wallis (New York 1996b, no. 7, repr. in color) and, it may be argued, has certain features in common with the series in the Thaw Collection.

The Thaw group does have some affinity with a relatively large group of sketches acquired about 1996 by the London dealer James Mackinnon (New York 1996b and New York 1998c). The latter are not unrelated in style to the sketches in the Thaw Collection and share with them a number of physical characteristics, such as the presence on the versos of traces of green sealing wax, perhaps intended to affix the sheets to the pages of an album. Among the sketches purchased by Mackinnon was a second version (now in the Fitzwilliam Museum, Cambridge) of *The Marmore Waterfalls* in the Thaw Collection. In addition to sketches in oil on paper, the works acquired by Mackinnon comprised a large, unsigned pen-and-wash drawing of a wooded landscape also in the Fitzwilliam Museum. Mackinnon considered the drawing comparable in style to sheets that are signed by Wallis and on this basis attributed the entire group to the British artist.

A year or so after the acquisition of the Mackinnon group, still another series of oil sketches surfaced in the south of France and was purchased by the Paris dealer Eric Coatalem (Paris 1998, twenty-six of the relevant sketches are reproduced). Although most were landscapes, the group also included a portrait in oil on paper of a young woman, which, in John Lishawa's opinion, resembles works by Wallis. Because of this, Lishawa went on to ascribe the numerous other sketches in the group to the same artist.

All three groups belong to the period during which painters began to venture into the countryside regularly to sketch in oil on paper. That all the works in question are by the same artist is less certain. The sketches in the Coatalem group, in particular, vary markedly in quality, and the fact that some bear original inscriptions in French seems surprising if they really are the work of an Englishman who spent most of his life in Italy and Germany. Moreover, while the existence among the sketches purchased by Mackinnon of a second version of *The Marmore Waterfalls* indicates some connection between that series and the Thaw group, differences in paper and paint application further complicate the attribution.

Such uncertainty continues to plague the study of early plein-air sketches, few of which are signed or fully documented. Clearly the facts do not warrant the wholesale reattribution of all three divergent groups to a single artist, let alone to a painter of Wallis's apparently modest stature. Further study is needed.

WMG and CDD

SIMON-JOSEPH-ALEXANDER-CLEMENT DENIS

Antwerp 1755–1813 Naples

72 *Paysage de Tivoli*

Oil on paper. 12¾ x 11½ in. (262 x 218 mm). Signed with initials on verso at lower right, inscribed, and numbered, *a Tivoli. Sn Denis | 30.*

PROVENANCE: Sale, Monte Carlo, Sotheby's Monaco, 19 June 1992, lot 204, repr.; Galerie de Bayser, Paris.

Denis first studied in his native Antwerp with the landscape and animal painter H.-J. Antonissen. In the early 1780s Denis moved to Paris and worked with the genre painter and dealer Jean-Baptiste Lebrun, who supported his 1786 journey to Rome, where he received high praise in the Italian press of the day for one of his landscapes and his special ability to handle effects of light as well as for his convincing use of detail. He married a Roman in 1787 and was considered part of the French artistic community in Rome, accompanying Elisabeth-Louise Vigée Le Brun, wife of his protector, and M. Ménageot, then director of the French Academy, on an excursion to Tivoli in December 1789.

The cascade at Tivoli was a picturesque subject, popular with artists for generations, and one that Denis painted often. In this view, he slightly offset the falls to show how the Aniene River flows through a hilly landscape and curves through some large rocky formations to make at least three small cascades. The artist's palette consists mainly of silvery greens for the landscape in the background and the river itself, topped with brilliant slashes of white to suggest the effect of sunlight as well as the swirling water playing on the rocks. He also used dark bottle greens for the foliage on the rocky outcroppings cast into the shade and a reddish brown for the rocks. He was to return to Tivoli often to paint. By 1806 he had established himself as court painter to Joseph Bonaparte in Naples.

CDD

SIMON-JOSEPH-ALEXANDER-CLEMENT DENIS

Antwerp 1755–1813 Naples

73 *A Roman Sunset on the Campagna*

Oil on paper. 8½ x 10½ in. (202 x 265 mm). Signed with initials on verso, inscribed, and numbered, *a Rome* /
S. Ds / *54.*

PROVENANCE: Sale, Paris, Hôtel Drouot, 20 December 1996, lot 137, repr. in color; Hazlitt, Gooden & Fox,
London.

EXHIBITIONS: London 1998a, no. 37, repr. in color; Paris and Mantua 2001, no. 84, repr. in color.

While the subject of this oil sketch is the sunset, most of the composition is a study of the
sky set off or anchored by a strip of land in the very immediate foreground with the sil-
houettes of a villa, a tower, and some trees. Denis's landscapes were written about as early
as 1806 when G. A. Guattani (in *Memorie Enciclopediche Romane sulle Belle Arti, Antichità, . . . ,*
Rome, 1806–8) wrote of one of his sunsets, "une chute de soleil . . . lorsque la planète se
couche, encombrée de nuages sombres" or "du soleil qui transperce les nuages . . . surgis-
sent différents jeux de lumière, qui produisent des effets étranges" (Guattani 1806–8, p. 116).

As Anna Ottani Cavina rightly observed, this kind of landscape has much in common
with the sort of thing Valenciennes did in so many of his studies—he also constructed a
disproportionate relationship between the sky and the buildings defining the edge of the
earth (Paris and Mantua 2001). By doing this the artist may achieve a "portrait de ciel et de
nuages," according to one of Denis's favorite formulas. There is no evidence that Denis
ever met Valenciennes, but it is possible that he may have encountered him in Paris between 1784 and 1786, just after Valenciennes's return from Rome. The numerals on the
verso of these oils on paper suggest that the artist produced a series of variations executed en plein air.

CDD

SIMON-JOSEPH-ALEXANDER-CLEMENT DENIS

Antwerp 1755–1813 Naples

74 *Landscape near Rome During a Storm*

Oil on paper. 9¼ x 14⅛ in. (235 x 357 mm). Signed and inscribed on verso, *L'Arc en Ciel, visible ou le soleil eclaire | e traversé par la pluie ou l'ombre commence | peint apres l'etude du dessin fait pres de Rome | Sn Denis.*

PROVENANCE: Private collection, New York; W. M. Brady and Co., New York, 1996.

EXHIBITIONS: New York 1996c, no. 2, repr. in color; Paris and Mantua 2001, no. 82, repr. in color.

The inscription on the back of this sketch indicates that Denis made it after an earlier drawing. Less sky is visible here than in No. 73; the artist was studying the weather, made especially interesting by the appearance of a rainbow. In the distance the sun has already broken through, and the earth is brilliantly illuminated, while the storm continues to darken the middle distance and foreground. To lend an air of romantic immediacy to the picture, Denis added two horses racing along a curved road along the lower edge. This work provides an excellent example of the artist's virtuosity, especially evident in the way he evoked the warm atmosphere of the saturated ground as well as the bright golden light of the Campagna beyond the storm.

CDD

JEAN-ANTOINE CONSTANTIN, called CONSTANTIN D'AIX

La Loubière, Marseille, 1756–1844 Aix-en-Provence

75 *View of Aix-en-Provence*

Oil on paper, laid down on board. 8¼ x 11 in. (210 x 279 mm).

PROVENANCE: By descent from the artist; Antoine Laurentin, Paris; Didier Aaron, Inc., New York.

While serving as an apprentice in the ceramic industry, Constantin attracted the attention of one M. Blanchard, a painter of faïence who encouraged him to pursue the study of art. In 1771 Constantin entered the Academy of Painting and Sculpture at Marseille and eventually settled in Aix-en-Provence. During the late 1770s he spent three years in Italy, during which he created numerous drawings and oil sketches of the environs of Rome. After returning to France, he executed historical landscapes but continued to work en plein air, producing sketches in oil on paper of the countryside near Aix and other sites in Provence. Constantin also was a gifted teacher, whose best-known pupil, François-Marius Granet, is represented in the Thaw Collection by a watercolor and two oil sketches (Nos. 33, 79–80).

This work depicts the artist's hometown, with the Gothic spire of the church of Saint-Jean-de-Malte visible to the left. Begun in graphite and freely worked up in oil, *View of Aix-en-Provence* has been dated about 1805 by John Lishawa and may be compared to another, similarly unfinished sketch, *View of a Church,* recently on the art market in London (London 2001, no. 20, repr.).

WMG

ANTOINE CHARLES HORACE VERNET,
called CARLE VERNET

Bordeaux 1758–1836 Paris

76   *Landscape*

Oil on paper, mounted on canvas. 8 x 10½ in. (203 x 267 mm). Signed with initials at lower right, *C. V.*
PROVENANCE: Artemis Fine Arts, Ltd., London.

This work apparently is the only known pure landscape by Carle Vernet, an artist best known for his paintings of horses and amusing series of drawings and prints of Parisians during the Directoire: *Les Incroyables, Les Merveilleuses, Cris de Paris,* and *Costumes.* The youngest son of the marine painter Joseph Vernet, Carle was a pupil of Nicolas-Bernard Lépicié. He won the Prix de Rome in 1782, and after returning to France the following year, he embarked upon a highly successful career as a painter of battle and hunting scenes, horse races, and equestrian portraits.

Although unparalleled in the artist's oeuvre, this sketch indisputably bears his monogram and is by no means incompatible with the landscape backgrounds in his paintings of other subjects. That he should have made independent landscape studies is hardly surprising, and his documented contact with his exact contemporary Jean-Joseph-Xavier Bidauld (No. 65), with whom he sometimes collaborated, adding figures to Bidauld's landscapes, may have prompted him to experiment with painting outdoors in oil on paper.

WMG

JOHANN GEORG VON DILLIS

Grüngiebing, Bavaria, 1759–1841 Munich

77 *Beech Trees in the English Garden in Munich*

Oil over graphite on paper, laid down on cardboard. 10¼ x 7⅞ in. (254 x 193 mm). Watermark: None visible. Inscribed on reverse, *Buchen im englischen Garten nahe beim Aumeister.*

PROVENANCE: Galerie Zinckgraf, Munich (according to label on verso); Dr. Eugen Roth, Munich; by descent to an anonymous collector; Daxer & Marschall, Munich, 2000.

LITERATURE: Messerer 1961, p. 87, no. 34.

EXHIBITION: Munich and Dresden 1991–92, repr. in color (detail) p. 68, fig.5; pp. 104–5, no. 23, repr. in color.

After initial studies in philosophy and theology and four years as a priest, Dillis decided to become an artist, studying under Johann Jacob Dorner the Elder (1741–1813) and supporting himself by giving drawing lessons to children of aristocratic families. In 1790 he was appointed inspector of the newly created royal picture gallery in the Hofgarten, Munich. He also acted as the main advisor on artistic matters to Crown Prince Ludwig of Bavaria—later King Ludwig I—with whom he traveled to France and Italy. Despite his demanding career as a high-ranking administrator, Dillis continued to sketch and draw in private. One of the first artists in Germany to execute nature studies and to paint in watercolors, he also pioneered the plein-air oil sketch, the earliest of which date from the 1790s. Three exceptional freely drawn oil sketches of 1818 with panoramic views taken from the Villa Malta, the residence of Ludwig I in Rome, are perhaps his most famous works in that technique and predate Reinhart's (No. 17) more monumental and *veduta*-like views by almost two decades (Neue Pinakothek, Munich). Together with Wilhelm von Kobell (1766–1853) and Carl Rottmann (No. 94), Dillis is considered among the principal exponents of the Munich school of landscape painting.

Beginning in the 1790s the English Garden, a park that recently had been created in Munich, became one of Dillis's favorite motifs. Inspired by Dutch painters such as Jacob van Ruisdael (No. 9), he would regularly make studies of old, gnarled trees and other aspects of unspoiled nature there. The inscription, which translates as "Beech trees in the English Garden near the Aumeister" (a popular country inn still extant today), suggests that this oil sketch, which apparently was intended as an independent work of art rather than as a preparatory study, was made in the open. As Christoph Heilmann noted, the artist probably worked seated slightly in front of and below the two massive beech trees that dominate the composition and only later added from his imagination the smaller tree indicated at left, the only one depicted at eye level (Munich and Dresden 1991–92, p. 105). The *Prater Island near Munich,* a pendant oil sketch of identical dimensions belonging to the Oskar Reinhart Foundation, Winterthur, also includes a solitary figure dwarfed by beech trees, striding through the thicket (Los Angeles and elsewhere 1993–94, no. 46, repr. in color).

REP

171

ANTOINE-PIERRE MONGIN

Paris 1761–1827 Chatillon-sous-Bagneux

78 *Landscape*

Oil on prepared paper, laid down on canvas. 13⅝ x 11⅜ in. (346 x 289 mm).
PROVENANCE: Private collection, Paris; Emmanuel Moatti, Paris and New York; Stiebel, Ltd., New York.

Although little known today, Mongin was one of the most successful pupils of the naturalistic landscape painter Louis Gabriel Moreau the Elder (1740–1805). Mongin exhibited regularly at the Salon from 1791 to 1824. His gouaches are perhaps better known than his few surviving paintings in the collection at Versailles, which consist of landscapes, genre scenes, and several depictions from Napoleonic history.

Like those by Moreau, Mongin's landscapes are characterized by a naturalism that departs from the more formally structured, eighteenth-century tradition of the classical landscape epitomized by the work of his contemporary Pierre-Henri Valenciennes (Nos. 66–71). In the present oil sketch, the artist depicted an intimate spot where a low retaining wall meets an embankment. Broken sunlight streams onto the intersection of two dirt paths leading to the stone wall, in which there is a small, grated window slightly off center. The composition, with its lush foliage and dazzling sunlight, is actually highly structured: the bush at the right balances the wall at the left, and the paths, which are bordered by stones, lead directly to the center of the composition. While the date of this work is not known, its stylistic divergence from some of the artist's more rococo works suggests that it dates to his maturity.

JT

FRANÇOIS-MARIUS GRANET

Aix-en-Provence 1775–1849 Aix-en-Provence

79 *Vault Inside the Colosseum*

Oil on canvas. 8¼ x 8¼ in. (210 x 210 mm).
PROVENANCE: Antichità Alberto Di Castro, Rome.

A native of Aix-en-Provence, Granet began his artistic career in the studio of Jacques-Louis David in 1798. After an initial, brief visit to Italy in 1802 with his colleague Auguste de Forbin, the following year Granet returned to Rome, where he would remain for more than two decades. He became part of the circle of artists surrounding Ingres and at first earned his living through the sale of small paintings depicting antique sites.

The Colosseum had been a source of fascination for foreign artists in Rome since the sixteenth century; by the nineteenth century, it was requisite for artists to visit the ruins, which were then overgrown with vegetation and in picturesque decrepitude. One of Granet's first stops on his initial tour of the city, the monument occupied an important role among his early works in Rome. He established his reputation as a painter with such works as *L'Interno del Colosseo,* 1804 (Musée du Louvre, Paris), which he presented at the Salon of 1806. Granet recalled in his memoirs that on his first visit to the city he and Forbin, led by Guillaume Guillon Lethière (1760–1832), director of the French Academy in Rome, "went . . . to the Colosseum, by way of the Campo Vaccino [Roman Forum]. There, all of ancient Rome spread itself out before our eyes. The temples, the arches of triumph, the handsome vaults of the Temple of Peace [Basilica of Maxentius] with their magnificent coffers. I felt that I was no longer of this world. I arrived under that spell . . . at the foot of the Colosseum, without uttering a word. We wandered through the midst of all those monuments like shades come down from heaven" (New York and elsewhere 1988–89, p. 20).

Once Granet had familiarized himself with the major sites of the city, he began to work. He recounted in his diary, "Finally, after visiting all there was to see, I decided to begin with some studies from nature. I chose the Colosseum. That monument had struck me as so handsome both for its remarkable form and for the vegetation that enveloped its ruins, and it produced such enchanting effects against the sky! . . . Alongside this natural wealth, you have shadowy passageways, with a light so well contrived that no painter with a modicum of taste for color and effect could resist the urge to do studies of it" (New York and elsewhere 1988–89, p. 21).

Indeed, Granet produced numerous studies of the Colosseum, including this oil sketch depicting one of the corridors half-filled with soil and rubble. Light streams into the tunnel from a row of windows in the barrel vault as well as through an opening in the wall at the left. The subtle drama of the play of light on architecture characterizes much of Granet's best Roman work.

JT

FRANÇOIS-MARIUS GRANET

Aix-en-Provence 1775–1849 Aix-en-Provence

80 *View from the Villa Medici, Rome*

Oil on paper, laid down on board. 5⅛ x 11¼ in. (130 x 286 mm).

PROVENANCE: Galerie de Bayser, Paris; Dr. Tobias Crist, Basel; Baron Robert von Hirsch, Zurich; sale, New York, Sotheby's, 13 October 1993, lot 239.

During his stay in Rome, Granet produced a vast number of watercolors, paintings, and oil sketches of sites in the city and the Campagna. This study has been identified by Denis Coutagne as a view from the Villa Medici. The central building is located in the gardens of the villa, behind the church of SS. Trinità dei Monti, the rear buildings of which are visible at the right. To the right of the center in the distance is the tower of the Villa Malta. Views from the windows and gardens of the Villa Medici, the site of the French Academy in Rome since 1803, were common during the 1820s. The area around SS. Trinità dei Monti—a French church in Rome—was frequented by artists for centuries. During the late eighteenth century, depictions of the church were popular, especially among artists living in the foreign quarter around the Piazza di Spagna. Many, including Corot (Nos. 90–92), depicted similar views from the Villa Medici, although none seemingly from the same vantage as this study, which omits the facade and tower of SS. Trinità dei Monti and focuses instead on a nondescript building in the villa's gardens (see Paris and Mantua 2001, nos. 112, 113, 114, p. 180).

Because Granet spent the majority of his career in Rome, it is difficult to date this study. The artist, however, recounted in his memoirs that he took rooms in "a little palazzo called the Arco della Regina" from which "I could see through my windows the most beautiful panorama in the world. . . . I had in the foreground the obelisk of Trinità dei Monti, the pretty façade of that church, the Villa Medici surmounted by its two handsome loggias . . . " (New York and elsewhere 1988–89, p. 28). This scene is unusual as the viewpoint is oblique and the facade of the church is not visible. It was not taken from Granet's rooms but demonstrates his familiarity with the grounds and vistas of the Villa Medici.

JT

JOHN CONSTABLE

East Bergholt, Suffolk, 1776–1837 Hampstead

81   *Hampstead Heath with Bathers*

Oil on canvas. 9¾ x 15¾ in. (247 x 400 mm).

PROVENANCE: Charles Golding Constable, the artist's son; J. P. Heseltine; his sale, London, Sotheby's, 27 May 1935, lot 15; Thos. Agnew & Sons, London; Sir Malcolm Robertson, 1936 and thence by descent; Agnew's, London, 2000.

LITERATURE: Heseltine 1914, no. 2, repr.; Hoozee 1979, p. 125, no. 380; Reynolds 1984, p. 110, no. 22.45, pl. 303a.

EXHIBITION: London 2000, no. 37, repr. in color.

By late 1816 Constable had moved from Suffolk to London and frequently took his family to Hampstead. In 1821 and 1822 he produced a series of remarkable paintings and sketches, including this sweeping landscape of the heath with some bathers in a pond in the foreground. Most of the canvas is taken up by the sky, which Constable always considered one of the most important parts of his landscapes and about which he wrote to his friend and frequent correspondent, John Fisher of Salisbury. After remarking that he had not been idle and had done more work than ever in one summer, Constable went on to say, "I am anxious to get to my London painting room, for I do not consider myself at work unless I am before a six-foot canvas—I have done a great deal of skying—I am determined to overcome all difficulties and that more arduous than the rest, and now talking of skies. . . . The sky is the source of light in nature and governs everything" (23 October 1821; see Beckett 1968, pp. 76–78). Because of his meticulous efforts to depict different types of clouds, his paintings of skies are exact meteorological studies, unprecedented in art.

When Heseltine owned the picture, it was inscribed on the back, —*July—Hampstead Heath—Looking north—wind South east.* Although Graham Reynolds dates the work to 1822, it has been suggested that it must be a little earlier because of its close relationship to another work, an oil on board *Hampstead Heath with Pond and Bathers.* Depicting virtually the same subject from a somewhat different point of view, the work is inscribed on the verso *Evening of Coronation July 19, 1821. Westward by North—cloudy and tempestuous looking but it did not turn out so* (private collection; Reynolds 1984, p. 79, no. 21.40, pl. 246). There is a good deal of sky in this superb oil sketch; perhaps as much as two thirds of the composition is taken up with Constable's close observation of how the sky looked that day. It apparently was very blue, and Constable filled it with large masses of clouds, including some little dashing, broken clouds suggestive of a sultry, windy day in July, hot enough for bathing.

CDD

178

179

LANCELOT THÉODORE, COMTE DE TURPIN DE CRISSÉ

Paris 1782–1859 Paris

82 *The Arch of Constantine Seen from the Colosseum,* 1818–38

Oil on paper, laid down on canvas. 11½ x 8½ in. (292 x 216 mm). Signed with the artist's initials and coronet and dated at right center, *T.T / 1818 / 1838.*

PROVENANCE: Private collection, France; sale, Paris, Hôtel Drouot, 25 February 1929, lot 62; sale, New York, Sotheby's, 10 November 1998, lot 65.

The son of an amateur painter and bankrupt aristocrat, the comte de Turpin de Crissé was able to study painting first in Switzerland and then in Rome supported by his patron, the comte de Choiseul-Gouffier (1752–1817). The artist's reputation was established with his early success at the Salon; he received a gold medal for his submissions in 1806. Shortly thereafter, he returned to France and rapidly became an important member of the Napoleonic court; the empress Josephine purchased his painting *View of Città Castellana* in 1809 and subsequently appointed him chamberlain and art advisor, an office he held until her death in 1814. He later was made inspecteur générale des beaux-arts from 1824 until 1830.

In this richly detailed study, a shady corridor of the Colosseum yields to a sunlit view of the upper register of the Arch of Constantine. Turpin de Crissé depicted the overrun Colosseum in great detail: a soft carpet of moss covers the stones at the left, weeds and flowers sprout from the cracked masonry, and a heap of stone fragments are enmeshed by weeds at the right. The Colosseum was a popular subject among artists in Rome and one of the most frequently depicted ruins. The conceit of including a view of the Arch of Constantine from inside the Colosseum has a long tradition. Turpin de Crissé exploited the structure's picturesque potential, using the arcade to frame the view beyond, intimating Rome's endless riches.

The artist is known to have traveled Italy in 1818, when he must have begun this work. He returned to Rome at least twice—in 1830 and 1838. After his first trip to the city in 1808, he wrote, "c'était une récolte indispensable, elle devait devenir la base de ma petite fortune pittoresque, une réunion de précieux matériaux à exploiter plus tard" (Levron 1937, p. 78). As Vincent Pomarède noted, Turpin de Crissé continued to exploit these souvenirs of Rome throughout his career; the present sketch was not finished until 1838 (Paris and Mantua 2001, p. 164). That this highly finished work was executed largely in the studio accounts for the precision and careful attention to light and shadow that makes the scene so fresh and striking.

JT

181

JOHAN CHRISTIAN CLAUSEN DAHL

Bergen 1788–1857 Dresden

83 *Mausoleum of San Vito near Pozzuoli,* 1820

Oil on paper laid down on artist board. 8½ x 13¾ in. (216 x 349 mm). Inscribed on reverse of old backing in graphite at center, *Volant | Fru- Dr. Bull | Lf olarsgh 35 III;* at upper left, *550* (?; the zero partially obscured by tape); on a label at center, *Fru | Tha | Bull;* in pen and black ink, on a label at lower right, *N°34 | Prof. Dahl Italiensk Studie | Privatz* (?) *Collection a.*

PROVENANCE: The artist's studio; by descent to Justitiarius Georg J. Bull (the artist's grandson); private collection, Trondheim, Norway; Galerie Jean-François Heim, Paris.

LITERATURE: Possibly Aubert 1920, p. 453 (as *Italian Temple*); Bang 1987, II, p. 107, no. 242, III, pl. 103bis.

EXHIBITION: Oslo 1907.

Dahl was the first Norwegian painter of international acclaim. He trained as a house painter and interior decorator in Bergen from 1803 to 1809 while taking private drawing lessons. In 1811 he traveled to Copenhagen on a stipend from a group of wealthy Bergen patrons to study at the Kunstakademi, where he remained until about 1817 and where he decided to devote himself to landscape painting. He studied with the landscape and history painter Christian August Lorentzen (1746–1828), with whom Caspar David Friedrich had studied about 1790. He copied after paintings in the Norwegian royal collections by the Dutch landscape artists Allart van Everdingen (1621–1675) and Jacob van Ruisdael (No. 9), and he made studies directly from nature.

In 1818 Dahl set out on what was to be a study tour of Europe, but he remained in Dresden, where he met Friedrich, until 1820. That same year, at the invitation of Prince Christian Frederik (later King Christian VIII of Denmark), he traveled to Naples, making excursions to Sorrento, Pompei, Capri, and Ischia, sometimes in the company of the German artist Franz Catel (1778–1856). From Naples he traveled to Rome, mingling with the circle of Bertel Thorvaldsen (1768/70–1844) as well as Achille-Etna Michallon (No. 93) and François-Marius Granet (Nos. 33 and 79–80).

Dahl's Italian sojourn lasted less than a year, but the experience was decisive for his career. As Marie Lødrup Bang has observed, "In Italy Dahl learned to approach nature more directly in his nature studies—to analyse colour and mass, light and atmosphere, independently of what he had seen in the works of the Old Masters" (Bang 1987, I, p. 63). Although he had begun plein-air painting in Denmark, he devoted himself to the practice in Italy. During his six-month stay in Naples in particular, he developed a style that was much freer and richer than that of the artists who preceded him there and much freer than he had produced hitherto.

The present oil sketch belongs to this fertile period. In his diary entry from 8 November 1820 Dahl noted, "I have been with Catel at Potsolo and painted a mausoleum which is now inhabited by some poor people" (Bang 1987, II, p. 106, under no. 241). The sketch is executed in rapid brushstrokes, with flashes of white paint to suggest a shaft of sunlight in the gloom and cream pigment in the upper right corner to evoke the damp seaside air.

It is one of two oil sketches Dahl executed of the subject; the second, in a private collection in Oslo (Bang 1987, II, no. 241, pl. 103), is a bit more finished than the Thaw work and depicts the scene from a slightly different angle.

Pozzuoli was a popular destination for such artists as Hubert Robert (1733–1808) and Giovanni Battista Piranesi (1720–1778), whose classicizing depictions of Roman ruins with tiny staffage figures emphasized their grand scale and heroic allusions (see, for example, *Ruins at Pozzuoli* by Giovanni Battista Piranesi, Montreal 1993–94, no. 46). In contrast, Dahl emphasized the humanness of the subject, and he represented it as he saw it—shrouded by trees, illuminated by natural light, populated with real (poor) people, the scene viewed at eye level and on a naturalistic scale.

KS

JOHAN CHRISTIAN CLAUSEN DAHL

Bergen 1788–1857 Dresden

84   *Cloud Study*

Oil on paper, mounted on board. 4 ¹³/₁₆ x 7⅝ in. (122 x 193 mm). Inscribed in pen and black ink on reverse, *N°*
227 12" h. - 19" L. | Johann Chr. Cl. Dahl fec. | [geb.?] Bergen in Norw. d 24 Febr. 1788 |† Dresden d. 14 Octbr. 1857 | Papier auf
Pappe aufgezogen Natur | Skizze | Luftstudie mit Horizont | mit Franz. Firn. gefirnisst | 2 28/3 1889.

PROVENANCE: The artist's studio; by descent to Siegwald Dahl (the artist's son); sale, Munich, Sotheby's, 22
June 1999, lot 30, repr.

Marie Lødrup Bang confirms the attribution of this work to Dahl because the reverse of
the support bears an inscription that is very close to that on the reverse of other oil
sketches signed and dated by the artist (correspondence, 1 October 2001). Such inscriptions likely were made by Dahl's son Siegwald after his father's death. They include the
artist's birth and death dates, a description of the subject, the media and dimensions, and
the date on which the artist's son applied French varnish (Bang 1987, I, p. 26).

Cloud studies form an important part of Dahl's oeuvre. He seems to have made them
throughout his career both for his pleasure and in preparation for more finished works.
Because they constituted "studio material for the painter," in Bang's words, they were
not considered works of art in their own right and rarely were sold during Dahl's lifetime (correspondence, 1 October 2001).

The artist executed his first nature studies while a student in Copenhagen and continued during his sojourn in Dresden, where he recorded the movement of clouds from
inside his studio. But it was in Italy, particularly during a six-month sojourn in Naples,
that his study of nature intensified. Enthralled with the moisture-laden atmosphere of
the Bay of Naples, he executed great numbers of land- or seascapes heavy with clouds
(see Bang 1987, II, nos. 238, 243–44, 250–51, 281–82).

Because Dahl's cloud style did not change much over the course of his career, dating
uninscribed works is problematic. Thus, the present sketch corresponds equally to
works from the 1820s, 1830s, and 1840s in the form of the clouds, the way in which they appear to roll across the sky, and in the alternation of quickly applied dabs of paint with
long sweeping strokes. See, for example, a study dated about 1820 from the Göteborgs
Konstmuseum, Gothenburg (Bang 1987, II, no. 262, pl. 112); a study signed with initials and
dated 11 July 1835, in a private collection in Oslo (Bang 1987, II, no. 786, pl. 332); and another
signed with initials and dated 7 August 1846, in a private collection in Bergen (Bang 1987,
II, no. 1046, pl. 445).

As Bang has observed, "Dahl's interest in clouds and weather was primarily the con-
sequence of his wish to give a thorough characterization of a given region." Although in
the 1820s he likely had been exposed to the meteorological theories of cloud formation
developed by Luke Howard (1772–1864), his "scientific interest was subordinated to his *le-
centia poetica*—his sense of the pictorial effect" (Bang 1987, I, pp. 69–71).

KS

185

JOHAN CHRISTIAN CLAUSEN DAHL

Bergen 1788–1857 Dresden

85   *A Birch Tree in a Storm,* 1849

Oil on cardboard. 8⅜ x 7¹/₁₆ in. (213 x 178 mm). Signed at lower right with monogram and dated, *D. 1849.*

PROVENANCE: Artemis Fine Arts, Inc., New York, 1997.

EXHIBITIONS: New York 1997, no. 11, repr. in color and in color on cover; New York 1999a, no. 18, repr. in color.

This work is a reduced variant of the same date made by the artist of his most famous painting, *Birch Tree in a Storm,* now in the Billedgalleri, Bergen (Fig. 1; correspondence with Marie Lødrup Bang, 1 October 2001). Two other variants by Dahl of the painting, both dated 1849, are cited by Bang in her catalogue raisonné of the artist: a pendant depicting the tree in sunlight (formerly E. W. Coopmanns, Brussels/Copenhagen), now lost and known only through a record drawing by the artist (Billedgalleri, Bergen; Bang 1987, II, no. 1092, pl. 466bis), and a reduced variant in oil on paper, also lost and known through a drawn copy by Dahl (Billedgalleri, Bergen; Bang 1987, II, no. 1090, pl. 466). Although the Bergen painting is dated 1849, the compositional idea and the tree itself appear in a drawing by the artist dated 1823 (Nasjonalgalleriet, Oslo; Bang 1987, I, p. 131, fig. 68).

As Bang has observed, Dahl frequently made copies of his work in the form of small paintings and drawings that repeated the subjects of his larger ones, which he then sold or gave away as *Album-blatt,* or "album leaves," for scrapbooks assembled by ladies of his day (correspondence, 1 October 2001). The lost oil sketch noted above was executed for a Miss von Serger, and in 1849 a watercolor drawing of a birch tree was sent to a dealer in Weimar for the Schiller Album (Bang 1987, II, under no. 1090).

The present oil sketch is very close to the Bergen painting compositionally and in handling. In both a large birch tree all but fills the surface of the support, its trunk bending to the left as it appears to grow out of a rocky headland. Tangled lower branches resemble roots more than tree limbs, creating the impression that the tree has been partially uprooted. The chief difference between the two is that the tree trunk in the Thaw sketch angles more sharply, emphasizing its precariousness.

In the Thaw sketch, Dahl dragged a fine, almost dry brush across wet paint to create the illusion of heavy rain, especially along the left third of the composition. The leaves in the Bergen painting are more abundant and fully described than in the Thaw sketch, which overall is brushier and more freely rendered. In the oil sketch a fury of quickly applied, very fine brushstrokes suggests tremulous, windblown leaves.

The image of the windswept birch has long had symbolic importance among Norwegians for whom

FIG. 1. Johan Christian Clausen Dahl, *Birch Tree in a Storm*, Billedgalleri, Bergen

the tree signified their nation enduring in its fight for independence from Denmark, which was won in 1814 (Bang 1987, II, p. 326). The tradition of the single heroic tree derives from Jacob van Ruisdael (No. 9), whose landscapes in turn were inspired by Allart van Everdingen (1621–1675). Van Everdingen, who traveled to Norway and Sweden in 1644, is credited with introducing and popularizing Northern landscape in the Netherlands (Ashton et al. 1982, pp. 5, 8, 11). Dahl copied after the paintings of these Dutch masters in the Norwegian royal collections during his student years.

KS

187

CARL GUSTAV CARUS

Leipzig 1789–1869 Dresden

86 *An Overgrown Shaft*

Oil on paper, laid down on cardboard. 11¼ x 8¼ in. (286 x 210 mm). Watermark: None visible. Inscribed on a label pasted onto the verso, *SAMMLUNG GEORG SCHÄFER SCHWEINFURT* | *73* (encircled) | *6513442.*

PROVENANCE: Lahmann Collection, Dresden; Georg Schäfer, Schweinfurt; his sale, Düsseldorf, Christie's, 31 January 2000, lot 72, repr. in color.

LITERATURE: Grashoff-Heins 1926, p. 48; Prause 1968, p. 138, no. 230, repr.; Papendorf 1970, p. 1640.

EXHIBITION: Schweinfurt 1970, p. 17, no. 7, repr. in color.

After Caspar David Friedrich (1774–1840), Carus is considered the leading figure of nineteenth-century German Romantic landscape painting. A physician, philosopher, and amateur painter, Carus was appointed professor of obstetrics and director of the maternity clinic in Dresden in 1814. He first exhibited as an artist at the Dresden Academy in 1816, though it was his meeting with Friedrich the following year that was to have the most profound impact on his painting. The two men quickly formed a close friendship, traveling the countryside of Saxony together in search of suitable motifs. Carus, however, eschewed the symbolic and allegorical overtones in Friedrich's landscapes and in the 1820s increasingly embraced realistic tendencies such as those in the work of the Norwegian painter Johan Christian Dahl (Nos. 83–85). Johann Wolfgang von Goethe, whom he had met in Weimar in 1821, also encouraged this inclination toward pictorial realism, characteristic of the transition from Romanticism to the more objective early realism of the Biedermeier period.

Carus's art was accompanied by personal theories on nature and landscape painting, which he sought to convey in his *Nine Letters About Landscape Painting* (Neun Briefe über Landschaftsmalerei), written in 1815–26 (Prause 1968) and first published in 1831. In these he developed the concept of the "earth-life image" (*Erdlebenbild*), which defines nature not as a fixed form or a mythical or religiously laden place but as a living organism characterized by dynamic processes and subject to scientific examination.

The artist's preference for fluid brushstrokes and close-range subjects, as well as his meticulous interest in detail, is apparent in this oil sketch, which Prause dates to about 1824, the same year as the painting *Fox in a Forest, Before a Ruined Gothic Wall*, which remains in the Schäfer collection in Schweinfurt (Schweinfurt 1970, no. 8, repr. in color). The small format and unassuming subject matter reveal the increasing influence of Dahl, who specialized in studies of landscape details. The viewer's interest is captured by the strong diagonal defined by the roof of the structure and the slope of the hill; this diagonal slices off a triangular area of sky from the dominant dark greens and browns of the foliage and stones. The strict geometry of the rectangular door and window surrounds along with the trapezoidal slabs in the foreground serve as a counterpoint to the organic growth of the brambles and bushes.

REP

FERDINAND VICTOR EUGÈNE DELACROIX

Charenton-Saint-Maurice 1798–1863 Paris

87   *Landscape with Rocks, Augerville*

Oil on paper, laid down on board. 11¼ x 14⅜ in. (281 x 372 mm). Verso: Stamped wax seal, *E D.*

PROVENANCE: The artist's studio; estate sale, Paris, Hôtel Drouot, 17–29 February 1864, probably part of lot 219; Henri Haro; his sale, 8 February 1912, lot 5 (for 110 fr.); sale, 27 January 1923, lot 42 (for 380 fr.); Dr. Paul Steiner, Berlin; Peter Nathan, Zurich, 1969; sale, London, Sotheby's, 20 March 1985, lot 101, repr.; Natan Saban, Miami; sale, New York, Christie's, 11 February 1997, lot 5, repr.

LITERATURE: Johnson 1981, p. 255, no. 484, pl. 286.

Delacroix's journal contains frequent references to Augerville, near Malesherbes, which is about fifty miles from Paris to the southeast of Fontainebleau. Delacroix's cousin Pierre Antoine de Berryer, a lawyer, had some property there that Delacroix had visited from childhood on. The artist had the fondest recollections of the place, and going back there always reminded him of his youth. In May 1854 Delacroix wrote at length in his journal about one of these visits. Having left Paris on 20 May, he returned eight days later. He traveled from Paris to Estampes by train and then went east by carriage to Augerville, passing through what he referred to as *"vraie campagne,"* of the sort that was not to be found in the immediate environs of Paris and made him think of all the good times he had so many years before.

> The arrival was charming: this place was especially arranged for him, it is full of ancient things that I adore. I do not know any impression more delightful than that of an old country house; in the cities one no longer finds even a trace of ancient customs: the old portraits, the old woodwork, the turrets, the pointed roofs, everything that pleases the imagination and the heart, even to the odor that one breathes in these ancient houses. One finds there quantities of forgotten picture-books such as delighted our childhood and that were new at that time. There is a room here which was dwelt in by the great Condé, and where the paintings in distemper still exist. These paintings are of an astounding freshness; the burnished gilding is intact (Pach 1948, p. 384).

Delacroix also walked about the grounds quite a bit and in several places in the journal commented on the rocks and Italian pines. On the morning of 26 May, for instance, he drew the pine trees in the rocks.

These remarks also indicate Delacroix's interest in the rocks themselves. During the course of this visit he was to make enough drawings to fill an entire sketchbook (Bibliothèque municipale, Grenoble) and to begin another, which he worked on at Champrosay as well over the course of a number of years, between 1847 and 1854 (collection of Claude Aubry, Paris; according to Johnson 1981).

In this oil sketch—which really is such a close detail of some rocks as to suggest a gorge—Delacroix's characteristic color harmonies are unmistakable. He used a cool turquoise blue for the sky, while the rocks of the foreground were heavily painted in greenish browns, heightened with white. The background was more lightly painted in the same dark brown and bright golden yellow accents were used throughout, highlighting the bit of earth in the foreground as well as the foliage.

CDD

THALES FIELDING

Yorkshire 1793–1837 London

88   *View of Sarnen over the Lake*

Oil on light brown paper. 7 ^{1}/$_{16}$ x 10 ^{7}/$_{16}$ in. (179 x 273 mm). Inscribed by the artist on verso (according to collector's files) in graphite at left, *Stanzerhorn;* at center, *View of Sarnen over the lake;* at right, *Thales Fielding—about 1825 or / —30;* at center, *S;* inscribed directly beneath, in another hand, *Stanzerhorn View of Sarnen over the Lake.*

PROVENANCE: William Drummond, London.

Born into a family of artists, Fielding was the fourth son of Nathan Theodore Fielding (active 1775–1819), a portrait and landscape painter, from whom he likely received his first instruction. From 1821/22 Fielding worked in Paris, where he collaborated with two of his brothers in making engravings for Baron Isidore-Justin-Severin Taylor's monumental *Voyages pittoresques et romantiques dans l'Ancienne France* (1820–63). In Paris Fielding became a member of the so-called Bonington circle, a group of British and French artists that included Richard Parkes Bonington (1801–1828) and Eugène Delacroix. Fielding worked alongside both artists in Paris and Normandy, and he and Delacroix painted each other's portraits; Fielding's portrait of the French artist (sale, Paris, Hôtel Drouot, 4 June 1999, lot 62, repr.) was exhibited at the Royal Academy in 1827. It has been suggested that Fielding's watercolor *Macbeth and the Witches* (untraced), one of three works he exhibited at the Salon of 1824, may have influenced Delacroix's lithograph of the same subject begun the following year (Pointon 1985, p. 73).

Fielding, who in 1829 became an associate of the Old Water-Colour Society, exhibiting eighty-eight works over the course of his brief career (Fisher 1972, p. 78), is best known as a watercolorist. It is not known to what extent he sketched in oil en plein air nor who inspired him to try his hand. He may have been influenced by John Constable (see No. 81), an avid practitioner of the oil sketch, whose paintings were widely known in artistic circles in Paris by the mid-1820s (Pointon 1985, pp. 80–82). Constable's influential painting *The Hay Wain* (National Gallery, London; Reynolds 1984, no. 21.1, pl. 213) won a gold medal in the 1824 Salon.

It is to Bonington, however, that Fielding's style as a painter of oil sketches and as a watercolorist is most indebted. Similarities in composition may be observed, for example, in a large, finished watercolor by Fielding, *Crossing Solway Sands* (Whitworth Art Gallery, Manchester; Manchester 1993, no. 135, p. 101, repr.), and a painting by Bonington, *View on the Beach* (Johnson collection, Philadelphia; Boston 1946, no. 203, repr.). Both works depict an expanse of shoreline on which groups of figures are gathered, with a horse-drawn carriage at the center of the composition, all beneath a broad, atmospheric sky. Likewise, Bonington's oil study *Boulogne—Low Tide* (National Gallery of Victoria, Melbourne; Nottingham 1965, no. 261, pl. 30) corresponds to the present work in its broad brushwork, quickly sketched figures, and the use of slender vertical brushstrokes to suggest shadows in the water. The stylistic hallmarks of Fielding's work—impressionistic, fluid, and expressive—are found as well in his watercolors, for example, *Old Breakwater, Plymouth* (British Museum, London; Hardie 1967, no. 213, repr.).

The Thaw study depicts a view of Sarner See, a small lake in Unterwalden, south of Lucerne. Fielding visited Switzerland in the summer of 1824 (Pointon 1985, p. 77), and the freshness and spontaneity of the present work suggest that it was executed on this trip. The artist used a high-key palette to suggest the brilliant light of midday. The foreground, including the near edge of the boat, dissolves into abstraction, with long strokes of brown pigment and dabs of gray to suggest the shoreline. Topographical details are indicated in a shorthand of minimalist brushstrokes: small dabs of paint define a row of deciduous trees along the ridge at the left and along the distant shore; slender vertical strokes suggest pine trees climbing the slope of the mountain at left. Fielding's economy of stroke extends to the figure of the fisherman, with tiny dabs of white pigment indicating his sleeves, and a single slender stroke for each oar.

KS

GILLES-FRANÇOIS-JOSEPH CLOSSON

Liège 1796–1853 Liège

89 *A View in the Dolomites, Italy*

Oil over graphite on paper, laid down on canvas. Sketches in oil and graphite on reverse. 4⅜ x 9½ in. (107 x 242 mm).

PROVENANCE: Sale, New York, Christie's, 24 January 2001, lot 137, repr. in color (as French school, early nineteenth century).

Closson only recently has been recognized as one of the most important Belgian landscape painters of the nineteenth century. After studying briefly in Tournai with the French neoclassical painter Philippe-Auguste Hennequin (1762–1833), Closson moved to Paris in 1817 to study with the history painter Antoine-Jean Gros (1771–1835), with whom he apprenticed for seven years (Brussels 1994, p. 3). In 1824, on a grant from the Darchis Foundation, he began a five-year sojourn in Italy during which he abandoned history painting and took up the subject of landscape. Returning to Liège in 1829, he brought with him several hundred drawings and scores of oil sketches devoted almost entirely to the Italian landscape and scenes of daily life. Although he exhibited Italian views in the Brussels Salon during the 1830s, there was little enthusiasm for his vision of landscape, and he began teaching at the Liège Academy in 1837, a position he held until his death.

The attribution of this oil sketch to Closson is convincing. It was first suggested by Régine Rémon, curator of the Cabinet des Estampes et des Dessins of the Musée des Beaux-Arts, Liège, Belgium (collector's files; correspondence, 23 May 2001). The museum's collections comprise approximately fifty oil sketches by Closson as well as about three hundred of his drawings, the gift of his widow. In *Mountain Landscape,* an oil sketch in the collection of the Musée des Beaux-Arts, Liège (Fig. 1), the alternation of bare rock and forested hillside is comparable to that of the Thaw oil sketch, as is the use of dabs and short strokes of white paint to suggest sunlight striking the landscape. Likewise, the treatment of rocky cliffs and a crystalline sky lit by the midday sun in the present work also may be observed in an oil sketch formerly with Galerie d'Arenberg, Brussels, *Study of Rocks* (Brussels 1994, no. 28, p. 6, repr.).

The Thaw oil sketch represents the distinctive limestone cliffs of the Dolomites, a mountainous region in northeastern Italy along the Austrian border. It is not known when Closson traveled the area, but the rugged terrain of steep escarpments, alternately fissured and sheer, no doubt appealed to him. In the present work he positioned himself at a point opposite and eye level with the tree-lined ridge along the horizon. Although the precise location is difficult to ascertain, the form of the ridge is comparable to that of a 10,000-foot-high mountain group north of Cortina d'Ampezzo, comprising Mount Cristallo at the right, Popena Peak at the left, and Cristallo Pass between them.

FIG. 1. Gilles-François-Joseph Closson, *Mountain Landscape,* Musée des Beaux-Arts, Liège

KS

JEAN-BAPTISTE-CAMILLE COROT

Paris 1796–1875 Paris

90 *Cività Castellana plateaux sur les montagnes*

Oil on paper, laid down on canvas. 7⅜ x 11⅝ in. (189 x 294 mm). Signed and inscribed at lower left, *Corot T Bardon*.

PROVENANCE: Given to T[héodore(?)] Bardon by the artist; sale, London, Christie's, 21 November 1997, lot 178, repr.

LITERATURE: Robaut 1905, p. 62, no. 173 (sketch by A. Robaut).

After a relatively late start at the age of twenty-five, Corot began studying under his exact contemporary, Achille-Etna Michallon (No. 93), who was then considered the most promising landscape artist of his generation. Michallon, himself Valenciennes's pupil, had been the first recipient of the Prix de Rome in landscape and made drawings and paintings of Rome and its environs while he was studying there. After Michallon's untimely death, Corot studied with another disciple of Valenciennes, Jean-Victor Bertin (1767–1842). It was not, however, until 1825 or 1826 that Corot, already thirty years of age, arrived in Rome for his first visit. Since he had independent means supplemented by his family, he was able to stay in the city for about three years, returning in 1834 and 1843.

The present work dates to Corot's first Italian sojourn, when he was quickly developing the remarkable skills that would set him apart from other artists for the rest of his career. Although he would follow a familiar itinerary, often in the company of other young artists, he brought to the art of landscape painting a sense of structure and form that, as Baudelaire wrote, helped to close "the gap between the empirical freshness of outdoor painting and the organizing principles of classical landscape composition" (Baudelaire 1965, p. 24). The artist was especially attracted to Cività Castellana in the Sabine Hills to the north of the city, just south of Viterbo. Located on a plateau overlooking deep ravines formed by the convergence of three rivers, the Treja, Maggiore, and Vicano, this ancient Etruscan city, with its famous twelfth-century duomo and imposing fortified castle, provided the artist with many picturesque opportunities and he often drew and painted the town in all its variety, making at least thirty oil sketches (see, for example, Paris and Mantua 2001, no. 120) as well as numerous drawings (see, for example, New York and elsewhere 1975–76, no. 77, repr.), many of which are in public and private collections. This site also provided Corot with a rich palette of colors that he was quick to explore. Here, for instance, he used mostly pale green, with ocher, black, bottle green, and gray as well as occasional touches of salmon and white. He must have executed this relatively small study rapidly in thin layers—everything is indicated in just a few cursory but telling strokes. The dark mountains in the background precede an even more distant landscape that almost disappears into the clouds. A few villas and a road are barely visible in the distance. A similar view of Cività Castellana is in the Phillips Collection (Washington 1985, p. 42, no. 307). The "T Bardon" of the inscription probably was Théodore Bardon (dates unknown), a landscape painter specializing in views of Normandy, who exhibited in the Salons of 1839, 1848, and 1849.

CDD

196

JEAN-BAPTISTE-CAMILLE COROT

Paris 1796–1875 Paris

91 *The Hills of Genzano with a Rider and Peasants*

Oil on paper, laid down on cardboard. 7 x 11¼ in. (183 x 292 mm). Signed at lower left, *C. Corot.* Numbered on reverse in black ink at upper left margin, *P. L. 4169.*

PROVENANCE: M. Alexis Le Go; by direct descent to previous owner; Galerie Hopkins-Thomas, Paris.

Corot visited Italy twice after his first sojourn from 1825/6 to 1828, during which time, in accordance with Valenciennes's recommendation, he painted many oil sketches outdoors, including this little view at Genzano, probably executed in the summer of 1826. Genzano is one of a group of towns known as the Castelli Romani that includes Frascati, Ariccia, Marino, Castel Gandolfo, Albano, and Nemi. Located just south of Rome in the Alban Hills near Lake Nemi, Genzano was to remain a favorite spot for the artist, and in 1843 he spent much of July there and at Ariccia before returning to Rome in early August.

Italy provided the artist with a distinctive palette. Here he used different shades of light and dark green for the foliage and gray for the buildings accented with a soft pink to suggest their terra-cotta roofs. The pale blue sky is striated with white and wispy black clouds. Below a horseman is poised atop the hill, and peasants populate the middle ground. Corot presented this work to M. Alexis Le Go (1798–1883), whom Ingres had appointed librarian of the French Academy in gratitude for the care he received at the villa, after a sudden illness. This work, which was unknown by Robaut when he published his catalogue raisonné of Corot's work in 1905, is to be included in the forthcoming fifth edition of Robaut's catalogue being edited by Martin Dieterle and André Pacitti.

CDD

JEAN-BAPTISTE-CAMILLE COROT

Paris 1796–1875 Paris

92 *The Hills of Genzano*

Oil on paper, laid down on canvas. 7 x 11⅞ in. (165 x 285 mm).

PROVENANCE: Corot sale, 26 May 1875 (Lugt 461 b), lot 97; M. Hurquebie, Paris; Henri Rouart, Paris; Ernest Rouart, Paris; Galerie Schmit, Paris.

LITERATURE: Robaut 1905, no. 454, p. 163, repr.

EXHIBITIONS: Paris 1934, no. 84; Paris 1938, no. 58; Paris 1947, no. 38; Paris 1957, no. 12; Berne 1960, no. 39; Paris 1975, no. 45, repr. in color p. 52; Paris [1994; *XVIIième exposition Biennale Internationale,* no. 101, repr. in color].

On his third and last trip to Italy in 1843 Corot revisited many of the places he had visited during his earlier sojourns, including Genzano. Benouville (No. 106) welcomed Corot later that summer, when he returned to Rome, and lent him his studio. By this time Corot was on the verge of fame. In 1845 no less a writer than Charles Baudelaire would write that Corot was "at the head of the modern school of landscape . . . " (Baudelaire 1965, p. 24). Corot apparently was so taken with this view that he painted it very much as he had some eighteen years earlier (No. 91). The two works are strikingly similar in size and perspective. Here, however, the approaching horseman, peasants, and large tree were omitted. Since this work remained in the artist's studio, it was included in the sale after his death and its subsequent history is well documented. For this reason it appears in the literature as early as 1905 (with Robaut), while the earlier work has only recently come to light and will be published in the next edition of Robaut.

CDD

ACHILLE-ETNA MICHALLON

Paris 1796–1822 Paris

93 *Vue de Châtenay*

Oil on paper, mounted on board. 10½ x 15¾ in. (267 x 400 mm). Inscribed on reverse, in pen and brown ink, *Vue de Chatenay—1er essai de Michalon d'après Nature*.

PROVENANCE: Marie-Madeleine Aubrun (?); Galerie de Bayser, Paris.

The only son of Claude Michallon (1751–1799), who had won the Grand Prix de Rome for sculpture in 1785, and Marie-Madeleine Cuvillon (d. 1813), stepdaughter of the sculptor Guillaume Francin (1741–1830), Achille-Etna Michallon was raised among artists and appears to have taken up drawing at a very early age. As a young man, he received instruction from Jacques-Louis David, Pierre-Henri de Valenciennes (Nos. 66–71), and Jean-Victor Bertin. In 1812 he exhibited two paintings at the Salon. Five years later, he became the first recipient of the newly established Prix de Rome for historical landscape painting, and on 24 December 1817 he arrived at the French Academy in Rome. He was to remain in Italy for three and a half highly productive years. When finally he returned to Paris in 1821, he promptly opened a studio, where for a short time he taught, among others, Jean-Baptiste-Camille Corot (Nos. 90–92). Although Michallon died the following year, he is regarded not only as one of the most accomplished French landscape painters of his generation but also as the link between Corot, on the one hand, and the art and theory of Valenciennes, on the other.

This work is one of two views of Châtenay formerly with the Galerie de Bayser, in Paris (verbal communication from James Mackinnon, 2001). Located southwest of Paris, very near Sceaux, Châtenay probably is best known as the birthplace of Voltaire. In his youth, Michallon seems routinely to have depicted the landscape outside Paris. That he should have made the short trip to Châtenay is by no means surprising.

According to the inscription on the reverse, this sketch represents Michallon's very first attempt to paint en plein air. While the inscription perhaps should not be taken literally, the charming naïveté of the sketch suggests it might indeed have been executed at the beginning of the artist's career—which, in the case of Michallon, would imply it was made while he still was a child. The catalogue of the sale of the contents of Michallon's studio, which took place in Paris in December 1822, includes "Deux paysages des commencemens de l'auteur" (nos. 382–83) and "Deux petits paysages, composés et exécutés par Michallon, à l'âge de onze ans" (nos. 394–95). While this work cannot definitely be identified with one of these early sketches, its style, the inscription, and the circumstances of Michallon's life all suggest a date as early as 1807 or 1808 and in any event little later than about 1812.

WMG

CARL ROTTMANN

Handschuhsheim, near Heidelberg, 1797–1850 Munich

94 *The Cemetery at Pronoia near Nauplia*

Oil on canvas. 10 x 12 in. (250 x 305 mm). Inscribed in dark brown paint on reverse, *Der Kirchhof in der Vorstadt | Pronia von Nauplia | von | Carl Rottmann.*

PROVENANCE: William Karrmann; Cincinnati Art Museum; private collection; Artemis Fine Arts, Ltd., London (on consignment), 2001.

EXHIBITIONS: Heidelberg and Munich 1998, no. 120, repr. in color p. 256; Munich 1999–2000, no. 365, repr. in color.

Rottmann treated the subject of this oil sketch at least six times in various media. The motif originated on a journey through Greece undertaken by the artist in 1834–35 at the behest of his patron, King Ludwig I of Bavaria. Just previously the artist had painted a series of frescoes of Italian landscape subjects beneath the arcades of the Munich Hofgarten (palace garden) and in 1834 Ludwig I commissioned a complementary series of thirty-eight Greek sites. The monarch's interest in and love of all things Greek was reinforced by the fact that in 1832, after a long and bitter war that freed Greece of Turkish dominion, his son had ascended the Greek throne as Otto I, king of the Hellenes. It was at Pronoia, a suburb of Nauplia, where Otto I had first set foot on Greek soil; it also was the burial site for Bavarian soldiers.

One of Rottmann's earliest studies of Pronoia is a watercolor now in the Kurpfälzisches Museum in Heidelberg (Fig. 1). It was probably created in situ in 1834 and depicts rocky mountains and chalk cliffs rising steeply from a plain with the houses of Pronoia nestled on a slope at right. This was followed by a compositional drawing in graphite, now in a private collection, that introduces the motif of the lone tree at lower left (Heidelberg and Munich 1998, no. 122, repr.). A subsequent detailed watercolor of 1841 (Staatliche Graphische Sammlung, Munich; Heidelberg and Munich 1998, no. 119, repr.) brings into the composition a large rainbow arching the scene and a darker, more dramatic mood: a storm is moving off to the right, and, though the foreground still is in deep shadow, the first rays of sunshine appear at upper left, illuminating the mountain range. The rainbow— the biblical symbol of God's covenant with man after the Flood—which touches the houses of Pronoia, and the unnaturally bright passage at center, impart an almost sacred aura to the scene. The final version was not completed until 1846/47 (Fig. 2). In order to avert vandalism and weather damage, it was decided to hang the entire series in a special

FIG. 1. Carl Rottmann, *Pronoia*, Kurpfälzisches Museum, Heidelberg

FIG. 2. Carl Rottmann, *Pronoia*, Bayerisches Nationalmuseum, Munich

room in the Neue Pinakothek, instead of having them executed in fresco beneath the Hofgarten arcades.

In comparison with the other versions, the present oil sketch is particularly free in handling; thick horizontal brushstrokes alternate with dabs of white and yellow, which pick out the crown of the tree in the foreground and the froth on the rivulet snaking through the plain. The stream leads into a dark pond at lower right, a motif that originated in a sketch by the artist of the spring Callirhoe near Athens. Unlike the final version and the late Munich watercolor, in which groups of travelers dot the plain, here the scene is entirely given over to the landscape.

REP

ROBERT-LÉOPOLD LEPRINCE

Paris 1800–1847 Chartres

95 *Interior of a Wood at Pierrefitte*

Oil on cardboard. 11 x 16 in. (279 x 406 mm). Signed, dated, and inscribed on reverse, *R. Leopold Leprince 1822 a pierre-f..tte.*

PROVENANCE: Galerie Fischer-Kiener, Paris.

EXHIBITION: Paris 1995, no. 9, repr. in color.

Although his name is little known today, Leprince exhibited regularly at the Salon from 1822 until 1844, winning a first-place medal in 1824 for his landscape *Moulin à eau, à Honfleur,* which was purchased by Louis XVIII (1823; Musée du Louvre, Paris). Born into a family of artists that included his father, Anne-Pierre, and his brothers, Auguste-Xavier (1799–1826) and Gustave (1810–1837), Leprince devoted his career to landscape painting. During the 1820s he worked at Fontainebleau and at nearby Chailly alongside the landscape painter Alexandre Pau de Saint Martin, a cousin of Théodore Rousseau (Nos. 38 and 105). Sometime after 1830 Leprince settled in Chartres, where he maintained a productive career as a painter of landscapes, specializing in forest scenes. Like his elder brother Auguste-Xavier, with whom he first studied, Leprince had an affinity for seventeenth-century Dutch landscape paintings and painted a number of rustic scenes with figures and animals as well as pure landscapes.

The site of this dense, lush forest view is likely Pierrefitte-sur-Seine, just outside of Paris, north of St. Denis, although the inscription is inconclusive. Leprince often represented thickly forested scenes, focusing not on a clearing but on the trees, which are usually cropped and close to the picture plane. In this fresh and luminous study, the artist depicted a stand of trees surrounding the edge of a small stream. The central knot of trees is highlighted by their trunks contrasting with the glimmering surface of the water. Leprince captured the atmosphere of the cool, moist heart of the woods. The sky is not visible, only a vast number of trunks and a green canopy of foliage.

The date on the reverse of this work reveals that the artist was only twenty-two years old when it was made. At the same time he executed his first canvases for the Salon, including two scenes of the cloister at Saint-Etienne du Mont and a historic landscape subject.

JT

THOMAS FEARNLEY

Frederiskshald 1802–1842 Munich

96 *Landscape Sketch with Monolith and Trees*

Oil on canvas, laid down on card. 4¾ x 6¹³⁄₁₆ in. (121 x 173 mm); trimmed irregularly. Inscribed on reverse, in pen and blue ink, *Dette maleri h. 12 bredde 17.5, | Landskap med to traer og en stor sten. | i forgrunden, er et ungdomsmaleri | av. Tho. Fearnley. | Oslo | 14.11.51 | Th. Ma[?]teson.*

PROVENANCE: Private collection, Oslo, 1951; Artis Fine Arts, London.

Fearnley is considered, with Johan Christian Dahl (Nos. 83–85), one of the most important Norwegian landscape painters of the nineteenth century. The grandson of a Yorkshire merchant who settled in Norway in 1753, Fearnley began his training in 1819 at the Royal School of Drawing in Christiania (present-day Oslo) and later studied at the art academies in Copenhagen (1821–23) and Stockholm (1823–27). In 1826 he met Dahl while traveling in Norway, and in 1829 he moved to Dresden to study with him. Fearnley, whom Dahl called his most talented pupil (Manchester and Cambridge 1993, p. 22), trained with the older artist for eighteen months and remained in close contact with him throughout his short life. The influences on his style were various, however, because he traveled widely and rarely stayed in one place for more than a few years.

This work has been plausibly dated to the artist's sojourn in Dresden because of the similarity in handling to that of other works he produced at that time (collector's files). In *A Forest Track with a Crucifix,* for example, an oil study of 1830 (Nasjonalgalleriet, Oslo; Manchester and Cambridge 1993, no. 24, repr.), the free, spontaneous manner and broad brushwork describing the rock surfaces are very close to that of the Thaw study, as is the palette of brown, gray, gold, and green and the practice of applying pigment alternately in single, isolated strokes with one tone on top of another.

Further support for dating the present sketch to Fearnley's stay in Dresden may be adduced from the similarity between *Landscape Sketch with Monolith and Trees* and the work not only of Dahl but of Dresden's other principal artist, Caspar David Friedrich (1774–1840). Both Dahl and Friedrich depicted rocky landscapes with spruce trees in numerous paintings, among them an oil sketch by Dahl of 1822, *Study of Clouds at Full Moon* (Fine Arts Museums of San Francisco; Ottawa and elsewhere 1999–2000, no. 16, repr.), and a painting by Friedrich, *View of the Elbe Valley* (Gemäldegalerie, Dresden; Börsch-Supan and Jähnig 1973, no. 163, repr.).

FIG. 1. Caspar David Friedrich, *Megalithic Grave in Spring,* Staatliche Kunstsammlungen, Dresden

The present study is also suggestive of Friedrich in the ambiguous, unidentifiable landscape setting with its sloping hillside that falls away in the distance as well as in the hieratic composition with the two trees standing like sentinels behind the monolith, elements that recur frequently in paintings by Friedrich, for example, *Cross in the Mountains* (Schlossmuseum, Gotha; Börsch-Supan and Jähnig 1973, no. 308, repr.). Moreover, in its centrality and isolation in the composition, and its closeness to the picture

plane, the huge rock in Fearnley's sketch assumes totemic power in the manner of the isolated, centrally placed subject in Friedrich's painting of about 1820 *Megalithic Grave in Spring* (Fig. 1).

KS

AUGUST LUCAS

Darmstadt 1803–1863 Darmstadt

97 *View of Monte Sant'Angelo from the Villa Auriemma near Sorrento*

Oil on paper, laid down on canvas. 9½ x 17¼ in. (235 x 435 mm). Watermark: None visible. Inscribed and dated on a piece of paper pasted onto the back of the wooden frame in pen and black ink, *dalla Villa Auriemma a Sorento / viso al monte St Angelo / 18 AL* (ligated) *32.*

PROVENANCE: Frankfurt art market; Busche Collection, Dortmund, Germany; C.G. Boerner Inc., New York, 1998.

LITERATURE: Franzke 1972, p. 38, no. G17, repr.

EXHIBITIONS: Darmstadt 1953, no. 65; Dortmund 1956, no. 89; New York and Düsseldorf 1999, no. 17, repr. in color.

Lucas belongs to the second generation of German Romantic painters. After early training in drawing at Darmstadt, he briefly went to Munich in 1825 to study with Peter Cornelius (1783–1867). Funded by a stipend provided by Ludewig I, grand duke of Darmstadt, Lucas traveled via Milan to Rome in October 1829. There he executed his first landscapes, a genre in which he excelled, though he also treated figural subjects. In the company of other members of the German artistic community, Lucas would often work en plein air, sketching in Rome itself, as well as in the surrounding Alban and Sabine hills. He was in close contact with Joseph Anton Koch (Nos. 18–19), whose heroic ideal landscapes proved to be a strong influence, and must also have been acquainted with Friedrich Overbeck, whose portrait he executed. Lucas spent the summer and autumn of 1832 touring southern Italy, visiting Naples, Pompeii, Sorrento, and Capri, before returning to Darmstadt in 1834.

The technique of the present study—oil on paper—its diminutive size, and the free handling of the brushwork, which preserves the freshness and the soft color harmonies of the natural scenery, indicate that the sketch was executed out of doors. Most of the artist's earlier plein-air sketches are landscape details; it was not until 1831 that these occasionally evolved into more comprehensive works, such as this one. His four other known plein-air landscapes are *Civitella in the Sabine Hills, View of Civitella, View of the Bay of Naples,* and *Landscape near Ariccia* (Collection Kuntz, Darmstadt; Collection Lade, Giessen; Collection Kuntz, Darmstadt; and Städtische Kunstsammlung, Darmstadt; Franzke 1972, nos. G 10, 11, 15, and 19). In their astonishing economy of means and open brushwork, they differ notably from the artist's larger studio paintings, which are more heavily influenced by Koch.

As witnessed by the old label on the verso, the sketch dates from Lucas's 1832 tour of the Bay of Naples. The view is taken from high and depicts the mountain range of the Monti Lattari and the Monte Sant'Angelo a Tre Pizzi in the background. The Villa Auriemma, which, as Professor Nicola Spinosa and Dottore Antonino De Angelis kindly inform me, still exists in Sorrento on the corner of vico I Rota and the corso Italia, is featured in two

other works by Lucas. One, a drawing from the same year in the Hessisches Landesmuse-um, Darmstadt, is similarly annotated *Villa Auriemma a Sorento* (Hamm and elsewhere 1984, p. 25, repr. p. 23). It shows, beneath a vine-covered pergola and against a backdrop of distant mountains and the sea, a friendly gathering that includes a woman peeling fruit, a mother spinning, and a young man playing the lute while two others look on from behind a wall. The second, entitled *Villa Auriemma in Sorrento,* is a lost painting on canvas dated 1844, of which we have no visual record (Franzke 1972, p. 55, no. VG 43, no repr.)

REP

WILHELM BENDZ

Odense 1804–1832 Vicenza

98   *Study of Light Under a Roof*

Oil on paper, laid down on canvas. 6⅛ x 8½ in. (157 x 210 mm). Signed at lower right, *Bendz.*
PROVENANCE: Private collection, Denmark; Galerie Jean-François Heim, Paris.

Bendz studied in Copenhagen from 1820 to 1831, taking classes at the Kunstakademi (1820–26) and studying privately with C. W. Eckersberg (No. 28) in 1822 and again from 1827 to 1831. In 1831, on a grant from the Kunstakademi, he embarked for Germany, stopping in Hamburg, Berlin, Dresden (visiting with Johan Christian Dahl; Nos. 83–85), Nuremberg, and finally Munich. He settled there for a year, enjoying much success, and may have intended to return permanently after a sojourn in Italy. He died, however, in Vicenza of typhoid fever at the age of twenty-eight, not long after he had left for Italy in the fall of 1832.

Bendz's earliest works reveal Eckersberg's influence in their straightforward recording of what the artist saw. The direct study of nature, a gift from Eckersberg following his return from Italy in 1816, was new to Danish art, which had been dominated by neoclassicism and academic practice. In *View of Nyhavn,* a painting of about 1822 (Den Hirschsprungske Samling, Copenhagen; Ottawa and elsewhere 1999–2000, p. 52, no. 1, repr.), Bendz described the view from the first floor of the Kunstakademi in Copenhagen looking north across the Nyhavn Canal.

He is perhaps best known for his portraits. Their quiet naturalism influenced his contemporary Christen Købke (1810–1848); see, for example, the closely observed pencil study of Bendz's boyhood friend Peter Gemzøe, dated 1830 (Statens Museum for Kunst, Copenhagen; New York and elsewhere 1995–96, no. 34, repr.).

The artist is noted as well for his interest in complex light effects, exemplified in an oil sketch made during the last year of his life, *A Coach House, Partenkirchen* (Statens Museum for Kunst, Copenhagen; Ottawa and elsewhere 1999–2000, no. 2, repr.). The work, made soon after he arrived in Munich, is a study of the gradations of tone as light illuminates different parts of the coach house, from a range of blacks and grays in the shadowed foreground to ocher and cream in the central room to brown and tan in the pointed shadows that follow the ribs of the vaulted ceiling.

In the present oil sketch, moodily atmospheric in tone and almost abstract in form, Bendz studied light effects in a vaulted interior. Sunlight falling at an angle from the arched doorway shines on the back wall of the chamber, dissolving the materiality of the surface. A similar abstracting of form may be found in a rare landscape, *View Towards Hoher Göll from Ramsau* (private collection; Ottawa and elsewhere 1999–2000, no. 3, repr.), one of a group of eight oil studies Bendz made on a sketching trip in the Austrian Alps, in the company of Thomas Fearnley (No. 96) and Joseph Petzl (1803–1871), two months before his death. In the mountain landscape, as in the present work, forms are flattened and space is compressed by broad brushwork and the absence of descriptive detail. The parallels with the Austrian landscape suggest that the present study may also date from very late in the artist's life.

KS

FRANÇOIS-ANTOINE LÉON FLEURY

Paris 1804–1858 Paris

99 *View of Tivoli, near S. Maria del Giglio*

Oil on paper mounted on canvas. 7¾ x 10 ^{7}/$_{16}$ in. (197 x 267 mm). Signed at lower right, *Fleury;* inscribed on the stretcher, . . . *Vue prise à Tivoli . . . (L. Fleury) (9)*.

PROVENANCE: Fleury estate sale, Paris, 22–23 April 1844 (no. 41, *Vue prise à Tivoli,* or no. 43, *Vue prise dans la campagne de Rome, route de Tivoli*); W. M. Brady and Co., New York.

Fleury was a student of the academic landscape painter Jean-Victor Bertin (1767–1842), in whose atelier he met Corot (Nos. 90–92). He later studied briefly with Achille-Etna Michallon (No. 93) who instilled him with the need to work en plein air. Like many landscape painters, Fleury did not compete for the Prix de Rome but nonetheless traveled to Italy in 1827, where he joined his friend Corot. The two artists traveled the Roman Campagna, supported largely by Corot's father, and remained close following their return to France (Corot in 1828, Fleury in 1829). The importance of oil sketches in Fleury's work is evident in the catalogue of his 1844 sale, "Nous espérons donc que MM. les amateurs saisiront avec empressement cette occasion de se rendre possesseurs de ces jolies productions, toujours si rares à se procurer, parce qu'elles sont la base des travaux des artistes qui les font, et l'auteur ne s'en séparerait pas s'il n'avait l'intention de faire de nouveaux voyages pour se procurer de nouveaux sites."

During his brief, intensely productive Roman sojourn, Fleury worked closely with Corot, who wrote to his friend Abel Osmond, "I have no time for society . . . Fleury is at Rome with me. He works from morning to night, then sleeps and is ready to do the same the next day. That's the life" (letter, 2 February 1828, Département des Arts Graphiques, Musée du Louvre, Paris; AR8 L10). The two artists visited Tivoli on 23 August 1827 before traveling north of Rome to Cività Castellana; the present study may have been executed on this visit. Constantino Centroni identified this idealized view as depicting the Campagna, around Tivoli, with the city visible in the background, taken from the road from Rome to Tivoli in the vicinity of Santa Maria del Giglio. The broad, rapidly executed brushstrokes suggest that this study was made on site. Since Fleury lived in Italy from 1827 until 1829, and never returned thereafter, this oil sketch can be securely dated to that period. This view was possibly among the group of studies by the artist exhibited in the Salon of 1831 (Gutwirth 1979, no. 11), which secured his success and were subsequently purchased for Louis-Philippe.

JT

(CARL CHRISTIAN) CONSTANTIN HANSEN

Rome 1804–1880 Frederiksberg

100 *Columns of the Temple of Neptune at Paestum*

Oil on canvas. 12⅝ x 10 in. (321 x 254 mm). Signed with monogram at lower right, *CH;* inscribed on reverse, *Constantine Hansen To soijler fra Neptuntemplet I Paestum June 1838;* inscribed on old label on stretcher, *Gram Vendesgade 28.*

PROVENANCE: Mrs. Christmas Dirckink-Holmfeld; sale, Copenhagen, Rasmussen, Auction 463 (1984), lot 3; private collection, Denmark; Artemis Fine Arts, Ltd., London.

LITERATURE: Hannover 1901, no. 139; Jensen (forthcoming).

EXHIBITION: New York 1999a, no. 7, repr.

Although born in Rome and baptized in Vienna, Hansen was raised in his native Denmark, where in 1816 he entered the Kongelige Akademi for de Skønne Kunster, Copenhagen, to study architecture. He soon became more interested in painting, however, and in 1825 he enrolled in the Modelskole. From 1828 until 1833, he worked under Christoffer Wilhelm Eckersberg (No. 28) and his gifted pupil Christen Købke. Hansen's familiarity with the work of the two leading painters of Denmark's golden age had a profound impact upon the development of his style, as did the eight years he spent in Italy, from 1835. When finally he returned to Copenhagen in 1843, he enjoyed tremendous success, both as a painter of carefully constructed figural compositions and for his smaller-scale portraits and architectural subjects.

Hansen journeyed from Rome to Naples in 1838. While in the south of Italy, he was captivated by the solemn grandeur of the Greek temples at Paestum, and he created a series of studies of these and other ancient ruins. This work, executed in summer 1838, depicts a view from inside the so-called Temple of Neptune, which was constructed about 450 B.C. The composition is anchored by two monumental Doric columns, through which another temple may be seen in the sun-drenched distance.

A view of the temple of Poseidon at Paestum, painted by Hansen a year later than this sketch, is in the Thorvaldsens Museum, Copenhagen (B220).

WMG

217

ALEXANDRE DESGOFFE

Paris 1805–1882 Paris

IOI *Cloud Studies Above a Mountain Landscape*

Oil on paper, laid down on cardboard. 5¾ x 12 in. (146 x 305 mm). Numbered on reverse of old mount, *219.*
PROVENANCE: By descent through the family of the artist; Bob P. Haboldt & Co., New York and Paris.

Having initially studied with Louis-Etienne Watelet (1780–1866) in 1826 and then with Charles Rémond (1795–1875), Desgoffe spent his early career traveling the Auvergne, Switzerland, and the Jura. The artist was one of Ingres's first pupils following the master's return from Rome in 1828. Desgoffe was joined in Ingres's studio by the Flandrin brothers, Hippolyte (1809–1864), and Paul (No. 103), the following year. He traveled Italy extensively on his first trip in 1834 and visited Capri with the composer Charles-François Gounod before stopping in Rome. On his second trip to Rome in 1839, Desgoffe again worked with Ingres, who was then director of the French Academy. Upon their return to France in 1842 the two artists continued to collaborate on projects: in 1843 Desgoffe painted the landscape background for Ingres's *L'Age d'Or* at the château de Dampierre, and in 1856 he painted the rocky background of *La Source.*

Desgoffe regularly participated in the Salon from 1834 until 1868. The first painting he exhibited was a landscape titled *Les Bruyères d'Arbonne,* which Louis Flandrin later described as "une vaste lande couverte de bruyères et de rochers, éclairée par les feux rasants du soleil couchant. Le site n'était pas fait pour charmer beaucoup le public, mais il plaisait au peintre par sa sauvagerie même" (Flandrin 1888, cited in Paris 1996, p. 8). Indeed, Desgoffe preferred to depict nature in its roughest guise, often working in dangerous mountainous conditions. He continued to travel the scenic regions of France, including the Auvergne, the Allier, the Loire valley, and Calvados.

In this oil sketch Desgoffe concentrated on the drama of a cloudy sky over a low-lying range of mountains. Several small cumulus clouds are subsumed by a large gray moving mass of cloud at the center. Although less violent than many of his depictions of nature, this study reflects the artist's interest in the dramatic mutability of the sky and nature's less placid side.

JT

ALEXANDRE DESGOFFE

Paris 1805–1882 Paris

102 *Italian Landscape,* 1837

Oil on paper. 7⅜ x 16 in. (191 x 406 mm). Stamped signature at lower right; inscribed at lower right, *1838;* numbered on verso, *202.*

PROVENANCE: Estate of the artist; Louis Flandrin; by descent to Yves Froidevaux; Galerie de Bayser, Paris.

Although Desgoffe is little known today, his obituary in the *Gazette des Beaux-Arts* attests to his many achievements and honors:

> Ses "verdures" exécutées à l'ancien Hôtel de Ville, à la Bibliothèque Sainte-Geneviève et à la salle d'études de la Bibliothèque nationale, quelques compositions pour diverses églises de Paris, et notamment pour l'église Saint-Nicolas du Chardonnet, et deux tableaux exposés au Salon de 1857 . . . sont les oeuvres qui contribuèrent à donner à Alexander Desgoffe quelque réputation. Après avoir obtenu des médailles aux Salons de 1842, 1843, 1845 et 1848, il fut décoré de la Légion d'honneur en 1857 (*Gazette* 1882, p. 203).

After three years in Italy, Desgoffe returned to France in spring 1837 and remained until autumn 1839. On 18 May 1838, he wrote from Paris to the brothers Hippolyte (1809–1864) and Paul Flandrin (No. 103), who were working in Naples, "J'ai terminé des tableaux que vous aviez vus commencés à Rome; à présent, je commence à travailler sur deux grandes ébauches de la campagne de Rome dont vous ne vous rappelez probablement pas [*sic*]" (Aubrun 1988, p. 54). At the Salon of 1838 Desgoffe exhibited only two historic landscapes, *Argus gardant la vache Io,* and *Hercule combattant le lion de Némée.* The following year, however, he showed four paintings of the Roman Campagna, all now lost.

A departure from his usual rocky landscapes, this subtle panoramic view of gently rolling hills in the Campagna includes a church or monastery at the lower right, and a small town is discernible in the valley at the left. The date *1838,* inscribed in the lower right corner, was added by a later hand: Desgoffe remained in France that year. It seems likely that the sketch dates slightly earlier and belongs to the group of works the artist brought back to France in 1837, many of which he continued to develop in his studio.

JT

PAUL FLANDRIN

Lyon 1811–1902 Paris

103 *Landscape with Mont Ventoux*

Oil on paper, mounted on canvas. 9⅝ x 14¼ in. (244 x 362 mm). Signed at lower right, *Paul Flandrin;* inscribed on reverse of stretcher, *1842.*

PROVENANCE: Private collection, Lyon; Bob P. Haboldt and Co., New York and Paris.

Paul Flandrin belonged to a family of artists that included his older brothers, the painters Auguste and Hippolyte. In 1829, after a period of study in Lyon, Paul and Hippolyte moved to Paris, where they became pupils of Ingres (No. 34). About a year after Hippolyte had won the Prix de Rome, in 1832, Paul followed his brother to Italy, remaining there from December 1833 until 1838. It was in Italy that Paul seems to have decided once and for all to specialize in historical landscape painting, and after returning to Paris, he exhibited a number of Italian landscapes in the Salon of 1939. He continued to exhibit in the Salon for many years, although as the century progressed, his devotion to Ingres would seem increasingly anachronistic, and by the time he died, the younger Flandrin was all but forgotten.

In France Paul painted in Normandy, Brittany, the Dauphiné, and Provence as well as in the forest of Fontainebleau, where he often worked with Desgoffe (Nos. 101–2), whose daughter he married in 1852. This work, dated on the stretcher to the year of the death of his eldest brother, Auguste, was painted just outside Orange. The town's famous second-century Roman theater is visible to the right of center, while the slopes of Mont Ventoux dominate the distant horizon.

WMG

EDWARD LEAR

Holloway, London, 1812–1888 San Remo

104 *Study of Rocks, Shrubs, and Tree Trunks at Monte Casale near Sansepolcro, Tuscany*

Oil with traces of graphite on blue paper mounted to canvas. 9 x 12⅞ in. (229 x 327 mm). Penciled outline of a duck at lower right, inscribed and dated in brown ink, *M^te. Casale. | 18.October.1842;* inscribed in graphite at upper right, *the . . . large & small | & very blue green. | there should be more black and | greys . . . & darker Bitumen | yellow (?) moss, B. Sienna pale | ferns . . .*

PROVENANCE: Sale, London, Phillips, 30 September 1997, lot 102, repr.; Thos. Agnew & Sons, Ltd., London.

EXHIBITION: London 1998b, number 96, repr. in color.

This oil sketch was made a year after Lear published the first of his seven travel books, *Views in Rome and Its Environs,* London, 1841. Lear, who made his living as a topographical draftsman, had set off for Italy in 1837, his trip and expenses underwritten by his patron Lord Derby and his cousin Robert Hornby. Before that time he was known primarily as an ornithological illustrator; by the time he was twenty, Lear had already published his first book, *Illustrations of the Family of Psittacidae or Parrots.* He spent most of the rest of his life abroad, initially based in Rome, making walking tours of southern and central Italy in the 1840s. Apparently almost from when he arrived in Italy, Lear aspired to become a serious painter in oils and began to use the medium in 1838. Lacking real technique, he had to return to London for study and also sought the advice of the great Pre-Raphaelite painter William Holman Hunt.

In this oil sketch of 1842 Lear focused on some rocks and tree trunks that might have been used as compositional elements in a larger work. The fact that it is painted on a sheet of blue paper rather than on canvas suggests it was executed outdoors and later mounted to canvas. Even though Lear used oil pigments here, he included his customary color notes as well as the notation about the day and location. It is interesting to compare this sketch with a study of tree roots executed in oil on paper in 1838 (The Forbes Magazine Collection, New York; see London 1985, no. 45, repr. in color). The Forbes study was executed at Corpo di Cava, a summer retreat near Naples. It may be that Lear's interest in such details in both these works look back to the minute observation of detail demanded by his ornithological and animal studies of the early 1830s. In 1842, when Lear painted the present study, he spent the summer at Monte Casale in Sicily.

CDD

THÉODORE ROUSSEAU

Paris 1812–1867 Barbizon (Seine-et-Marne)

105 *A Stream in the Auvergne*

Oil on paper, laid down on canvas. 11½ x 14½ in. (292 x 368 mm). Numbered in black paint on reverse, *no. 4.*
PROVENANCE: Hazlitt Gallery, London; sale, London, Sotheby's, 4 July 1974, lot 221, repr.; sale, London, Sotheby's, 19 November 1997, lot 134, repr.; J. Duncan collection; Salander-O'Reilly Galleries, New York.
LITERATURE: Schulman 1999, no. 67, p. 105, repr.

As a schoolboy Rousseau showed such aptitude for landscape painting that his family sent him to study with one of the leading neoclassical landscape painters of his day, Charles Rémond (1795–1875). He also would study with Guillaume Guillon Lethière (1760–1832) but did not remain long with either master. Rousseau had already become so involved in the depiction of unadorned nature that he really was not interested in the neoclassical landscape painting then so much in vogue, a genre that sought to embellish nature with mythological subject matter. Rousseau's dislike of contrivance was confirmed by an unsuccessful attempt at the historical landscape painting prize in 1829. Although he had become familiar with the area around Fontainebleau as early as 1827, he journeyed to the relatively faraway rugged mountainous country of the Auvergne in 1830. The young artist soon became absorbed by the unfettered nature of this region with its strange volcanic rock formations and mountain streams, and he began to paint these forms in a series of sketches and oils executed en plein air. This oil sketch is such a work. Consisting only of some boulders and a mountain stream, the site would not be readily identifiable but for the existence of a nearly duplicate and somewhat larger work entitled *Cours d'eau à travers les roches a Dampiere; vallée de Chevreuse* (present location unknown; Schulman 1999, no. 66, repr.). Since this other sketch was exhibited as early as 1867, it may be assumed that the identification of the site in Dampierre is correct as Rousseau himself would have titled it (Paris 1867, no. 10). The artist's creation of two such similar works is not too surprising given his evident interest in depicting the play of water over rocks. He made at least four other related studies of the stream and its rocky bed around the same time (Schulman 1999, nos. 64, 65, 68, 69, repr.).

The young artist was fascinated by the Auvergne and produced many drawings and oil sketches during his stay of nearly six months. Schulman reproduces some fifty-eight paintings and oil sketches dating to this sojourn. These sketches and canvases are much the same size, rather compact, and would have been ideal for carrying along on some of Rousseau's painting expeditions into the rugged countryside. Judging from his oeuvre, it is fair to say that Rousseau explored all sorts of compositional modalities and viewpoints. They included sweeping vistas of the mountains and valleys of the region, close-up nature studies, such as the present work, as well as rustic cottages, or *chaumières,* bridges, and views of entire small villages. One of his contemporaries called Rousseau's Auvergne sojourn "sa petite révolution." He was energized by the region to such a degree that it gave him the confidence to continue working along the same lines when he returned to Paris. A year later, in 1831, Rousseau made his debut at the Salon with a painting, simply entitled *Auvergne Site* (present location unknown). He then moved on to the area around Fontainebleau and became one of the prime movers of the Barbizon school.

CDD

JEAN-ACHILLE BENOUVILLE

Paris 1815–1891 Paris

106 *View of the Villa Medici Park, Rome*

Oil on paper. 10¼ x 8¾ in. (250 x 218 mm). On verso, atelier stamp and *no. 115.*

PROVENANCE: Galerie Fischer-Kiener, Paris.

EXHIBITION: Paris 1995, no. 27, repr. in color.

Benouville was the pupil of the history painter François-Édouard Picot until he went to study at the École des Beaux-Arts in Paris in 1837. As early as 1834 he had enjoyed some success when he exhibited at the Salon landscapes of the park at Versailles and Ville d'Avray, Saint-Cloud, Compiègne, and Fontainebleau concurrently with Barbizon artists Rousseau (Nos. 38 and 105), Jules Dupré, and Charles-François Daubigny. He won the Prix de Rome for historical landscape painting in 1845 with *Ulysses and Nausicaa* (École des Beaux-Arts, Paris) and went to Rome to study at the French Academy with his younger brother Léon, who won the Prix de Rome for historical painting the same year. The French academy was already in its familiar location, the Villa Medici on the Pincio. Benouville remained in Rome until 1870, frequently submitting to the Salon Roman views, such as *View of St. Peter's* in 1863, and *View of the Villa Borghese* (1864).

In the present work Benouville chose to depict the view from the front of the Villa Medici overlooking Rome. It probably dates to the same time as the artist's full-scale (550 x 910 mm) painting of the same subject signed and dated 1864 (sale, London, Sotheby's, 17 March 1995, lot 209), which came from the collection of Princesse Mathilde. In this landscape set in the late afternoon, Benouville demonstrated his particular sensitivity to variations in light and atmosphere. From the gardens of the Villa Medici, the dome of St. Peter's is seen in faint silhouette against an almost mauve sky. Benouville chose to evoke a rather poetic moment between late afternoon and evening when there was sufficient light in the foreground to contrast the bright yellow greens of the grass and low-lying shrubs. The soft silver green leaves of an agave plant in an urn on a pedestal are also discernible, while the umbrella pines in the middle distance are beginning to disappear in the gathering dusk. There is also a suggestion of some low clouds in the middle distance and background. Benouville's work is more detailed and carefully composed than that of the Barbizon artists.

CDD

JOHAN THOMAS LUNDBYE

Kalundborg 1818–1848 Bedsted

107 *An Evening Beside Lake Arresø,* ca. 1837

Oil on canvas. 9 x 11¾ in. (229 x 298 mm).

PROVENANCE: Generalkonsul Johan Hansen; Hans Tobiesen; his sale, Winkel and Magnussen, 1953, lot 631.

LITERATURE: Madsen 1931, pp. 8–9, fig. 4; Bramsen 1935, p. 77; Madsen 1949, no. 38a, repr. p. 327; Nørregård-Nielsen (forthcoming).

EXHIBITIONS: Stockholm 1922, no. 144; Copenhagen 1931, no. 21.

One of the youngest artists of the last generation of the Danish golden age painters, Lundbye began his education at the Kongelige Akademi for de Skønne Kunster, Copenhagen, at the age of fourteen. He was a student of Johan Ludvig Lund (1777–1867) and the animal painter Christian Holm (1804–1846). His eventual decision to pursue landscape painting, however, was strongly influenced by his long exposure to the work of Christen Købke, a fellow resident of the Citadel, Copenhagen, where Lundbye lived with his family. Lundbye exhibited his first painting in 1835, but it was not until 1838, when his *Landscape at Arresø with the Dunes of Tisvilde* (1838; Thorvaldsens Museum, Copenhagen) was shown at Charlottenberg Palace that he received significant critical attention. In a review of the exhibition, the art historian Niels Laurits Høyen remarked that Lundbye's introduction of clouds and staffage figures into his previously sparse landscapes marked the young artist's transition to a mature style.

In 1836 Lundbye's family moved from their official residence at the Citadel to Zealand, where the artist's father was stationed as chief of the Raketkorpset at the port city of Frederiksvaerk near Lake Arresø. While his family lived north of the town with a view of the lake, Lundbye remained in Copenhagen, although he frequently visited his family. Frederiksvaerk is located on the canal leading from the lake, Denmark's largest, to Roskilde Fjord, and the town and its environs were predominant subjects among Lundbye's earliest depictions of pure landscape, such as *View of Frederiksvaerk Before Sunrise, Late Autumn,* painted and exhibited in 1837 (subsequently destroyed by the artist), when the artist was nineteen years old. The present oil sketch was probably executed the same year during one of Lundbye's stays at Frederiksvaerk.

Set at dusk, this scene depicts a man in hunting dress carrying a rifle, with a hound close at his heels, walking along the marshy edge of the lake. The branches of a barren shrub on the bank are silhouetted in the left foreground. The dunes of Tisvildeleje, along the coast north of Lake Arresø, are visible in the distance. Inspired by the work of Caspar David Friedrich and Johan Christian Clausen Dahl (Nos. 83–85), and motivated by Høyen's call for a style that captured the Danish character, Lundbye has virtually eliminated the narrative element to focus on light, infusing the familiar low-lying landscape with a certain nostalgia. It is possible that the young hunter in the scene was one of the artist's six brothers. Lundbye likewise may have represented two of his brothers in another oil sketch from 1837, *A Sunken Road near Frederiksvaerk* (Statens Museum for Kunst, Copenhagen).

JT

GIOVANNI BATTISTA CAMUCCINI

Rome 1819–1904 Rome

108 *A Path in the Roman Countryside*

Oil on paper, mounted on canvas. 11 x 16⅜ in. (280 x 415 mm).

PROVENANCE: By descent to the family of the artist, Cantalupo, near Sabina; Emmanuel Moatti, New York and Paris.

EXHIBITION: New York 2000–2001a, no. 20, repr.

The son of Vincenzo Camuccini (1771–1844), a neoclassical history painter and portraitist of international repute, Giovanni Battista Camuccini presumably received his earliest instruction in the atelier of his father, although by 1839 he had entered the studio of the landscape painter Giambattista Bassi (1784–1852). Bassi was among the relatively few Italian artists who routinely worked en plein air, and it must have been with Bassi's encouragement that the young Camuccini began painting in the countryside near Rome. In 1844 Camuccini's father retired to Albano, where he died two years later. This loss was compounded in 1851 by the death of Camuccini's wife Candida Mazzetti after just five years of marriage, and in 1852 by that of his teacher Bassi. He thereafter painted very little, and his latest known work is dated to that year.

This exceptionally vigorous sketch of a path winding into the distance is one of a number of works in oil on paper that were discovered about 1980 at the villa of the Camuccini family at Cantalupo. The brevity of Camuccini's activity as an artist and the fact that a related sketch (New York 2000–2001a, no. 6, repr.) is dated *24 luglio 184*[?] combine to suggest that the entire group was created during the 1840s. Two other sketches from the same source also were acquired by Mr. and Mrs. Thaw (New York 2000–2001a, nos. 15, 25), while the three works by Camuccini in the Gere Collection were purchased directly from the artist's descendants in 1983 (Christopher Riopelle, in London 1999, nos. 9–11).

WMG

JEAN-MICHEL CELS

The Hague 1819–1894 Brussels

109 *Clouds and Blue Sky*

Oil on brown paper, mounted on card. 10 5/16 x 14⅜ in. (263 x 365 mm). Inscribed on reverse, in pen and brown ink at upper left, *V[ernis]: cop[al] étendu de téréb[enthine]:.*

PROVENANCE: Private collection, Belgium, about 1950; sale, London, Christie's South Kensington, 16 April 1997, part of lot 310; W. M. Brady and Co., New York.

This is one of a group of about twenty recently discovered oil sketches of cloud and tree studies by Cels. No other works of this Belgian artist are known. He received instruction from his father, Cornelis Cels (1778–1859), a neoclassical painter who studied in Italy for seven years and later served as director of the Académie de Tournai. During the period in which the elder Cels was in Italy, sketching landscapes in oil en plein air became established practice, particularly through the efforts of Pierre-Henri de Valenciennes, who was working in Rome at the time (Nos. 66–71).

Cloud studies in oil were among the exercises Valenciennes recommended in his influential treatise *Elémens de perspective pratique* of 1800. Apart from his own examples, however, such works were rare before the first decades of the nineteenth century. One of the early practitioners was Simon Denis (Nos. 72–74), a Belgian artist whose delicately painted cloud studies with their narrow strip of earth anchoring the bottom of the composition follow the formula advocated by Valenciennes; see, for example, *Cloud Study in Rome* (about 1800, private collection, New York; Washington and elsewhere 1996–97, no. 37, repr.). Cels's cloud studies, by contrast, are more abstract in form, with thickly impastoed surfaces contrasting with areas of thinly brushed tone; see, for example, the group of four studies recently with James Mackinnon (New York 1998c, nos. 33–36, repr.).

In the present sketch, the artist dragged an almost dry brush across sections of the middle of the sheet, leaving small areas of unpainted tan paper showing through, creating the effect of streaks of yellowish tan pigment among the deep gray of the undersides of cloud. The modulation in tone helps give the undersides definition, enhancing the illusion that the clouds recede into depth. Cels's brushstrokes and density of pigment are varied throughout, providing both visual interest and, paradoxically, greater illusionism. He used long, thinly applied strokes of yellow and blue across the bottom third of the composition, thick dabs of pigment applied with a full brush across the center, and short, midweight strokes of blue at the top.

Several of the recently discovered cloud studies are signed and dated between 1838 and 1842, and their locations are identified as in and around Brussels. Some are inscribed by the artist with the time of day. Cloud forms extremely close to those in this sketch are found in another study from this group, now in the Gere collection, which is signed and dated on the verso *JM Cels 1842 Bruxelles* and is drawn on a sheet of almost the same dimensions as those of this sketch (London 1999, no. 12, repr.). As in the Gere oil sketch, in the present work Cels used areas of blank paper to lend tone. Also, as he did in the Gere sketch, Cels omitted the narrow strip of landscape at the bottom edge of the composition, conventional in the cloud studies by Valenciennes. Because of the illusionism of this sketch, however, the viewpoint is not from midair but from the ground looking up.

KS

234

235

HENRI-JOSEPH HARPIGNIES

Valenciennes (Nord) 1819–1916 Saint-Privé (Yonne)

110 *Environs de Rome*

Oil on laid paper, mounted on canvas. 5⅛ x 10⅛ in. (130 x 262 mm). Signed at lower left, *h Harpignies,* and inscribed and dated at right, *Rome 1851.*

PROVENANCE: Galerie Fischer-Kiener, Paris.

Harpignies studied with Jean Achard, who took his pupil to Lyons and taught him how to paint from nature. He went to Rome via Germany for the first time in 1849, returning to Paris in 1852. He was dazzled by the city and its environs and wrote the following in his journal:

> C'était bien là le pays qui j'avais rêvé. L'impression a été grande, heureuse pour moi, elle est gravée dans ma mémoire en lettres d'or. J'aimais la forme, elle existe là par excellence comme partout dans la campagne romaine, c'est là que je l'ai bien comprise, et elle a été mon guide pendant toute ma carrière (Journal d'Harpignies, unpublished, November 1849).

The site has not been identified, but it would appear that Harpignies was sketching and painting in the Campagna, somewhere perhaps in the Alban or Sabine hills, northwest of the city. This work exemplifies the importance Harpignies gave to structure and to simplification of the subject. He seems to have been very much caught up with form in this work, which is dominated by the gentle mountain rising above a small town or villa. It is a very volumetric—even uncharacteristic—work for Harpignies, whose familiar work is suffused with atmosphere and a certain limpidity of touch that gives his later watercolors such a poetic cast or feel. Following in the footsteps of Benouville (No. 106) and Corot (Nos. 90–92), the artist was fascinated by the open countryside surrounding Rome.

Although he did not actually meet Corot until after his return to Paris, in this work Harpignies used very much the same palette as that artist. The paint, however, is much more thickly applied, and the clouds are well defined as contrasted with the vague, quick indications of the older master. While Corot's style may have influenced him, Harpignies was to remain independent of the Barbizon artists, although his passion for light and nature has much in common with their oeuvre. In order to encourage the younger artist, Corot purchased two of his watercolors during this period (Moreau-Nélaton and Robaut 1905, I, p. 232).

CDD

FRANÇOIS-AUGUSTE BONHEUR

Bordeaux 1824–1884 Bellevue

III   *Landscape with Mountains*

Oil on paper, laid down on canvas. 6¾ x 14⅜ in. (171 x 365 mm). Stamped at lower left, *A. Bonheur.*
PROVENANCE: The artist's studio, Magny-les-Hameaux, near Versailles; W. M. Brady and Co., New York.

Born into a family of artists, his sister Rosa (1822–1899) having been the most famous, Auguste Bonheur was a pupil of their father, the landscape painter Raymond Bonheur. Like his sister, he was a painter of animalier subjects and exhibited regularly at the Salon from 1845 until 1868. In fact all four Bonheur children became artists, having trained in their father's studio: Isidore was a painter and sculptor, and Juliette also became a painter. In 1853 Auguste, Rosa, Isidore, and Juliette all had works on view at the Salon. Louis Auvray, in his review of the 1859 Salon, commented, "M. Auguste Bonheur, le frère de Rosa Bonheur, est un peintre qui réussit avec talent les animaux et le paysage. Sa couleur est solide et brillante tout à la fois; son pinceau est plus ferme, plus hardi que celui de sa soeur."

Bonheur preferred rocky and mountainous sites and traveled France working en plein air in the forest of Fontainebleau as well as the rougher terrain of the Auvergne, Normandy, Bretagne, the Pyrénées, and Calvados. This study belongs to a large group of works recently discovered at the artist's studio in Magny-les-Hameaux. Although the site is unidentified, it may be a view of the mountains in the Auvergne or the Pyrénées, which the artist often visited.

JT

Appendix A

Head of a Bear (No. 5)
Attributed to Frans Snyders
Transcription by M. Montias and E. Haverkamp-Begemann

Obverse

1.	___		*f 2020*
2.	*36*_____		
3		*Cornelis Ver*	
4.	*15 f 3296* [?]		
5.	*350 pds*		
6.	*450 pds*		
7. (?)			
8. (?)			
9. (?)			
10. (?)			
11. (?)			
12. (?)			
13. (?)			
14. (?)	*29*		
15. (?)	*99*		
16. (?)	*36*		
17. (?)			
18. (?)			*f 2-12*
19. (?)			
20. (?)			*f 100.10.10*
21.			
22.		*sijn*	*f 65.3.8*
23.		*bennich* [?] *debet aen Winckel*	
24.		*op ses maenten vercoft hebbe als*	
25.		*stuck 3½ ghuldens*	*f 912*
26.	*winckel debet aen pieter Jacobsz de goÿer*	*f 1900 voor*	
27.	*witte denser oor* [?] *zayen stuck 23¾ gh* _____		*f 1900*
28.	*betaeld acht maenten naer dato deses*_____		

1.	<u>63</u>	Ghÿsbarto tholinx Debet aen Francisco boudewij[ns]		
2.	2610[?]	f 2125 voor soe veel [hem?] op boudewÿns hebbe		
3.		Laetten rescontreren procuderende van 1000 fl bÿ		
4.		myn van ditto boudewÿns opde paesmisse getrocken		
5.		tegen 85 p[onds] vlaems per Dierick van hetter gedaen		f 2125

6.	<u>124</u>	Cassa Debet aen Jan lambers tot Venlo	f 200	
7.	2	door Jan France van Koekercken ontfangen		f 200

8.	<u>121</u>	Winckel debet a die 17 ditto aen Raphael Baesie		
9.	100	f 494 _____ voor 13. dosÿnen stuck 3 $^1/_6$ ghulden		f 494

10.	<u>115</u>	Jacob Wÿntges tot Niemegen Debet aen Winckel		
11.	22[?]	f 847:4:0 hem gesonden bÿ onsse boode _____		
12.		28¼ ellen bruijn coluer d elle 22st	f 184:16	
13.		een osestere silvere hortmans 38 [pond Vlaams]	f 228:0:	
14.		een Casselcoens Jan Allenes 32 gh tot 29p	f 174.0:	
15.		vier coluer dosÿnnen stuck 42 gh	f 268:0:	
16.		drie voeringen swart 2 root a 17½ gh stuck	f 52:10:	
17.		een Essix [graee?] dosÿn tot	f 39:0:	
18.		voor 9. vaen touw a 2 stuvers de vaen	f :18:	
19.			f 847:4:	f 847.4

20.	<u>22</u>	Winckel Debet aen Isack Sollemans f 48 voor		
21.	17	een root ende twee swarte voeringe a 16 gh het stuck		f 48

22.	<u>22</u>[?]	Winckel Debet aen Henderick van Cuÿck f 48:12		
23.	20	voor 46 ellen blaeue duffels d ellen 21 stuuers		f 48:12

24.	<u>23</u>	Isack van Haelmael Debet aen Cassa f 187: 13 —		
25.	14[?]	[aen] sÿn knecht michael betaelt		f 187:13

26.		Rembolt Brewer tot Nuÿs Debet aen winckel f 247:11—	
27.		[h]em gesonden ouer niemegen aen driessen met ordre ons	
28.		te senden op Venlo aen Dirck van Dael [. . . . . .]	

Appendix B

Vincent van Gogh (No. 54)
Letter to Paul Gauguin
[17 October 1888]

mon cher Gauguin   merci de votre lettre et merci surtout de votre promesse de venir déjà le vingt. Certes cette raison que vous dites doit ~~vous~~ ne pas contribuer à faire un voyage d'agrément du trajet en chemin de fer et ce n'est que comme de juste que vous retardiez votre voyage jusqu'à que vous puissiez le faire sans emmerdement. Mais à part cela je vous l'envie presque ce voyage qui va vous montrer en passant des lieue, et des lieues de pays de diverse nature avec les splendeurs d'automne.

J'ai toujours encore présent dans ma mémoire l'émotion que m'a causé le trajet cet hiver de Paris à Arles. Comme j'ai guetté si cela était déjà du Japon! Enfantillage quoi

Dites donc je vous écrivais l'autre jour que j'avais la vue étrangement fatiguée   Bon je me suis reposé deux jours + demi et puis je me suis remis au travail mais n'osant pas encore aller en plein air J'ai fait toujours pour ma décoration une toile de 30 de ma chambre à coucher avec les meubles en bois blanc que vous savez

Eh bien cela m'a énormément amusé de faire cet intérieur sans rien. D'une simplicité à la Seurat   A teintes plates mais grossièrement brossées en pleine pâte   les murs lilas pâle   le sol d'un rouge rompu + fané les chaises + le lit   jaune de chrôme   les oreillers et le drap citron vert très pâle   la couverture rouge sang   la table à toilette orangée   la cuvette bleue   la fenêtre verte. J'avais voulu exprimer un <u>repos</u> [obliterated] <u>absolu</u> par tous ces tons très divers vous voyez et où il n'y a de blanc que la petite note que donne le miroir à cadre noir (pour fourrer encore la quatrième paire de complémentaires dedans)

Enfin vous verrez cela avec les autres et nous en causerons   car je ne sais souvent pas ce que je fais   travaillant presqu'en somnambule.

Il commence à faire froid surtout les jours de mistral.

J'ai fait mettre le gaz dans l'atelier pour que nous ayons une bonne lumière en hiver.

Peut être serez vous désenchanté d'Arles si vous y venez par un temps de mistral mais attendez . . . C'est à la longue que la poésie d'ici pénètre

Vous ne trouverez pas encore la maison aussi confortable que peu à peu nous chercherons à la rendre   Il y a tant de dépenses et cela ne peut pas se faire d'une seule haleine Enfin je crois qu'une fois ici vous allez comme moi être pris d'une rage de peindre dans les intervalles du mistral les effets d'automne. et que vous comprendrez que j'ai insisté pour que vous veniez ~~avant~~ maintenant qu'il y a de bien beaux jours. Allons   au revoir

t a v

Vincent

Works Cited in Abbreviated Form
LITERATURE

AARON 1985

Olivier Aaron, *Dessins insolites du XVI-IIᵉ français,* Paris, 1985.

AMSTERDAM 1976

All the Paintings of the Rijksmuseum in Amsterdam: A Completely Illustrated Catalogue, Amsterdam, 1976.

ARISI 1986

Ferdinando Arisi, *Giovanni Paolo Panini e i fasti della Roma del '700,* Rome, 1986.

ARSLAN 1952

Edoardo Arslan, "Due disegni e un dipinto di Carpaccio," *Emporium,* vol. 116, 1952, pp. 109–13.

ARTEMIS ANNUAL REPORT 1995–96

Artemis Fine Arts, *Artemis S. A. Consolidated Annual Report,* 1995–96. London, published 1997.

ARTEMIS ANNUAL REPORT 1997–98

Artemis Fine Arts, *Artemis S. A. Consolidated Annual Report,* 1997–98, London, published 1999.

THE ART QUARTERLY 1961

The Art Quarterly 24, no. 1, 1961.

ASHTON ET AL. 1982

Peter Shaw Ashton, Seymour Slive, and Alice Davies, "Jacob van Ruisdael's Trees," *Arnoldia* 42, no. 1, winter 1982, pp. 2–31.

AUBERT 1920

Andreas Aubert, *Maleren Johan Christian Dahl. Et stykee av forrige Aarhundredes Kunst-ock Kulturhistorie,* Oslo, 1920.

AUBRUN 1988

Marie-Madeleine Aubrun, "Une correspondance d'Alexandre Desgoffe," *Bulletin du Musée Ingres* 59–60, 1988, pp. 53–77.

BAILLY-HERZBERG 1980

Janine Bailly-Herzberg, *Correspondance de Camille Pissarro,* 5 vols., Paris, 1980.

BANG 1987

Marie Lødrup Bang, *Johan Christian Dahl, Life and Works,* 3 vols., Oslo, 1987.

BANTZER ET AL. 1994

Andreas Bantzer, Bernhard Lauer, and Karin Mayer-Pasinski, *Gerhardt von Reutern (Willingshäuser Hefte* 4), 1994.

BARON 1973

Wendy Baron, *Sickert,* New York, 1973.

BAUDELAIRE 1965

Charles Baudelaire, *Art in Paris, 1845–1862; Salons and Other Exhibitions Reviewed by Charles Baudelaire,* Jonathan Mayne, trans., London, 1965.

BECKETT 1968

R. B. Beckett, *John Constable's Correspondence,* vol. 6, Ipswich, 1968.

BELL AND GIRTIN 1935

C. F. Bell and Thomas Girtin, "The Drawings and Sketches of John Robert Cozens," *Walpole Society* 23, 1935, pp. 1–87.

BENESCH 1935

Otto Benesch, *Rembrandt: Werk und Forschung,* Vienna, 1935.

BENESCH 1954–57

Otto Benesch, *The Drawings of Rembrandt,* 6 vols., London, 1954–57.

BENESCH 1973

Otto Benesch, *The Drawings of Rembrandt,* 6 vols., revised and enlarged by Eva Benesch, London and New York, 1973.

BERNARD 1911

Émile Bernard, *Lettres de Vincent Van Gogh à Émile Bernard,* Paris, 1911.

BINYON 1925

L. Binyon, *The Followers of William Blake,* London, 1925.

BIRNBAUM 1960

Martin Birnbaum, *The Last Romantic,* New York, 1960.

BLUNT 1954

Anthony Blunt, *The Drawings of G. B. Castiglione & Stefano della Bella in the Collection of Her Majesty the Queen at Windsor Castle,* London, 1954.

BÖRSCH-SUPAN AND JÄHNIG 1973

Helmut Börsch-Supan and Karl Wilhelm Jähnig, *Caspar David Friedrich: Gemälde, Druckgraphik und bildmässige Zeichnungen,* Munich, 1973.

BRAMSEN 1935

Henrik Bramsen, *Landskabsmaleriet i Danmark, 1750–1875,* Copenhagen, 1935.

BREESKIN 1970

Adelyn Dohme Breeskin, *Mary Cassatt: A Catalogue Raisonné of the Oils, Pastels, Watercolors, and Drawings,* Washington, D.C., 1970.

BREESKIN 1979

Adelyn Dohme Breeskin, *Mary Cassatt: A Catalogue Raisonné of the Graphic Work,* Washington, D.C., 1979.

BRETTELL AND LLOYD 1980

Richard Brettell and Christopher Lloyd, *A Catalogue of the Drawings by Camille Pissarro in the Ashmolean Museum, Oxford,* Oxford and New York, 1980.

BROOK 1923

A. Brook, "Henri de Toulouse-Lautrec," *The Arts,* September 1923.

BROOS 1981

Ben Broos, *Rembrandt en tekenaars uit zijn omgeving: Oude tekeningen in het bezit van de Gemeentemusea van Amsterdam waaronder de collectie Fodor,* Amsterdam, 1981.

BROOS 1987

Ben Broos, "'Notitie der teekeningen van Sybrand Feitama,' III: Der verzameling van Sybrand I Feitama (1620–1701) en van Isaac Feitama (1666–1709)," *Oud Holland* 99, 1987, pp. 171–213.

BROOS 1989

Ben Broos, "Improving and Finishing Old Master Drawings: An Art in Itself," *Hoogsteder-Naumann Mercury* 8, 1989, pp. 34–55. ,

CANCOGNI AND PEROCCO 1967

Manlio Cancogni and Guido Perocco, *L'opera completa del Carpaccio,* Milan, 1967.

CANTOR 2000

Jay E. Cantor, "Mary Cassatt: Drawing on Drawing," in *Mary Cassatt: Prints and Drawings from the Artist's Studio,* catalogue by Marc Rosen and Susan Pinsky, Princeton, 2000, pp. 127–33.

CARRÉ 1939

Jean-Marie Carré, *La Vie aventureuse de J.-A. Rimbaud*, nouvelle édition, revue et augmentée, Paris, 1939.

CASSOU AND LEYMARIE 1973

Jean Cassou and Jean Leymarie, *Fernand Léger: Drawings and Gouaches*, Greenwich, 1973.

CLAYTON (in preparation)

Martin Clayton, "Domenico Campagnola's Drawings After Giusto de Menabuoi's Apocalypse Cycle" (in preparation).

COGNIAT AND GEORGE 1950

Raymond Cogniat and Waldemar George, *Oeuvre complète de Roger de la Fresnaye*, Paris, 1950.

COMPIN 1964

Isabelle Compin, *Henri-Edmond Cross*, Paris, 1964.

DAVIES 1992

Alice Davies, *Jan van Kessel (1641–1680)*, Doornspijk, 1992.

DE HAUKE 1961

César M. De Hauke, *Seurat et son œuvre*, 2 vols., Paris, 1961.

DELACROIX 1981

Eugène Delacroix: Journal 1822–1863, Paris, Edition Plon, 1981.

DELÉCLUZE 1855

E. J. Delécluze, *Louis-David: Son école et son temps*, Paris, 1855.

DELTEIL 1906

Loys Delteil, *Le Peintre-graveur illustré, XIXe et XXe siècles, J.-F. Millet et al.*, vol. 1, Paris, 1906.

DELTEIL 1923

Loys Delteil, *Camille Pissarro: L'Oeuvre gravé et lithographie*, Paris, 1923; rev. ed., *Camille Pissarro: The Etchings and Lithographs*, supplemented by Jean Cailac, San Francisco, 1999.

DE VRIES 1915

R. W. P. de Vries, *Cornelis Ploos van Amstel et ses élèves: Essai d'une iconographie*, Amsterdam, 1915.

DOBROKLONSKY 1955

M. V. Dobroklonsky, *Drawings of the Flemish School: 17th–18th Centuries*, Moscow, 1955.

DORTU 1971

M. G. Dortu, *Toulouse-Lautrec et son oeuvre*, New York, 1971.

DOVER ART LIBRARY 1982

Dover Art Library, *Klee: Drawings*, New York, 1982.

EBERTSHÄUSER 1976

Heidi Ebertshäuser, *Adolph von Menzel, Das graphische Werk*, Munich, 1976.

ENGEN 1983

Rodney Engen, *Richard Doyle*, Stroud, 1983.

FEITAMA 1746–58

Sybrand II Feitama, *Notitie der teekeningen van Sybrand Feitama*, MS. 1746–58, Rijksbureau voor Kunsthistorische Documentatie, The Hague, 1746–58.

FEUCHTMAYR 1975

Inge Feuchtmayr, *Johann Christian Reinhart, 1761–1847: Monographie und Werkverzeichnis*, Munich, 1975.

FIOCCO 1958

Giuseppe Fiocco, *Carpaccio*, Venice, 1958.

FISCHER 1972

Stanley W. Fischer, *A Dictionary of Watercolour Paintings, 1750–1900*, London, 1972.

FLANDRIN 1888

Louis Flandrin, *Alexandre Desgoffe*, Paris, 1888.

FRANZKE 1972

Andreas Franzke, "August Lucas, 1803–1863," *Kunst in Hessen und am Mittelrhein* 12, 1972, p. 38.

GALASSI 1991

Peter Galassi, *Corot in Italy. Open-Air Painting and the Classical Landscape Tradition*, New Haven and London, 1991.

GAUNT 1969

William Gaunt, "Jean-François Millet Comes as a Surprise," *The London Times*, 11 November 1969, p. 9.

GAUSS 1976

Ulrike Gauss, *Die Zeichnungen und Aquarelle des 19. Jahrhunderts in der Graphischen Sammlung der Staatsgalerie Stuttgart*, Stuttgart, 1976.

GAZETTE 1882

Obituary of Alexandre Desgoffe, *Gazette des Beaux-Arts* 26, supplement, 1882, p. 203.

GENSEL 1904

Julius Gensel, *Friedrich Preller*, Bielefeld, 1904.

GERSON 1936

Horst Gerson, *Philips Koninck*, Berlin, 1936.

GILTAY 1980

J. Giltay, "De tekeningen van Jacob van Ruisdael," *Oud Holland* 94, 1980, pp. 141–208.

GORDON AND FORGE 1988

R. Gordon and A. Forge, *Degas*, New York, 1988.

GRASHOFF-HEINS 1926

Gerda Grashoff-Heins, *Carus als Maler*, dissertation, Lippstadt, 1926.

GRIGSON 1947

Geoffrey Grigson, *Samuel Palmer: The Visionary Years*, London, 1947.

GROHMANN 1934

Will Grohmann, *The Drawings of Paul Klee*, New York, 1934.

GUATTANI 1806–8

G. A. Guattani, *Memorie Enciclopediche Romane sulle Arti, Antichità . . . ,* 4 vols., Rome, 1806–8.

GUTWIRTH 1979

Susan Gutwirth, "Léon-François-Antoine Fleury (1804–1858), peintre d'après nature," *Bulletin de la Société de l'histoire de l'art français*, 1979, pp. 191–209.

HANNOVER 1898

Emil Hannover, *Maleren C. W. Eckersberg, en studie I dansk kunsthistorie*, Copenhagen, 1898.

HANNOVER 1898a

Emil Hannover, *Maleren C. W. Eckersberg*, Copenhagen, 1898.

HANNOVER 1901

Emil Hannover, *Maleren Constantin Hansen*, Copenhagen, 1901.

HARDIE 1967

Martin Hardie, *Water-colour Painting in Britain*, II, *The Romantic Period*, New York, 1967.

HENKEL 1942

Max Ditmar Henkel, *Tekeningen van Rembrandt en zijn school. Catalogus van de Nederlandse tekenigen in het Rijksmuseum te Amsterdam*, The Hague, 1942.

HESELTINE 1914

J. P. Heseltine, *Drawings and Paintings by Artists of Norfolk and Suffolk in the Collection of J. P. H.*, London, 1914.

HOFSTEDE DE GROOT 1906

Cornelis Hofstede de Groot, *Die Handzeichnungen Rembrandts*, Haarlem, 1906.

HOOZEE 1979

Robert Hoozee, *L'Opera completa di Constable*, Milan, 1979.

HUFFEL 1921

N. G. Huffel, *Cornelis Ploos van Amstel Jacob Corneliszoon, en zijne medwerkers en tijdgenooten: Historische schets van de techniek der Hollandsche prentteekeningen gemaakt in de tweede helft der 18e eeuw*, Utrecht, 1921.

INGAMELLS 1985–92

John Ingamells, *The Wallace Collection Catalogue of Pictures*, 4 vols., London, 1985–92.

ISERMEYER 1940

Christian Adolf Isermeyer, *Philipp Otto Runge (Die Kunstbücher des Volkes 32)*, Berlin, 1940, p. 131.

ISOLA 1976

Maria Catelli Isola, *Disegni di Stefano della Bella dalle collezioni del Gabinetto Nazionale delle Stampe*, Rome, 1976.

JENSEN (forthcoming)

Hannemarie Ragn Jensen, biography of Constantin Hansen (forthcoming).

JOHNSON 1981

Lee Johnson, *The Paintings of Eugène Delacroix*, vol. 3, Oxford, 1981.

JOHNSON 1986

Lee Johnson, *The Paintings of Eugène Delacroix*, vol. 4, Oxford, 1986.

JOOSTEN AND WELSH 1998

Joop M. Joosten and Robert Welsh, *Piet Mondrian: Catalogue Raisonné*, 3 vols., Munich and New York, 1998.

JOSI 1821

Christian Josi, *Collection d'imitations de dessins d'après les principaux maîtres hollandais et flamands*, 2 vols., Amsterdam and London, 1821.

JOYANT 1927

Maurice Joyant, *Henri de Toulouse-Lautrec, 1864–1901, Dessins, estampes, affiches*, Paris, 1927.

KALKSCHMIDT 1943

Eugen Kalkschmidt, *Moritz von Schwind. Der Mann und das Werk*, Munich, 1943.

KENDALL 1998

Richard Kendall, *Degas and The Little Dancer*, with contributions by Douglas W. Druick and Arthur Beale, New Haven and London, 1998.

KRAFFT AND SCHÜMANN 1969

Eva Maria Krafft and Carl-Wolfgang Schümann, *Katalog der Meister des 19. Jahrhunderts in der Hamburger Kunsthalle*, Hamburg, 1969.

LACLOTTE 1956

Michel Laclotte, "Peintures italiennes des XIVe et XVe siècles à l'Orangerie," *Arte Veneta* 10, 1956, pp. 225–32.

LAFOND 1918

P. Lafond, *Degas*, Paris, 1918.

LAPAIRE 1991

Claude Lapaire, *Musée d'art et d'histoire, Genève*, Geneva, 1991.

LAURENTIUS ET AL. 1980

Th. Laurentius, J. W. Niemeijer, and G. Ploos van Amstel, *Cornelis Ploos van Amstel (1726–1798): Kunstverzamelaar en prentuitgever*, Assen, 1980.

LAUTS 1962

Jan Lauts, *Carpaccio: Paintings and Drawings. Complete Edition*, London, 1962.

LEMOISNE 1946

P. A. Lemoisne, *Degas et Son Oeuvre*, Paris, 1946.

LEPOITTEVIN 1973

Lucien Lepoittevin, *Jean-François Millet*, 2 vols., Paris, 1973.

LETTERS 1974

The Letters of Samuel Palmer, R. Lister, ed., Oxford, London, 1974.

LÉVÊQUE 1987

Jean-Jacques Lévêque, *L'art et la Révolution Française 1789–1804*, Neuchâtel, 1987.

LEVRON 1937

Jacques Levron, ed., *Lettre au conservateur de ses collections (Lancelot Théodore, comte Turpin de Crissé)*, Angers, 1937.

LIEVORE 1994

Pietro Lievore, ed., *Padua: Baptistery of the Cathedral. Frescoes by Giusto de Menabuoi*, 2d ed., Padua, 1994.

LIPPMANN 1882–92

F. Lippmann, *Original Drawings by Rembrandt*, 2 vols., Berlin and The Hague, 1882–92.

LISTER 1988

Raymond Lister, *Catalogue Raisonné of the Works of Samuel Palmer*, Cambridge and New York, 1988.

LUGT 1915

Frits Lugt, "Wandelingen met Rembrandt in Amsterdam," *Feest-Bundel Dr. Abraham Bredius*, Amsterdam, 1915.

LUGT 1920

Frits Lugt, *Mit Rembrandt in Amsterdam*, Berlin, 1920.

LUGT 1921

Frits Lugt, *Les Marques de collections de dessins et d'estampes . . .* , Amsterdam, 1921.

LUTTEROTTI 1940

Otto R. von Lutterotti, *Joseph Anton Koch, 1768–1839, Mit Werkverzeichnis und Briefen des Künstlers*, Berlin, 1940.

LUTTEROTTI 1985

Otto R. von Lutterotti, *Joseph Anton Koch, 1768–1839, Leben und Werk, Mit einem vollständigen Werkverzeichnis*, Vienna and Munich, 1985.

MADELEINE-PERDRILLAT 1990

Alain Madeleine-Perdrillat, *Georges Seurat*, Geneva, 1990.

MADSEN 1931

Karl Madsen, *Malerier af Johan Thomas Lundbye*, Copenhagen, 1931.

MADSEN 1949

Karl Madsen, *J. Th. Lundbye*, Copenhagen, 1949.

MATHEWS 1994

Nancy Mowll Mathews, *Mary Cassatt: A Life*, New Haven and London, 1994.

MEIER-GRAEFE 1920

J. Meier-Graefe, *Degas*, Munich, 1920.

MELLERIO 1913

André Mellerio, *Odilon Redon*, Paris, 1913.

MESSERER 1961

Richard Messerer, *Georg von Dillis*, Munich, 1961.

MEURICE 1898

Paul Meurice, ed., *The Letters of Victor Hugo from Exile and After the Fall of the Empire*, Boston and New York, 1898.

MICHEL 1893

E. Michel, *Rembrandt: Sa Vie, son œuvre et son temps*, Paris, 1893.

MIDDLETON 1983

Christopher Middleton, ed., *Johann Wolfgang von Goethe, Selected Poems*, Boston, 1983.

MIOTTI 1962

Tito Miotti, *Il collezionista di disegni*, Venice, 1962.

MONGAN 1969

Agnes Mongan, *Ingres as a Great Portrait Draughtsman*, in *Colloque Ingres* [1967], Montauban, 1969.

MORASSI 1937

Antonio Morassi, *Disegni antichi dalla Collezione Rasini in Milano*, Milan, 1937.

MOREAU-NÉLATON AND ROBAUT 1905

E. Moreau-Nélaton and Alfred Robaut, *L'Oeuvre de Corot*, Paris, 1905.

MORGAN LIBRARY ANNUAL REPORT 1995

The Pierpont Morgan Library, *Annual Report 1995*, New York, 1996.

MRC

Mellerio Redon Chronology (MRC), from Odilon Redon's documentation of his art, contained in the Mellerio Redon papers, in the collection of the Ryerson and Burnham Libraries at the Art Institute of Chicago (forthcoming).

MURARO 1966

Michelangelo Muraro, *Vittorio Carpaccio*, Florence, 1966.

MURARO 1977

Michelangelo Muraro, *I disegni di Vittore Carpaccio*, Florence, 1977.

NAEF 1956

Hans Naef, "Zwei unveröffentlichte Ingres-Zeichnungen," *Schweizer Monatshefte*, Zurich, March 1956.

NAEF 1958

Hans Naef, "Ein unveröffentlichtes Meisterwerk von Ingres im Städelschen Kunstinstitut," *Die Weltkunst*, Munich, 15 February 1958.

NAEF 1977–80

Hans Naef, *Die Bildniszeichnungen von J.-A.-D. Ingres*, 5 vols., Bern, 1977–80.

NÎMES 1940

Musée des Beaux-Arts, Ville de Nîmes: Catalogue, Nîmes, 1940.

NØRREGÅRD-NIELSEN (forthcoming)

Hans Edvard Nørregård-Nielsen, catalogue raisonné and biography of Johan Thomas Lundbye (forthcoming).

NUGENT 1925–30

M. Nugent, *Alla mostra della pittura italiana del sei e settecento*, 2 vols., San Casciano, 1925–30.

OPPÉ 1951

A. P. Oppé, ed., "Memoirs of Thomas Jones," *Walpole Society* 32, 1951, pp. 1–143.

OPPENHEIM 1986

Irving J. Oppenheim, "Domenico Campagnola and an Earthquake Fantasy," *Earthquake Spectra* 2, no. 3, 1986, pp. 631–34.

PACH 1948

Walter Pach, trans., *The Journal of Eugène Delacroix*, New York, 1948.

PALMER 1892

A. H. Palmer, *The Life and Letters of Samuel Palmer*, London, 1892 (reprinted 1972).

PAPENDORF 1970

Dr. Papendorf, review of the 1970 Schweinfurt C. G. Carus exhibition, *Die Weltkunst*, 1970, vol. 15, no. 24, p. 1,640.

PASQUALI (forthcoming)

Marilena Pasquali, *Catalogue raisonné of the work of Giorgio Morandi* (forthcoming).

PÉROUSE DE MONTCLOS 1994

Jean-Marie Pérouse de Montclos, *Étienne-Louis Boullée*, Paris, 1994.

PIGNATTI 1963

Terisio Pignatti, review of Jan Lauts, *Carpaccio: Paintings and Drawings*, London, 1962, *Master Drawings* 1, no. 4, 1963, pp. 47–54.

PIGNATTI 1972

Terisio Pignatti, *Carpaccio*, Milan, 1972.

PISSARRO AND VENTURI 1939

Lodovic Rodo Pissarro and Lionello Venturi, *Camille Pissarro: Son art—son oeuvre*, Paris, 1939.

POINTON 1985

Marcia Pointon, *The Bonington Circle: English Watercolour and Anglo-French Landscape, 1790–1855*, Brighton, Sussex, 1985.

POPHAM AND WILDE 1949

A. E. Popham and Johannes Wilde, *The Italian Drawings of the XV and XVI Centuries in the Collection of His Majesty the King at Windsor Castle*, London, 1949.

POTTER 1984

Margaret Potter, *The David and Peggy Rockefeller Collection*, vol. 1, *European Works of Art*, New York, 1984.

PRAUSE 1968

Marianne Prause, *Carl Gustav Carus: Leben und Werk*, Berlin, 1968.

REWALD 1944

J. Rewald, *Degas—Works in Sculpture*, New York, 1944.

REYNOLDS 1984

Graham Reynolds, *The Later Paintings and Drawings of John Constable*, 2 vols., New Haven and London, 1984.

RHEINISCHE MERKUR 1956

[Author unknown], "Zwei Ingres-Zeichnungen," *Rheinische Merkur* 13, Cologne, 1956, p. 8.

RIMBAUD 1955

Rimbaud: Pages choisies, Paris, 1955.

ROBAUT 1905

Alfred Robaut, *L'Oeuvre de Corot, par Robaut; catalogue raisonné et illustré, précédé de l'histoire de Corot et de ses oeuvres, par Etienne Moreau-Nélaton, orné de dessins et croquis originaux du maître*, Paris, 1905.

ROETHLISBERGER 1962

Marcel Roethlisberger, *Claude Lorrain: L'Album Wildenstein*, Paris, 1962.

ROETHLISBERGER 1962a

Marcel Roethlisberger, "Claude Lorrain: ses plus beaux dessins retrouvés," *Connaissance des Arts*, no. 130, December 1962, pp. 138–47.

ROETHLISBERGER 1968

Marcel Roethlisberger, *Claude Lorrain: The Drawings*, 2 vols., Berkeley and Los Angeles, 1968.

ROETHLISBERGER 1971

Marcel Roethlisberger, *The Claude Lorrain Album in the Norton Simon Inc. Museum of Art*, Los Angeles, 1971.

ROSENTHAL 1982

Michael Rosenthal, *British Landscape Painting*, Ithaca, New York, 1982.

ROYALTON-KISCH 1988

Martin Royalton-Kisch, *Adriaen van de Venne's Album in the Department of Prints and Drawings in the British Museum*, London, 1988.

RUCHAU 1946

François Ruchau, *Rimbaud: Documents iconographiques*, Geneva, 1946.

RUHMER ET AL. 1969

Eberhard Ruhmer with Rosel Gollek, Christoph Heilmann, Hermann Kuhn, and Regina Löwe, *Schack-Galerie: Vollständiger Katalog*, Munich, 1969.

SCHMID 1998

F. Carlo Schmid, *Naturansichten und Ideallandschaften: Die Landschaftsgraphik von Johann Christian Reinhart und seinem Umkreis*, Berlin, 1998.

SCHREIBER 1819

Aloys Wilhelm Schreiber, *The Traveller's Guide Down the Rhine: Exhibiting the Course of that River from Schaffhausen to Holland and Describing the Moselle from Coblentz to Treves*, translated from German, London, 1819.

SCHULMAN 1997

Michel Schulman, *Théodore Rousseau, 1812–1867: Catalogue raisonné de l'oeuvre graphique*, Paris, 1997.

SCHULMAN 1999

Michel Schulman, *Théodore Rousseau, 1812–1867: Catalogue raisonné de l'oeuvre peint*, Paris, 1999.

SELIGMAN 1947

Germain Seligman, *The Drawings of Georges Seurat*, New York, 1947.

SELIGMAN 1969

Germain Seligman, *Roger de la Fresnaye: With a catalogue raisonné*, Greenwich, 1969.

SELLARS 1974

James Sellars, *Samuel Palmer*, London, 1974.

SGARBI 1994

Vittorio Sgarbi, *Carpaccio*, Milan, 1994.

SHACKELFORD 1984

G. Shackelford, *Degas: The Dancers*, Washington, 1984.

SHAPIRO 1991

David Shapiro, *Mondrian: Flowers*, New York, 1991.

SLIVE 1965

Seymour Slive, *Drawings of Rembrandt*, New York, 1965.

SLIVE 2001

Seymour Slive, *Jacob van Ruisdael: A Complete Catalogue of His Paintings, Drawings, and Etchings*, New Haven and London, 2001.

THE ST. LOUIS ART MUSEUM 1975

The St. Louis Art Museum, *The St. Louis Art Museum: Handbook of the Collections*, St. Louis, 1975.

SUMOWSKI 1979–92

Werner Sumowski, *Drawings of the Rembrandt School*, 10 vols., New York, 1979–92.

SUMOWSKI 1983–90

Werner Sumowski, *Die Gemälde der Rembrandt-Schüler*, 6 vols., Landau in der Pfalz, 1983–90.

TALBOT 1971

Charles W. Talbot, ed., *Dürer in America. His Graphic Work*, Washington, D.C., 1971.

TERRASSE 1976

Antoine Terrasse, *L'Univers de Théodore Rousseau*, Paris, 1976.

THOMPSON 1957

Francis Thompson (foreword), *Old Master Drawings at Chatsworth: Reproductions of Thirty of the Drawings by Rembrandt van Rijn (1606–1669)*, Derby, 1957.

TIETZE AND TIETZE-CONRAT 1944

Hans Tietze and Erika Tietze-Conrat, *The Drawings of the Venetian Painters in the Fifteenth and Sixteenth Centuries*, New York, 1944.

TRAEGER 1975

Jörg Traeger, *Philipp Otto Runge und sein Werk*, Munich, 1975.

VAD 1992

Poul Vad, *Vilhelm Hammershøi and Danish Art at the Turn of the Century*, Kenneth Tindall, trans., New Haven and London, 1992.

VALLOTTON AND GOERG 1972

Maxime Vallotton and Charles Goerg, *Félix Vallotton: catalogue raisonné de l'oeuvre gravé et lithographie*, Geneva, 1972.

VAN GOGH 1978

Vincent van Gogh, *The Complete Letters of Vincent van Gogh*, Greenwich, Connecticut, 2d ed., 1978.

VARNHAGEN VON ENSE 1865

Karl August Varnhagen von Ense, *Tagebücher*, Zurich, 1865.

VIATTE 1974

Françoise Viatte, *Inventaire général des dessins italiens. II. Dessins de Stefano della Bella*, Paris, 1974.

WAETZOLDT 1951

Stephan Waetzoldt, *Philipp Otto Runge, "Vier Zeiten,"* dissertation, Hamburg, 1951.

WEIGMANN 1906

Otto Weigmann, *Schwind: Des Meisters Werke in 1265 Abbildungen* (Klassiker der Kunst, vol. 9), Stuttgart and Leipzig, 1906.

WEIGMANN 1925

Otto Weigmann, "Schwinds Entwürfe für ein Schubertzimmer," *Münchner Jahrbuch der Bildenden Kunst*, vol. 2, 1925.

WEINRAUTNER 1997

Ina Weinrautner, *Friedrich Preller d. Ä. (1804–1878): Leben und Werk*, Münster, 1997.

WILDENSTEIN 1992

Alec Wildenstein, *Odilon Redon: Catalogue raisonné, I, Portraits et figures*, I, Paris, 1992.

WIRTH 1965

Irmgard Wirth, *Mit Adolph Menzel in Berlin*, Munich, 1965.

ZAMPETTI 1966

Pietro Zampetti, *Vittore Carpaccio*, Venice, 1966.

EXHIBITIONS

AMSTERDAM 1969

Rijksmuseum, Amsterdam, *Rembrandt 1669/1969*, catalogue by P. J. J. van Thiel, ed., 1969.

AMSTERDAM AND OTTERLO 1990

Rijksmuseum Vincent van Gogh, Amsterdam, and Rijksmuseum Kröller-Müller, Otterlo, *Vincent van Gogh*, 1990.

AMSTERDAM AND PARIS 1998–99

Amsterdam Municipal Archives, and Institut Néerlandais, Paris, *Landscapes of Rembrandt: His Favorite Walks*, catalogue by Boudewijn Bakker, 1998–99.

BALTIMORE 1964

The Baltimore Museum of Art, *1914: An Exhibition of Paintings, Drawings, and Sculpture. In Celebration of the 50th Anniversary of The Baltimore Museum of Art*, 1964.

BERLIN 1955

Nationalgalerie, Berlin, *Adolph Menzel Zeichnungen*, catalogue by Werner Schmidt, 1955.

BERNE 1960

Kunstmuseum Berne, *Corot*, 1960.

BIELEFELD AND ELSEWHERE 1983–84

Kunsthalle Bielefeld, Staatliche Kunsthalle Baden-Baden, and Kunsthaus Zurich, *Seurat, Zeichnungen*, 1983–84.

BOSTON 1919–20

Museum of Fine Arts, Boston, [loan exhibition, title unknown], 1919–20.

BOSTON 1946

Museum of Fine Arts, Boston, *An Exhibition of Paintings, Drawings and Prints by J. M. W. Turner, John Constable, R. P. Bonington*, 1946.

BOSTON 1984

Museum of Fine Arts, Boston, *Jean-François Millet*, catalogue by Alexandra R. Murphy, 1984.

BREMEN 1977–78

Kunsthalle Bremen, *Zurück zur Natur: Die Künstlerkolonie von Barbizon: Ihre Vorgeschichte und ihre Auswirjung*, 1977–78.

BROOKLYN 1957

The Brooklyn Museum, *Trends in Watercolors Today: 19th Biennial International Watercolor Exhibition*, 1957.

BRUSSELS 1994

Galerie d'Arenberg, Brussels, *Souvenirs d'Italie (1825–1829) de Gilles-François-Joseph Closson (Liège 1796–1842)*, exhibited at The European Fine Art Fair, Maastricht, 1994.

BRUSSELS 1999

Musée d'Ixelles, Brussels, *Victor Hugo dessinateur*, 1999.

BRUSSELS AND ELSEWHERE 1968–69

Bibliothèque Albert I, Brussels; The Boijmans Van Beuningen Museum, Rotterdam; Institut Néerlandais, Paris; and Musée des Beaux-Arts, Bern, *Dessins de paysagistes hollandais du XVIIᵉ siècle à l'Institut Néerlandais à Paris*, catalogue by Carlos van Hasselt, 1968–69.

BUENOS AIRES 1971

Galeria Wildenstein, Buenos Aires, *J-F. Millet*, 1971.

CAMBRIDGE 1929

Fogg Art Museum, Harvard University, Cambridge, Massachusetts, [title unknown], 1929.

CAMBRIDGE 1958

Fogg Art Museum, Harvard University, Cambridge, Massachusetts, *Drawings from the Collection of Curtis O. Baer*, catalogue by Agnes Mongan, 1958.

CAMBRIDGE 1967

Fogg Art Museum, Harvard University, Cambridge, Massachusetts, *Ingres Centennial Exhibition*, 1967.

CAMBRIDGE 1984

Fitzwilliam Museum, Cambridge, *Samuel Palmer and "The Ancients,"* catalogue by Raymond Lister, 1984.

CAMBRIDGE AND MONTREAL 1988

Arthur M. Sackler Museum, Harvard University, Cambridge, Massachusetts, and Montreal Museum of Fine Arts, *Landscape in Perspective: Drawings by Rembrandt and His Contemporaries*, catalogue by Frederik J. Duparc, 1988.

CHICAGO 1930–31

Art Institute of Chicago, *Loan Exhibition of Paintings, Drawings, Prints and Posters by Henri de Toulouse-Lautrec*, 1930–31.

CHICAGO 1935

The Renaissance Society of the University of Chicago, *Twenty-four Paintings and Drawings by Georges-Pierre Seurat*, 1935.

CHICAGO AND ELSEWHERE 1969–70

Art Institute of Chicago, Minneapolis Institute of Arts, and Detroit Institute of Arts, *Rembrandt After 300 Years*, catalogue by Egbert Haverkamp-Begemann, Anne-Marie Logan, and others, 1969–70.

CHICAGO AND ELSEWHERE 1994–95

Art Institute of Chicago, Van Gogh Museum, Amsterdam, and Royal Academy of Arts, London, *Odilon Redon: Prince of Dreams, 1840–1916*, catalogue by Douglas W. Druick et al., 1994–95.

COPENHAGEN 1931

Kunstforeningen, Copenhagen, [title unknown], 1931.

COPENHAGEN AND ELSEWHERE 1997–98

Ordrupgaard, Copenhagen, Musée d'Orsay, Paris, and Solomon R. Guggenheim Museum, New York, *Vilhelm Hammershøi (1864–1916): Danish Painter of Solitude and Light*, 1997–98.

DARMSTADT 1953

Hessisches Landesmuseum, Darmstadt, *August Lucas 1803–1863. Ausstellung zum Hundertfünfzigsten Geburtsjahr*, catalogue by Gisela Bergsträsser, 1953.

DARMSTADT AND MUNICH 1995–97

Hessisches Landesmuseum, Darmstadt, and Haus der Kunst, Munich, *Carl Philipp Fohr: Romantik-Landschaft und Historie*, catalogue by Peter Märker, 1995–97.

DETROIT AND PHILADELPHIA CA. 1968

Detroit Institute of Arts and Philadelphia Museum of Art, *Romantic Art in Britain: Paintings and Drawings 1760–1860*, ca. 1968.

DORTMUND 1956

Museum für Kunst und Kulturgeschichte, Schloss Cappenberg,

Dortmund, *Blick aus dem Fenster: Gemälde und Zeichnungen der Romantik und des Biedermeier*, 1956.

FLORENCE 1922

Palazzo Pitti, Florence, *Mostra della pittura italiana del seicento e settecento*, 1922.

FLORENCE 1931

Palazzo Vecchio, Florence, *Mostra del giardino italiano*, 1931.

FLORENCE 1965

Palazzo Strozzi, Florence, *70 pitture e sculture del '600 e '700 fiorentino*, catalogue by Mina Gregori, 1965.

FRANKFURT 2000

Städtische Galerie im Städelschen Kunstinstitut, Frankfurt-am-Main, *"Nach dem Leben und aus der Phantasie": Niederländische Zeichnungen vom 15. bis 18. Jahrhunderts aus dem Städelschen Kunstinstitut*, catalogue by Annette Strech, 2000.

GENEVA 1988

Musée d'Art et d'Histoire, Geneva, *Berggruen Collection*, 1988.

GENEVA AND PARIS 1992

Musée d'Art et d'Histoire, Geneva, and Musée du Louvre, Paris, *Dessins de Liotard*, catalogue by Anne de Herdts, 1992.

THE HAGUE AND CAMBRIDGE 1981–82

Mauritshuis, The Hague, and Fogg Art Museum, Harvard University, Cambridge, Massachusetts, *Jacob van Ruisdael*, catalogue by Seymour Slive and H. R. Hoetinck, 1981–82.

HAMBURG 1935

Kunstverein Hamburg, *Frühjahrsaustellung des Hamburger Künstlerverein im Kunstverein*, 1935.

HAMM AND ELSEWHERE 1984

Gustav-Lübcke-Museum, Hamm, Magistrat der Stadt and Kunstverein, Darmstadt, and Oberhessisches Museum, Giessen, *Zeichnungen Darmstädter Romantiker: Aus der Sammlung Hugo von Ritgen*, catalogue by Hans Wille, 1984.

HEIDELBERG 1925

Kurpfälzisches Museum, Heidelberg, *Carl Fohr und die Maler um ihn*, 1925.

HEIDELBERG 1968

Kurpfälzisches Museum, Heidelberg, *Carl Fohr 1795–1818, Skizzenbuch der Neckargegend Badisches Skizzenbuch*, 1968.

HEIDELBERG AND MUNICH 1998

Kurpfälzisches Museum, Heidelberg, and Kunsthalle der Hypo-Kulturstiftung, Munich, *Landschaft als Geschichte: Carl Rottmann, 1797–1850. Hofmaler König Ludwig I*, catalogue by Christoph Heilmann and Erika Rödiger-Diruf, eds., 1998.

HOUSTON AND ELSEWHERE 1989–90

The Museum of Fine Arts, Houston, The Phillips Collection, Washington, D.C., and The Brooklyn Museum, *The Intimate Interiors of Edouard Vuillard*, catalogue by Elizabeth Wynne Easton, 1989–90.

LAUSANNE 1985

Bibliothèque des Arts, Lausanne, *Vallotton*, with essays by Günter Busch, Bernard Dorival, Patrick Grainville, and Doris Jakubec, 1985.

LEIPZIG 1938

C. G. Boerner, Leipzig, *Deutsche Handzeichnungen Der Romantikerzeit*, 1938.

LIVERPOOL 1937

Walker's Galleries, Liverpool, *Early English Watercolours*, 1937.

LONDON 1787

Royal Academy of Arts, London, [untitled exhibition], 1787.

LONDON 1883

Grosvenor Gallery, London, [untitled exhibition], 1883.

LONDON 1929

Royal Academy of Arts, Burlington House, London, *Exhibition of Dutch Art*, 1929.

LONDON 1931

Alex Reid & Lefevre, Ltd., London, *Paintings and Drawings by Roger de la Fresnaye*, 1931.

LONDON 1964

Victoria and Albert Museum, London, *The Orange and the Rose: Holland and Britain in the Age of Observation, 1600–1750*, catalogue by A. G. H. Bachrach, ed., 1964.

LONDON 1964a

Arts Council of Great Britain, London, *Delacroix*, 1964.

LONDON 1969

Wildenstein & Co. Ltd., London, *J.-F. Millet*, 1969.

LONDON 1978

Hazlitt, Gooden & Fox, London, *Gerhardt Wilhelm von Reutern 1794–1865: Drawings and Watercolours*, 1978.

LONDON 1982–83

The Tate Gallery, London, *Richard Wilson: The Landscape of Reaction*, catalogue by David H. Solkin, 1982–83.

LONDON 1983–84

Victoria and Albert Museum, London, *Richard Doyle and His Family*, 1983–84.

LONDON 1985

Royal Academy of Arts, London, *Edward Lear: 1812–1888*, 1985.

LONDON 1991

National Gallery of Art, London, *Van Gogh to Picasso: The Berggruen Collection at the National Gallery*, catalogue by Richard Kendall, 1991.

LONDON 1994

Fine Arts Society, London, [title unknown], 1994.

LONDON 1996–97

Royal Academy of Arts, London, *From Mantegna to Picasso: Drawings from the Thaw Collection at The Pierpont Morgan Library, New York*, catalogue by Cara Dufour Denison et al., 1996–97.

LONDON 1998

Thomas Williams, London, *Old Master Drawings*, n.d. [1998].

LONDON 1998a

Hazlitt, Gooden & Fox, London, *Nineteenth- and Early-Twentieth-Century Drawings and Oil Sketches*, 1998.

LONDON 1998b

Thos. Agnew and Sons, Ltd., London, *English Watercolours, Drawings, and Small Oil Paintings: 125th Annual Exhibition*, 1998.

LONDON 1999

National Gallery of Art, London, *A Brush with Nature, The Gere Collection of Landscape Oil Sketches*, catalogue by Christopher Riopelle and Xavier Bray, with an essay by Charlotte Gere, 1999.

LONDON 2000

Thos. Agnew & Sons, Ltd., London, *Millennium Exhibition*, 2000.

LONDON 2001

Kate de Rothschild at Didier Aaron, London, *Master Drawings*, 2001.

LONDON AND ELSEWHERE 1999

National Gallery, London, National Gallery of Art, Washington, D.C., and The Metropolitan Museum of Art, New York, *Portraits by Ingres*, 1999.

LOS ANGELES 1959

Los Angeles Municipal Art Gallery, *The Collection of Mr. and Mrs. John Rewald*, 1959.

LOS ANGELES AND ELSEWHERE 1993–94

Los Angeles County Museum of Art, The Metropolitan Museum of Art, New York, and National Gallery of Art, London, *Caspar David Friedrich to Ferdinand Hodler: A Romantic Tradition, Nineteenth-Century Paintings and Drawings from the Oskar Reinhart Foundation, Winterthur*, catalogue by Peter Wegmann et al., 1993–94.

LUGANO 1980

Villa Malpensata, Lugano, [title unknown], 1980.

MANCHESTER 1961

Manchester City Art Gallery, *Old Master Drawings from Chatsworth*, catalogue by J. Byam Shaw, 1961.

MANCHESTER 1993

Whitworth Art Gallery, University of Manchester, *From View to Vision: British Watercolours from Sandby to Turner in the Whitworth Art Gallery*, 1993.

MANCHESTER AND CAMBRIDGE 1993

Whitworth Art Gallery, University of Manchester, and Fitzwilliam Museum, Cambridge, *"Nature's Way," Romantic Landscapes from Norway: Oil Studies, Watercolours and Drawings by Johan Christian Dahl (1788–1857) and Thomas Fearnley (1802–1842)*, catalogue by Jane Munro, ed., 1993.

MANCHESTER AND LONDON 1971

Whitworth Art Gallery, University of Manchester, and Victoria and Albert Museum, London, *Watercolours by John Robert Cozens*, 1971.

MONTREAL 1993–94

Canadian Centre for Architecture, Montreal, *Exploring Rome: Piranesi and His Contemporaries*, catalogue by Cara D. Denison et al., 1993–94.

MOSCOW AND ST. PETERSBURG 1998

Pushkin Museum, Moscow, and State Hermitage Museum, St. Petersburg, *French Master Drawings from The Pierpont Morgan Library*, (in Russian), 1998.

MUNICH 1927

Ludwigsgalerie, Munich, *Carl Philipp Fohr nebst einigen Arbeiten von anderen Künstlern seiner Zeit*, 1927.

MUNICH 1999–2000

Bayerisches Nationalmuseum, Munich, *Das neue Hellas: Griechen und Bayern zur Zeit Ludwigs I*, catalogue by Reinhold Baumstark, ed., 1999–2000.

MUNICH AND DRESDEN 1991–92

Neue Pinakothek, Munich, and Albertinum, Dresden, *Johann Georg von Dillis, 1759–1841: Landschaft und Menschenbild*, catalogue by Christoph Heilmann et al., 1991–92.

NEW HAVEN 1977

Yale Center for British Art, New Haven, *English Landscape 1630–1850, Drawings, Prints and Books from the Paul Mellon Collection*, catalogue by Christopher White, 1977.

NEW HAVEN 1980

Yale Center for British Art, New Haven, *The Art of Alexander and John Robert Cozens*, catalogue by Andrew Wilton, 1980.

NEW HAVEN 1982

Yale Center for British Art, New Haven, *Presences of Nature: British Landscape 1780–1830*, catalogue by Louis Hawes, 1982.

NEW YORK 1931

The Museum of Modern Art, New York, *Tenth Loan Exhibition, Lautrec–Redon*, 1931.

NEW YORK 1946

Wildenstein and Co., New York, *A Loan Exhibition of Toulouse-Lautrec for the Benefit of the Goddard Neighborhood Center*, 1946.

NEW YORK 1947

Buchholz Gallery/Curt Valentin, New York, *Seurat, His Drawings*, 1947.

NEW YORK 1951

Jacques Seligmann & Co., New York, *Master Drawings of Five Centuries*, 1951.

NEW YORK 1953

New School for Social Research, New York, *Drawings of the Past and Present Time*, 1953.

NEW YORK 1956

The Museum of Modern Art, New York, *Toulouse-Lautrec Paintings, Drawings, Posters, and Lithographs*, 1956.

NEW YORK 1959

The Metropolitan Museum of Art, New York, *French Drawings from American Collections: Clouet to Matisse*, 1959.

NEW YORK 1959a

Charles E. Slatkin Galleries, New York, *French Master Drawings*, 1959.

NEW YORK 1960–61

The Museum of Modern Art, New York, *One Hundred Drawings*, 1960–61.

NEW YORK 1962–63

The Museum of Modern Art, New York, *Drawings and Recent Acquisitions*, 1962–63.

NEW YORK 1964

Wildenstein and Co., New York, *Toulouse-Lautrec*, 1964.

NEW YORK 1968

Davis Galleries, New York, *Edward Lear, David Roberts*, 1968.

NEW YORK 1973

The Pierpont Morgan Library, New York, *Drawings from the Collection of Lore and Rudolf Heinemann*, catalogue by Felice Stampfle and Cara D. Denison, 1973.

NEW YORK 1984

The Metropolitan Museum of Art, New York, *Van Gogh in Arles*, catalogue by Ronald Pickvance, 1984.

NEW YORK 1986

Zangrilli and Brady Co., New York, *French and English Drawings, 1700–1875*, 1986.

NEW YORK 1991

Sidney Janis Gallery, New York, *Mondrian/Flowers in American Collections*, 1991.

NEW YORK 1992

Bob P. Haboldt & Co., New York and Paris, *Old Master Paintings: French, Northern and Italian Schools*, 1992.

NEW YORK 1992a

The Pierpont Morgan Library, New York, *Sketching at Home and Abroad:*

British Landscape Drawings, 1750–1850, catalogue by Evelyn J. Phimister, Stephanie Wiles, and Cara D. Denison, 1992.

NEW YORK 1994

The Pierpont Morgan Library, New York, *The Thaw Collection: Master Drawings and New Acquisitions,* catalogue by Cara D. Denison, Peter Dreyer, Evelyn J. Phimister, and Stephanie Wiles, 1994.

NEW YORK 1995

Bob P. Haboldt & Co., New York and Paris, *Fifty Paintings by Old Masters,* 1995.

NEW YORK 1995a

The Pierpont Morgan Library, New York, *Fantasy and Reality: Drawings from the Sunny Crawford von Bülow Collection,* catalogue by Cara Dufour Denison with contributions by Stephanie Wiles and Ruth S. Kraemer, 1995.

NEW YORK 1996

The Metropolitan Museum of Art, New York, *Genoa: Drawings and Prints, 1530–1800,* catalogue by Carmen Bambach, Nadine M. Orenstein, and William M. Griswold, 1996.

NEW YORK 1996a

Richard L. Feigen and Co., New York, *A Century of Landscape Painting: England and France, 1770–1870,* 1996.

NEW YORK 1996b

James Mackinnon at W. M. Brady and Co., New York, *Aspects of Landscape: 1760–1880,* 1996.

NEW YORK 1996c

W. M. Brady and Co., New York, *Drawings and Pictures: Recent Acquisitions,* 1996.

NEW YORK 1997

Artemis Fine Arts, New York, *Selected Nineteenth-Century Paintings & Works on Paper,* 1997.

NEW YORK 1997–98

The Pierpont Morgan Library, New York, *From Romanticism to Realism: German Drawings in The Pierpont Morgan Library,* 1997–98.

NEW YORK 1997–98a

The Pierpont Morgan Library, New York, *On Wings of a Song: A Celebration of Schubert and Brahms,* 1997–98.

NEW YORK 1998

Artemis Fine Arts, New York, *Nineteenth-Century Paintings and Works on Paper,* 1998.

NEW YORK 1998a

The Drawing Center, New York, *Shadows of a Hand: The Drawings of Victor Hugo,* catalogue by Florian Rodari, Pierre Georgel, Luc Sante, and Marie-Laure Prévost, 1998.

NEW YORK 1998b

The Pierpont Morgan Library, New York, *To Observe and Imagine: British Drawings and Watercolors, 1600–1900,* catalogue by Stephanie Wiles, 1998.

NEW YORK 1998c

James Mackinnon at W. M. Brady and Co., New York, *Paintings and Sketches 1780–1870,* London, 1998.

NEW YORK 1999

The Pierpont Morgan Library, New York, *New York Collects: Drawings and Watercolors, 1900–1950,* 1999.

NEW YORK 1999a

Artemis Fine Arts, New York, *Danish Paintings of the Golden Age,* 1999.

NEW YORK 2000

W. M. Brady and Co., New York, *Old Master Drawings,* 2000.

NEW YORK 2000a

Marc Rosen Fine Art, Ltd., New York, *From the Artist's Studio: Unknown Prints and Drawings by Mary Cassatt,* catalogue by Marc Rosen and Susan Pinsky, exhibited at Adelson Galleries, Inc., New York, 2000.

NEW YORK 2000–2001

The Pierpont Morgan Library, New York, *Claude Lorrain and the Ideal Landscape,* 2000–2001.

NEW YORK 2000–2001a

Emmanuel Moatti, New York, *Giovanni-Battista Camuccini: Oil Sketches of the Roman Countryside, 1840s,* 2000–2001.

NEW YORK 2001

The Pierpont Morgan Library, New York, *The World Observed: Five Centuries of Drawings from the Collection of Charles Ryskamp,* catalogue by William M. Griswold, Cara Dufour Denison, Kathleen Stuart, and Jennifer Tonkovich, 2001.

NEW YORK 2001a

Emmanuel Moatti, New York, *Master Drawings, 1600–1900,* 2001.

NEW YORK AND CHICAGO 1961–62

The Museum of Modern Art, New York, and Art Institute of Chicago, *Redon-Moreau-Bresdin,* 1961–62.

NEW YORK AND DÜSSELDORF 1999

Artemis Fine Arts, New York, and C. G. Boerner, Düsseldorf, *Neue Lagerliste 111 (1999), German Drawings, 1600–1900,* 1999.

NEW YORK AND PARIS 1977–78

The Pierpont Morgan Library, New York, and Institut Néerlandais, Paris, *Rembrandt and His Century: Dutch Drawings of the Seventeenth Century from the Collection of Frits Lugt, Institut Néerlandais, Paris,* catalogue by Carlos van Hasselt, 1977–78.

NEW YORK AND ELSEWHERE 1956–57

The Museum of Modern Art, New York, City Art Museum, St. Louis, and California Palace of the Legion of Honor, San Francisco, *Masters of British Painting, 1800–1950,* 1956–57.

NEW YORK AND ELSEWHERE 1972

The Pierpont Morgan Library, New York, Royal Academy of Arts, London, and the Yale Center for British Art, New Haven, *English Drawings and Watercolors, 1550–1850, in the Collection of Mr. and Mrs. Paul Mellon,* catalogue by John Baskett and Dudley Snelgrove, 1972.

NEW YORK AND ELSEWHERE 1975–76

The Pierpont Morgan Library, New York; the Cleveland Museum of Art; Art Institute of Chicago; and the National Gallery of Canada, Ottawa, *Drawings from the Collection of Mr. and Mrs. Eugene V. Thaw,* catalogue by Felice Stampfle and Cara D. Denison, 1975–76.

NEW YORK AND ELSEWHERE 1988–89

The Frick Collection, New York, the Cleveland Museum of Art, and the Fine Arts Museums of San Francisco, *François-Marius Granet, Watercolors from the Musée Granet at Aix-en-Provence, with the Memoirs of the Painter Granet,* catalogue by Edgar Munhall, Joseph Focarino, trans., 1988–89.

NEW YORK AND ELSEWHERE 1995–96

The Frick Collection, New York, The Frick Museum, Pittsburgh, and the Crocker Museum, Sacramento,

The Golden Age of Danish Art: Drawings from the Royal Museum of Fine Arts, Copenhagen, catalogue by Hans Edvard Nørregård-Nielsen, 1995–96.

NOTTINGHAM 1965

Castle Museum and Art Gallery, Nottingham, *R. P. Bonington, 1802–1828,* 1965.

OMAHA 1941

Joslyn Memorial Museum, Omaha, *The Tenth Anniversary Exhibition,* 1941.

OMAHA AND ELSEWHERE 1998

Joslyn Memorial Museum, Omaha, Walters Art Gallery, Baltimore, and Minneapolis Institute of Arts, *Degas: Little Dancer,* 1998.

OSLO 1907

Christiania Kunstforening, Oslo, *Retrospective Exhibition,* 1907.

OTTAWA AND ELSEWHERE 1976–77

National Gallery of Canada, Ottawa, National Gallery of Art, Washington, D.C., and Royal Academy of Arts, London, *The Graphic Work of Félix Vallotton,* 1976–77.

OTTAWA AND ELSEWHERE 1999–2000

National Gallery of Canada, Ottawa, Hamburger Kunsthalle, Hamburg, and Thorvaldsens Museum, Copenhagen, *Baltic Light: Early Open-Air Painting in Denmark and North Germany,* catalogue by Catherine Johnston, Helmut Börsch-Supan, Helmut R. Leppien, and Kasper Monrad, 1999–2000.

PARIS 1867

Cercle des arts, Paris, *Exposition des études peintes par M. Théodore Rousseau,* 1867.

PARIS 1934

Musée des Arts Décoratifs, Paris, *Les Artiste Français en Italie: De Poussin à Renoir,* 1934.

PARIS 1937

Musée de l'Orangerie, Paris, *Degas,* 1937.

PARIS 1938

Galerie Maurice Gobin, Paris, *Dessins et quelques peintures par Corot,* 1938.

PARIS 1939

Galerie André Weil, Paris, *Degas,* 1939.

PARIS 1947

Galerie Charpentier, Paris, *Paysages d'Italie,* 1947.

PARIS 1948

Galerie J. Dubourg, Paris, *Odilon Redon: Peintures, pastels, dessins,* 1948.

PARIS 1957

Galerie Hector Brame, Paris, *Exposition Corot,* 1957.

PARIS 1958–59

Musée de l'Orangerie, Paris, *De Clouet à Matisse, dessins français des collections américaines,* 1958–59.

PARIS 1960

Galerie Durand-Ruel, Paris, *Degas,* 1960.

PARIS 1966

Centre Georges Pompidou, Musée National d'Art Moderne, Paris, *Vallotton,* 1966.

PARIS 1973–74

Galerie de Bayser, Paris, *Pierre-Henri de Valenciennes,* 1973–74.

PARIS 1975

Orangerie des Tuileries, Paris, *Hommage à Corot: Peintures et dessins des collections françaises,* 1975.

PARIS 1982–83

Musée du Louvre, Paris, *L'Atelier de Desportes: Dessins et esquisses conservés par la Manufacture nationale de Sèvres,* 1982–83.

PARIS 1991

Musée d'Orsay, Paris, *A. Rimbaud: Portraits, dessins, manuscrits,* catalogue by H. Dufour and A. Guyaux, Les Dossiers du Musée d'Orsay, 1991.

PARIS 1991–92

Didier Imbert Fine Art, Paris, *Henry Moore—Intime,* 1991–92.

PARIS 1993

Musée du Petit Palais, Paris, *Chefs-d'Oeuvre du musée des Beaux-Arts de Leipzig,* 1993.

PARIS 1994

Musée Jacquemart-André, Paris, *Chefs-d'Oeuvre des collections françaises,* 1994.

PARIS 1994–95

L'Institut du Monde Arabe, Paris, *Delacroix—Le Voyage au Maroc,* 1994–95.

PARIS 1995

Galerie Fischer-Kiener, Paris, *Peintures de paysages de la revolution au second-empire,* catalogue by Jacques Fischer and Chantal Kiener, 1995.

PARIS 1996

Galerie Antoine Laurentin, Paris, *Alexandre Desgoffe (1805–1882),* 1996.

PARIS AND BALTIMORE 2000

Musée d'Orsay, Paris, and The Baltimore Museum of Art, *Manet: The Still-Life Paintings,* 2000.

PARIS AND MANTUA 2001

Grand Palais, Paris, and Centro Internazionale d'Arte e di Cultura di Palazzo Te, Mantua, *Paysages d'Italie: Les Peintres du plein air (1780–1830),* catalogue by Anna Ottani Cavina, ed., 2001.

PARIS AND NEW YORK 1991–92

Grand Palais, Paris, and The Metropolitan Museum of Art, New York, *Georges Seurat, 1859–1891,* catalogue by Robert Herbert, 1991–92.

PARIS AND NEW YORK 1993–94

Musée du Louvre, Paris, and The Pierpont Morgan Library, New York, *French Master Drawings from The Pierpont Morgan Library,* catalogue by Cara Dufour Denison, 1993–94.

PHILADELPHIA 1971

Philadelphia Museum of Art, *Giovanni Benedetto Castiglione: Master Draughtsman of the Italian Baroque,* foreword by Anthony Blunt, catalogue by Ann Percy, 1971.

POUGHKEEPSIE 1976

Vassar College Art Gallery, Poughkeepsie, New York, *Seventeenth-Century Dutch Drawings,* catalogue by Curtis Baer, 1976.

PRINCETON AND ELSEWHERE 1973

The Art Museum, Princeton University, Detroit Institute of Arts, and Philadelphia Museum of Art, *The Claude Lorrain Album in the Norton Simon Inc. Museum of Art,* 1973.

PROVIDENCE 1937

Rhode Island School of Design, Providence, [title unknown], 1937.

ROME 1980

Galleria Nazionale d'Arte Moderna e Contemporanea, Rome, *Félix Vallotton (1865–1925): Le incisioni su legno,* 1980.

ROTTERDAM 1958

The Boijmans Van Beuningen Museum, Rotterdam, *Van Clouet tot Matisse: Tentoonstelling von franse tekeningen uit amerikaanse collecties,* 1958.

ROTTERDAM AND PARIS 1974

The Boijmans Van Beuningen Museum, Rotterdam, and Institut Néerlandais, Paris, *Dessins flamands et hollandais du dix-septième siècle, Collections Musées de Belgium, Musée Boijmans Van Beuningen, Rotterdam, Institut Néerlandais, Paris,* catalogue by A. W. F. M. Meij, Jeroen Giltay, Maria van Berge, and Carlos van Hasselt, 1974.

SALZBURG 1990

Galerie Salis, Salzburg, *Fernand Léger,* 1990.

SAN FRANCISCO 1947

California Palace of the Legion of Honor, San Francisco, *Nineteenth-Century French Drawings,* 1947.

SCHWEINFURT 1970

Altes Rathaus, Schweinfurt, *Carl Gustav Carus und die zeitgenössische Dresdner Landschaftsmalerei: Gemälde aus der Sammlung Georg Schäfer,* catalogue by Konrad Kaiser, 1970.

SPOLETO 1996

Palazzo Racani Arroni, Spoleto, *Pierre-Henri de Valenciennes, 1750–1819,* catalogue by Bruno Mantura and Geneviève Lacambre, 1996.

STOCKHOLM 1922

Sveriges allmänna konstförening, Stockholm, *Danish Art of the Early Nineteenth Century,* 1922.

STUTTGART 1989

Staatsgalerie Stuttgart, *Joseph Anton Koch, 1768–1839: Ansichten der Natur,* catalogue by Christian von Holst, 1989.

SYRACUSE 1949

Syracuse University, College of Fine Arts, *Fifteen Impressionists,* 1949.

TOKYO 1998

National Museum of Western Art, Tokyo, *Claude Lorrain and the Ideal Landscape,* 1998.

TOKYO AND ELSEWHERE 1970

Seibu Department Store, Tokyo, Municipal Museum, Kyoto, and Cultural Center of Fukuoka, *Jean-François Millet et ses amis—peintres de Barbizon,* 1970.

TOKYO AND ELSEWHERE 1992–93

Sezon Museum of Modern Art, Tokyo; Kitakyushu Municipal Museum of Art; Hiroshima City Museum of Contemporary Art; and Oita Prefectural Museum of Art, *Henry Moore—Intime,* 1992–93.

VENICE 1963

Palazzo Ducale, Venice, *Vittorio Carpaccio,* catalogue by Pietro Zampetti, 1963.

VILLEQUIER AND PARIS 1971–72

Musée Victor Hugo, Villequier, and Maison de Victor Hugo, Paris, *Dessins de Victor Hugo,* catalogue by Pierre Georgel, 1971–72.

WASHINGTON 1985

The Phillips Collection, Washington, D.C., *The Phillips Collection: A Summary Catalogue,* 1985.

WASHINGTON 1990

National Gallery of Art, Washington, D.C., *Rembrandt's Landscapes: Drawings and Prints,* catalogue by Cynthia P. Schneider, 1990.

WASHINGTON AND ELSEWHERE 1962–63

National Gallery of Art, Washington, D.C.; The Pierpont Morgan Library, New York; Museum of Fine Arts, Boston; the Cleveland Museum of Art; National Gallery of Canada, Ottawa; Art Institute of Chicago; and California Palace of the Legion of Honor, San Francisco, *Old Master Drawings from Chatsworth,* catalogue by A. E. Popham and James Byam Shaw, 1962–63.

WASHINGTON AND ELSEWHERE 1977

National Gallery of Art, Washington, D.C., Denver Art Museum, and Kimbell Art Museum, Fort Worth, *Seventeenth-Century Dutch Drawings,* catalogue by Franklin Robinson, 1977.

WASHINGTON AND ELSEWHERE 1985–87

National Gallery of Art, Washington, D.C.; Indianapolis Museum of Art; The John and Mable Ringling Museum of Art, Sarasota; High Museum of Art, Atlanta; Walters Art Gallery, Baltimore; and Frederick Wight Gallery, University of California, Los Angeles, *Master Drawings from Titian to Picasso, The Curtis O. Baer Collection,* catalogue by Eric M. Zafran, 1985–87.

WASHINGTON AND ELSEWHERE 1996–97

National Gallery of Art, Washington, D.C., The Brooklyn Museum, and The St. Louis Art Museum, *In the Light of Italy: Corot and Early Open-Air Paintings,* catalogue by Philip Conisbee, Sarah Faunce, and Jeremy Strick, with Peter Galassi, guest curator, 1996–97.

WILLIAMSTOWN 1999

Sterling and Francine Clark Art Institute, Williamstown, Massachusetts, *Jean-François Millet: Drawn into the Light,* catalogue by Alexandra R. Murphy, 1999.

ZURICH 1949–50

Kunsthaus Zurich, *Gemälde der Ruzicka-Stiftung,* 1949–50.

ZURICH 2001

August Laube, Zurich, *Félix Vallotton,* 2001.

Index of Artists

Credits

Every effort has been made to trace copyright owners and photographers. The Morgan Library apologizes for any unintentional omissions and would be pleased in such cases to add an acknowledgment in future editions.

PUBLISHED BY THE PIERPONT MORGAN LIBRARY

Karen Banks, *Publications Manager*
Patricia Emerson, *Senior Editor*
Genna P. Patacsil, *Assistant*

PROJECT STAFF

Drawings and Prints

Egbert Haverkamp-Begemann, *Acting Director*
Cara Dufour Denison, *Curator*
Jennifer Tonkovich, *Assistant Curator*
Kathleen Stuart, *Frank Strasser Administrator and Assistant Curator*
Jan Leja, *Curatorial Assistant*

Marilyn Palmeri, *Manager, Photography and Rights*

Anita Masi, *Director of Institutional Development*

Designed by Jerry Kelly
Color consulting by Sally Fisher
Printed and bound by The Studley Press